80 Years after Bretton Woods

Federalism

VOLUME 16

80 Years after Bretton Woods

Relaunching Multilateralism
through Regional Monetary Unions

Edited by Fabio Masini

PETER LANG
Bruxelles · Berlin · Chennai · Lausanne · New York · Oxford

This book was made possible by the Centro Studi sul Federalismo (www.csfederalismo.it)

This publication has been peer reviewed.

Published by Peter Lang P.I.E. s.a. Éditions scientifiques internationales Bruxelles

Library of Congress Cataloging-in-Publication Data
Library of Congress Control Number: 2025904541

ISSN 2294-6969
ISBN 978-3-0343-5444-8
ePDF 978-3-0343-5449-3
ePUB 978-3-0343-5450-9
DOI 10.3726/b22421
D/2024/5678/65

Bibliographic information published by Die Deutsche Nationalbibliothek
Die Deutsche National Bibliothek lists this publication in the "Deutsche Nationalbibliografie"; detailed bibliographic data is available on the Internet at <http://dnb.de>.

www.peterlang.com

Contents

Bretton Woods at 80. Back to the Future

Fabio Masini

The year 2024 marks the 80th anniversary of the international monetary conference held at Bretton Woods (BW) in New Hampshire (USA) from 1st to 22nd July 1944, where the foundations of a new international economic and monetary order were laid down. WWII had not yet come to an end, the *Operation Overlord* was just reversing the hegemonic ambitions of the Nazi Germany over Europe, and the USA were about to demonstrate to the whole world their technological supremacy in military weapons, which would culminate in the nuclear bombing of Hiroshima and Nagasaki in August 1945.

In October 1945 the United Nations (UN) were established and in December 1945 two global economic institutions, agreed upon at BW, were born under its aegis: the International Monetary Fund (IMF) and the International Bank for Reconstruction and Development (IBRD), later become the World Bank (WB).

The system crystallized the US supremacy in economic and financial matters, relying on fixed-exchange rates based on a grid of bilateral parities with the US dollar, placed under the monitoring and short-term assistance of the IMF (whose decision making was under the control of the USA), and on the pivotal role of the dollar in international payments and reserves, being the British pound *de facto* subordinate reserve currency. The IBRD was meant to support long-term assistance to reconstruction and development projects and a negotiation process was initiated to reduce barriers to international trade within the General Agreement on Tariffs and Trade (GATT, since October 1947).

Despite the US supremacy in global institutions, the UN struggled to design an increasingly multilayered system of economic cooperation, based on five regional bodies to allow for greater convergence in economic policies and setting of broad macroeconomic goals; this is how the United Nations Economic Commission for Europe (UNECE) (its role was complemented in the context of the Marshall Plan of 1947 by the Organization for European Economic Cooperation, which became the OECD in 1961), the ones for

Latin America and the Caribbean (ECLAC, better known with its Spanish acronym CEPAL, in 1948) and for Africa (ECA, in 1958), and the Economic and Social Commission for Asia and the Pacific (ESCAP, in 1947) and for Western Asia (ESCWA, in 1973) were born.

One of the main protagonists of such regional cooperation processes was Robert Triffin, first hired by the IMF, designer of the European Payments Union (EPU, to multilateralize clearing within the Marshall Plan), and by OEEC until 1951, when he was hired as a Professor of Economics at Yale. Apart from the European attempt, on which he invested most of his advocacy skills, he had previous and subsequent extensive experience in regional integration advisory, especially in Latin America and East-Asia. Triffin was the single most important economist to advocate for a multilayered system of global governance, with both regional and global institutions, firmly believing in the need to compromise between centralizing a few key economic regulatory and policy framework and decentralizing, to a multipolar system of regional safety nets, the financial stabilization that he deemed to be impossible at the global level, under the US hegemony.

While in the post-WWII world, characterized by increasing international trade and liquidity requirements to support national paths to reconstruction, it seemed that dollars would soon become scarce, as balance of payments deficits had to be settled in dollars (or gold), in October 1959 Triffin noted before the US Congress that the twofold role of the dollar as a national currency and as provider of international liquidity was bound to fail, as it involved an inherent contradiction. Liquidity, required by increasing trade and domestic goals, could only be provided by a structural deficit in the US internal and external balance, thus eventually jeopardizing the credibility of the dollar pledge to convertibility into gold, and ultimately the functioning of the entire system.

The subsequent debate on the possible reforms of the international monetary system increasingly involved academics and policymakers, until the Group of Ten and the Bellagio Group were established to provide suggestions. The *liquidity* (credit expansion) versus *adjustment* (austerity measures) options led to the compromise emerged in 1969, with the first amendment to the Articles of Agreement of the IMF, in which a new reserve asset was designed, the Special Drawing Right (SDR), meant to supplement the dollar as a reserve asset. And to the establishment of a stricter system of conditionality through Stand-By Arrangements (SBAs), based on Polak's monetary approach to the balance of payments.

In 1970 a first tentative, small-scale general allocation of SDRs was implemented. Its amount and administrative constraints made it impossible to accomplish the task it had been designed for: saving the system. Triffin, disappointed by this evolution, had already resorted to attempt fostering regional monetary integrations, trying to advocate the establishment of a European Reserve Fund (Triffin 1970), and an Asian Monetary Fund (Triffin 1969). Regional integrations might have provided, in his thought, the necessary infrastructure to make global financial-assistance sustainable and more equitable in a two-tier logic.

These proposals came too late and lacked authoritative political ownership. In August 1971 the dollar convertibility with gold was suspended, leading to the adoption of generalized floating exchange rates since 1973. The Yom Kippur war and the subsequent rise of oil prices led to mounting global imbalances, with oil-exporting countries asymmetrically financing with balance-of-payment surpluses the current account deficits of oil-importing countries. This created a first dramatic clash of interests between the IMF and the USA, with IMF Managing Director Witteveen supporting a supranational solution to such imbalances through the intermediation of the IMF and the use of SDRs in energy invoicing, while the USA preferred to pursue a weaponization of the dollar and implemented bilateral agreements with a few oil-exporting countries, with the complacency of most Western allies who traded off their security against the dollar hegemony.

After the formal collapse of the fixed-rates regime, a *de facto* hegemony of the US dollar substituted its *de jure* hegemony, dominated by greater vulnerability of the world economy, due to the *built-in destabilizer,* i.e the asymmetric impact of the monetary and fiscal policy pursued by the dominant country, that characterizes each international monetary system relying on a national currency to provide global liquidity. A structural problem that occasionally resurfaced in times of extreme international geopolitical stress.

In this context, a political compromise emerged, again thanks mostly to Triffin's advisory work for the European Commission's President Roy Jenkins, that led to the adoption of the Exchange Rate Mechanism of the European

Monetary System in 1979 and the further process, thanks to the political leadership of Jacques Delors and diplomatic skills of Tommaso Padoa Schioppa, to the single currency in Europe.

The 1980s and 1990s, that saw the reshuffling of global geopolitical power with the collapse of the Soviet Union and block, was characterized by the explosion of the emerging countries debt, with recurrent balance of payments crises and default risks, followed by painful debt restructuring, paralleled by an increasing weaponization of the IMF by the USA, the so-called *Washington Consensus*, culminating in the humiliation of Japan's attempt to establish an Asian Monetary Fund in 1997, during the East-Asian currency crisis.

The rise of China as an export-led economy and the accumulation of new and unprecedented global imbalances suggested some to call for a New Bretton Woods. The financial crisis originating in the US subprime mortgage sector since 2007 further accentuated this demand, and in 2008 the United Nations appointed a Commission of experts, chaired by Joe Stiglitz, to tackle the issues concerning the shortcomings of — and solutions to — a reshaping of the world monetary order.

In parallel, Michel Camdessus, Tommaso Padoa Schioppa and Alexandre Lamfalussy launched in 2010 the Palais Royal Initiative, which brought together 20 high personalities, mostly former central bankers, including Paul Volcker, Edwin Truman from the US and Arminio Fraga from Brazil, and produced the Palais Royal Report with a blueprint and 18 suggestions for reform of the international monetary system. Unfortunately the launching of this report coincided with the onset of the sovereign debt crisis in the euro area, which completely absorbed the political decision makers.

Despite great political and academic debates, these various initiatives only led to a reconsideration of quotas and the insertion of the renminbi in the SDR basket, since 2016.

Ambitions for reforming the system were systematically frustrated by the USA. When the BRICS emerged as a block confronting the Western, US-based one, and the triple shock (Covid, Russian invasion of Ukraine, the return of inflation) hit the global economy we witnessed a new weaponization of the dollar, which is leading to a counter-weaponization of all other major currencies and to new initiatives within the BRICS+.

The slow but inexorable protagonism of China behind the scenes of global politics in the last few decades has successfully led to the multilateralization of the swaps agreement within the ASEAN+3 while attempts were initiated by China (with the China's Cross-Border Interbank Payment System), Russia (Russia's Financial Messaging System), and India (INR/Local Currency Settlement System) to establish alternative financial infrastructures to support local currencies for cross-border settlements.

An undeclared war between currency areas is currently in place, with the dollar still playing its hegemonic role in an increasingly difficult context, characterized by worsening problems to further expand the US public debt (i.e. heading towards the exorbitant amount of $40tn).

The triple shock and the emergence of the BRICS also triggered new demands by emerging market economies, trying to resist the old colonial logics of mono-production patterns (that exposed them to the variability of prices of their underlying exporting commodities) and in search for alternative financial and structural support to the usual US-led one. An unsuccessful attempt, until now, as refusal for old colonial models has led to acceptance of new colonial logics under the control of other major players.

The critical situation we are living now incites for creative designing of a new and more balanced international economic and monetary order, that would imply a geopolitical change in country weights, decision-making mechanisms, governance structures and institutions.

Pending such radical reform, what are the opportunities to improve the current flawed framework? Can we advance on multilateralism with significant steps towards greater regional economic and monetary cooperation and integration? Is there anything we can learn from European integration (both successes and failures) which might be inspiring for other regional contexts? What lessons have been learned so far from the regional or sub-regional initiatives of economic and/or monetary union and cooperation in Africa, Latin America and Asia? Could the introduction of Central Bank Digital Currencies (CBDCs), that might become interoperable, pave the way to regional payments unions and, subsequently, to greater regional monetary integration? What might be the consequences for the global monetary system?

Around these research questions the Robert Triffin International (RTI) association decided to organize in Lisbon a collective debate, convening a panel of experts under the title *80 years after Bretton Woods. Relaunching Multilateralism through Regional Monetary Unions*. Thanks to the organizational efforts of Banco de Portugal and the Academia de Ciencias de Lisboa and the support of the Fonds Gutt (Université Libre de Bruxelles) and Centro Studi sul Federalismo (Turin) more than thirty panelists — a large proportion of them from the Community of Portuguese-speaking Countries (CPLP) — provided their views on the critical elements and possible directions that might be taken to advance regional integration and transregional cooperation, with the ultimate aim of reforming the international monetary system. Let me briefly dwell on a critical policy knot that emerged.

This concerns the excess weaponization of the dollar, that many assessed as having gone too far, inducing attempts at counter-reactions of the same kind. Renato Flores warned that this might be the most effective instrument to bring the USA to reconsider their aggressive behavior in monetary matters. A radical alternative to further pursuing the general weaponization of all the currencies is emerging in the form of rehabilitating multilateralism. I suggested that a different perspective might compromise between the two, based on an increasing regionalization of a few, critical competences to limit the financial vulnerability of areas such as Africa and Central and Latin America (and I would add: increasing the internationalization of the euro, which I did not tackle in my intervention, reproduced almost at end of the volume, but on which I have written elsewhere).

I must acknowledge, nevertheless, that this might not be enough to convince the USA to see the advantages of a managed transition toward multilateralism over further weaponizing the dollar. And it might even not be enough to solve the inherent, structural problem posed by the Triffin Dilemma, as it can be generally ascribed to the (ab)use of any national liquid debt on the interbank/repo markets, not just for cross-border operations. Local currencies cannot become safe assets without their public authorities being a lender/consumer of last resort. Competition for becoming so would presumably result in a chaotic system of global liquidity and exchange rates, very difficult to manage. From this perspective, CBDCs would also not change the need for a single vehicle. Still, the global system is weakening, and no first-best solution is in sight.

As in other critical moments in the past, when radical reform was needed but political compromise seemed impossible to reach, a viable, pragmatic solution may lay in strengthening regional cooperation and integration. A two-layers system of financial assistance may help its long-term sustainability, before a radical rethinking of the whole global economic governance is pursued. This is the main legacy left by Triffin, an effort on which he spent most of his life. And this is the message we would like to convey to the international community. Let's move forward, building on our past: back to the future!

SECTION 1

Challenges to Multilateralism and Prospects for Regional Monetary Cooperation

Introductory Statement

Bernard Snoy

I would like first to thank Banco de Portugal and the Academia das Ciéncias de Lisboa, who are the co-organizers of this conference with Robert Triffin International (RTI). Thank you in particular to Prof. Jorge Braga de Macedo, former Minister of Finance of Portugal, who signed for Portugal the Treaty of Maastricht, and to Prof. Clara Raposo, Deputy Governor for their key role in preparing this conference. Thank you very much to the Centro Studi sul Federalismo and to the Gutt Fund of the Free University of Brussels, who commemorates the intellectual heritage of Camille Gutt, Minister of Finance who represented Belgium in Bretton Woods and was the first Managing Director of the IMF. Thank you also to Michel Camdessus, former Managing Director of the IMF who supports the conference without being able to attend. Michel Camdessus urges all of us to become more aware of the serious dangers of inaction in the face of the huge challenges facing us and the possibility of new systemic crises.

Bretton Woods, Multilateralism and Regional Monetary Unions are three terms closely related to the life, the academic research and teaching of the late Belgian-American economist Robert Triffin (1911–1993) and his concrete involvement in global and regional — particularly European — integration and governance processes. We recommend his biography by Ivo Maes. A few participants to this conference, among them Jorge Braga de Macedo, Rurik Ingram and Alain Camu have been students of Robert Triffin. The Robert Triffin International Association was created in 2002, under the chairmanship of Alexandre Lamfalussy, former Managing Director of the Bank for International Settlements (BIS), to perpetuate his intellectual heritage and to draw attention to the continuing relevance of his advocacy of reform of the international monetary system. A number of RTI publications, available in this room, illustrate our activities and the reports we have produced.

More than 60 years ago, Robert Triffin enunciated what has become known as the Triffin Dilemma, namely: "It is impossible for a national currency used as a world currency to serve properly both the needs of the national economy of the country issuing that currency and the needs of the international economy". There is an obvious tendency for the interests of the national economy to prevail over the needs of the global economy. We saw this with the explosion of budgetary and commercial deficits in the United States leading to the collapse Triffin had predicted of the original Bretton Woods system, based on mutual obligations of macroeconomic and financial discipline and a dollar convertible in gold. This collapse was a first defeat for the multilateral institutions set up after the end of World War II.

But the abandonment of a fixed anchor and the introduction of floating exchange rates did not eliminate the Triffin dilemma. The "exorbitant privilege" enjoyed by the United States under the de facto dollar system allowed an exponential development of debt and an uncontrolled proliferation of liquidity multiplying itself outside of the United States. We lost the notion that international liquidity was a public good that needed to be managed accordingly by a genuine Lender of Last Resort. The US Federal Reserve played only partially this role in times of crises, while the IMF was marginalized. As stressed by Jacques de Larosière, former Managing Director of the IMF, laxism, combined with the financialization of the economy and inadequate financial regulation, was at the root of the dramatic financial crises we have seen, in particular the great financial crisis of 2008, which provoked a huge loss of confidence in the elites of the Western world and the surge in populism. The problem has been compounded by unorthodox monetary operations of central banks, including quantitative easing and near-zero interest rates to fight recession, followed by significant tightening to deal with rising inflation.

Today the Triffin Dilemma is still with us. Its most obvious dimension is the potential loss of confidence given the imbalance between the amount of US dollar debt and the fiscal capacity of the US. The US federal debt is on an explosive path relative to GDP. As Martin Wolf wrote recently in the Financial Times of 10 April, "the tree of debt must stop growing"

But a second dimension already identified by Robert Triffin is the "built-in-destabilizer" resulting from the spillover effects of the US monetary policy on the rest of the world, particularly the destabilizing inflows and outflows of short-term capital to and from emerging and developing countries, preventing these countries from pursuing the fiscal and monetary policies most appropriate for them and forcing them to accumulate huge exchange reserves in a very unstable world. This is obliging these countries to pursue export-oriented policies that might not be optimal and to sterilize a high part of their savings which might otherwise be used to finance the huge investments required for their ecological transition and the attainment of the Sustainable Development Goals. We should not be astonished that emerging countries in the Global South are looking for alternatives. The unsustainability of the de facto dollar based international monetary system is a second defeat for genuine multilateralism.

Robert Triffin was not only a critic of what he saw as a very unequitable non-system. He advocated positively the move to another more rational and equitable multilateral system that would be based on a much stronger mandate given to the IMF and the move to a potential multilateral global reserve currency, the Special Drawing Rights. He was one of the conceptors of SDRs, created in 1969 under the first amendment to the statutes of the IMF. Unfortunately, under US pressure, the SDR was relegated only to be parked as a marginal reserve asset in Central Banks' balance sheet, instead of being used as the most important reserve instrument and ultimately as a multiplier for the financing of SDGs, ecological transition and other public goods.

The intellectual heritage of Triffin has found defenders in prominent personalities such as Michel Camdessus, Tommaso Padoa Schioppa and Alexandre Lamfalussy, who launched in 2010 the Palais Royal Initiative, which brought together 20 high personalities, including Paul Volcker, Edwin Truman from the US and Arminio Fraga from Brazil, and produced the Palais Royal Report with a blueprint and 18 suggestions for reform. This report was complemented by the proposal of a *sequenced agenda* written by Michel Camdessus with Anoop Singh, who will speak this afternoon in the second session, published in 2014. RTI has brought its contribution, as Christian Ghymers will surely explain to-day or to-morrow, explaining that an alternative exists to the present system and could combine in a creative way multilateral cooperation and national sovereignty.

Unfortunately, except for the creation of the Financial Stability Board and of some new banking regulations, very little has been accomplished. We missed a period where geopolitical tensions were less acute. Now with the war in Ukraine, we have entered a period where polarization is so intense that progress to reform at the global level looks almost impossible. Worse, we see an unravelling of the authority and relevance of the existing global multilateral institutions which had underpinned global prosperity since WWII. Nevertheless, we should not lose hope. It was in 1942, at a time when the outcome of WWII was far from certain, that Keynes started to build the intellectual foundations of the discussions in Bretton Woods on a new international monetary system. In the same way, we should prepare now for a time when the need to move to a new global system of monetary governance would become obvious, including in the interest of the US. But what would we do if this time does not come?

This is where the idea of redirecting our efforts to forms of regional trade and economic integration supported by monetary unions comes from. Robert Triffin himself, a very pragmatic man and inventive mind, always worked both at the international and at the regional level switching to initiatives at the regional level when conditions were not propitious at the global level. For instance, in 1970s and 1980s, he played a key role in the elaboration of the Exchange Rate Mechanism of the European Monetary System. This is why we proposed to you this theme of "Relaunching Multilateralism through Regional Monetary Unions."

Current wars notwithstanding, there is a renewed interest towards regional trade integration and monetary unions. Unavoidable economic and monetary interdependence and the continental dimension of most actors now playing in the global arena call for better regional integration as a compromise between the shortening of global value chains and the need for open economies. As Fabio Masini, Secretary General of RTI, will explain to us, regional integration could provide the key to the transition towards a global multipolar system. Equal dignity of each pole, at least in terms of future perspectives, is crucial for the sustainability of a multipolar system of global governance. This requires strengthening regional integration processes beyond and outside Europe, where regional integration is the most advanced and from which interesting lessons can be learnt.

The conference complements the collective endeavor of RTI of writing and publishing a book on the same themes. By joining forces with Banco de Portugal and ACL, the natural focus is on the Community of Portuguese-speaking Countries (CPLP) such that each institution provides a venue for debate on the models for regional integration, in the perspective of improving global economic and monetary governance. We are very proud of having in the conference speakers from almost all CPLP countries. Africa is of great importance to us, and it is a special honor to have Jean-Claude Kassi Brou, Governor of the BCEAO. He is the only governor of a multilateral central bank to be with us.

The conference is structured as follows: today we will address the subject through two roundtables, the first on challenges to multilateralism and the prospects for regional monetary cooperation; and the second more squarely on the issue of geo-economic fragmentation, asking ourselves if regional monetary unions provide an answer. We are very grateful to Banco de Portugal, who will host a dinner, where we will have the honor to listen to a keynote speech of H.E. Governor Mario Centeno.

Tomorrow, at the Academy of Sciences of Lisbon, we will review, in the morning, the state of regional economic and monetary cooperation in Africa, in Latin America and in Asia, asking ourselves what lessons we can draw from the past and what are the key issues for the future. After lunch, we will have the honor of listening to a keynote speech by Vitor Gaspar, former Minister of finance of Portugal, now Director of the Fiscal Department of the IMF on the subject: *The impact of geopolitics on fiscal policy*. Our session of tomorrow afternoon will wrap up the conference trying to answer the question: *Where do we go from here? 80 years after Bretton Woods, what kind of regional initiatives could contribute to a more stable and equitable international monetary system?*

Welcome Address: The Importance of Regional Monetary Arrangements

José Antonio Ocampo

I am very glad to participate in this meeting on the Regional Monetary System.

Let me thank the three organizers, one of them being the Robert Triffin International, with which I have a long history of collaboration.

The important thing to emphasize in relation to regional monetary institutions is that, in contrast to the system of multilateral development banks, the international monetary system essentially lacks a significant number of regional institutions. In the multilateral development banks, aside from the World Bank group, we have regional banks for all developing countries' regions and two new banks headquarter in China (the New Development Bank and the Asian Infrastructure Investment Bank).

But in the International Monetary System, we essentially have only three institutions that can be considered as relevant regional organizations:

- the European Stability Mechanism, which is by far the largest. It was created during the Euro crisis; of course you will refer to it widely during your meeting.
- the second mechanism is the Chiang Mai Initiative. It was created in the aftermath of the Asian financial crisis but then reformed during the 2007–2009 crisis (which I call North Atlantic financial crisis), when it was expanded significantly. It is a system of swaps but in the 2009 reform the swaps were broadened and multi-lateralized; previously they were bilateral.
- and the third mechanism is the one that we have in Latin America: the Latin American Reserve Fund, which was the expansion, in 1989, of the Andean Fund, that had been created in 1978 and had played a very useful role during the Latin American debt crisis. This is an institution that has nine members: the five Andean countries, three non-Andean — Uruguay, Costa Rica and Paraguay — and Chile, who rejoined the organization after having left it in the late 1970s. This is a very useful mechanism, although it is a small institution: it has a balance of payment support, liquidity financing — one-year loans — and debt restructuring financing. Basically,

it gives countries which are engaged in a debt restructuring process some lending. I am hopefully the largest Latin American countries, Brazil and Mexico, with eventually join it.

Let me say that there is a fourth institution, the Arab Monetary Fund, but when you look at its portfolio it looks more like a multilateral development bank and even a trade financing institution, rather than a monetary institution, so the monetary role of the institution can be questioned.

I think it is very important to develop a hopefully broader network of regional monetary institutions to complement the International Monetary Fund — that is, a network similar to the system of multilateral development banks.

Finally, let me say that one of the proposals I have made is that the contribution of countries to regional monetary institutions should be considered as part of the bases for the allocation of IMF Special Drawing Rights. This would generate a significant incentive to create these institutions.

I hope you have a fantastic meeting. I am sorry I cannot be present in person due to other commitments, but I am grateful for the invitation and for being able to participate virtually.

Towards a Regional Approach for Rebuilding the International Monetary System

Christian Ghymers

Introduction

The global economy has entered in a so-called "perma-crisis" *that is* a stage of extended global crisis generating permanent instability and insecurity threatening welfare, democracies and peace. One of its key-symptoms is the geopolitically driven fragmentation at the very moment that the world is facing major global challenges on intertwined problems that issue important spillovers which should only be tackled efficiently at multilateral level and with a strong improvement in international cooperation: climatic changes, global macroeconomic crisis and the consequent weakening of democracy are all expressions of the same incoherence of the present global economic system. This fundamental incoherence condemns to unsustainability our present socio-economic world.

A key-aspect of it, that all contemporaneous political regimes share, is the principle of unmanaged "market failures" *that is* those mispricing whose effects damage others and the future because the biased relative prices don't incorporate fatal external effects. This is obvious, from a microeconomic point of view, for the too low prices (or no price at all) for carbon emissions, as well as for the too high relative return for financial activities with respect to productive activities. It is, however, less obvious for the third kind of inappropriately managed spill-overs, which are essentially the macroeconomic externalities issued by the international role of US dollar as the main international reserve in the International Monetary System (IMS). From a microeconomic point of view, its visible effects are the too high prices for too scarce safe assets in US dollar (*i.e.* too low yields, see Caballero, R. & others, 2017)[1], while its macroeconomic effects are the empirically observed global financial cycle created by the US monetary

[1] Caballero R., Farhi E., Gourinchas P.O. [2017], "The Safe Assets Shortage Conundrum", *Journal of Economic Perspectives*, Vol. 31, No. 3, Summer 2017

policy (Shin H. S. 2012, Rey, H. 2013)[2], that we qualified as pro-cyclical global liquidity waves, provoking a global financial instability which implies damaging real economy crisis (Ghymers C. 2021)[3], but also an obstacle to financing de-carbonization Ghymers C. 2021,2024. Following Robert Triffin (1959), with RTI (2014) we identify the deeper cause to the systemic "built-in destabilizer" implicit to the use of a national currency, the dollar, as the main international currency.

The above-mentioned trilogy of systemic flaws in the working of the global economy, although generally observed or even acknowledged by economists, have remained amazingly untouched by policy-makers, despite existing multilateral institutions and available tools. The main reason is merely what Triffin (1957) already qualified as "the fundamental dilemma of international economic relations which lies in the inadequacy of national sovereignty as a framework for policy decisions [...] in an interdependent world"[4]. As regards the macro-monetary flaw, Triffin (1957) considered that the origin of this irrational paralysis lies in "the immense weight of inertia which always blocks international action" and in "the jealous zeal with which many central bank officials insist on safeguarding their full — even though often merely formal — independence of decision against international institutions [...]"[5]. This amazing status quo among monetary authorities remains all the stronger as financial risks increase in a world in the process of fragmentation and weakening of multilateralism, while, more than ever, a strengthening of international cooperation would be the only rational option to face the common global challenges. The geopolitical fragmentation adds a potential worsening to this typical 'Prisoner Dilemma' as far as it makes more difficult to improve the international cooperation necessary to preserve and

---

2 Shin H. S. (2012), "Global Banking Glut and Loan Risk Premium", *IMF Economic Review*, Vol. 60, No. 2; Rey H. (2013), *Dilemma not Trilemma: The Global Financial Cycle and Monetary Policy Independence*, Federal Reserve Bank of Kansas City Economic Policy Symposium.

3 Ghymers C. (2021), *The systemic instability of ballooning Global Liquidity as a symptom of the worsening of the Triffin Dilemma*, RTI Paper no. 15, Torino: Centro Studi sul Federalismo.

4 Triffin, R. (1957), *Europe and the Money Muddle*, New Haven: Yale University Press, p. 303.

5 *Ibid*, p.286

develop a multilateral order able to internalize the main spillovers between sovereign national policies and monetary systems.

Under conditions to draw upon some lessons from different past experiences in regionalism, a new dynamic regionalism could be able to emerge for contributing to solve the mentioned trilogy of systemic market failures. In particular a specific kind of cooperative monetary regionalism could be instrumental as a game-changer for updating and rebuilding a multilateralism coherent with the pressing economic and environmental constraints and adapted to the new geopolitical forces.

1. The main cause of the global macroeconomic instability: the Triffin's built-in destabilizer

In 1959, Robert Triffin warns in a hearing at the US Congress that the "use of national currencies as international reserves constitutes a totally irrational 'built-in destabilizer' in the present world monetary system [...]" which is bound "to endanger the stability of the whole monetary superstructure erected upon these key currencies" (Triffin 1959)[6]. Updating the Triffin's analysis — coined the Triffin Dilemma — we have been sustaining for many years [Ghymers C. 1986][7] and later thanks to RTI (2014)[8], that the growing amplitude of financial crisis is the direct consequence of the unsolved Triffin Dilemma through the development of an endogenous generation of global monetary waves that constitute a systemic cause for recurrent global crisis. This Triffin's 'built-in destabilizer' — due to the asymmetry inherent to the role of a national currency as international reserve — has been working with an increasing amplitude since the end of the sixties through two intertwined mechanical channels: first, as the growing world demand for dollar reserves is a growing indebtedness of the US economy, the external monetary discipline disappears together with the easing to finance US fiscal deficits with cheaper

6 Triffin's hearing before the Joint Economic Committee of the US Congress, 28 October 1959, Employment, Growth, and Price Levels (Google Books)

7 Ghymers C. (1986), "Réagir à l'emprise du dollar", in M. Aglietta, *L'Ecu et la Vieille Dame*, Paris: Economica, 1986.

8 Triffin International Foundation (2014), *Using the Special Drawing Rights as a Lever to Reform the International Monetary System*, RTI Paper No. 1, https://www.triffininternational.eu/images/RTI/articles_papers/SDR-WP_Final-Report-May-2014.pdf.

bonds demanded outside as foreign reserves; second by provoking significant monetary spillovers on global liquidity conditions, which tend to become suboptimal and difficult to manage by central banks. While the first channel (the lack of external constraint) explains that the asymmetric role given to the US $ tends to exacerbate macroeconomic imbalances increasing the US indebtedness, the second one (the multiplier effect on global monetary policy) explains the strong spillovers generated by the US monetary policy upon global liquidity conditions, and the combination of both channels provides a plausible explanation for the dangerous course of the world economy towards a process of crisis amplification, with boom-and-bust episodes, leading to huge losses of global welfare and consequent increased populism.

The combination of these two channels biases the policy-mix of the issuer of reserves. It creates a mutually supportive process of systemic imbalances, generating pro-cyclical excess of fluctuations in international liquidity, which in turn worsens the imbalances in a destabilizing and costly cycle: the US economy tends to suffer from a dollar over-valuation which implies the need for increased doses of Keynesian policies to support domestic demand. The inescapable spillovers taking the form of global liquidity waves generate a vicious circle which is a systemic cause for recurrent global crisis, with boom-and-bust episodes. Therefore, the loss of welfare for all countries is inevitable, including those issuing reserve currencies.

Furthermore, it is clear that the present IMS based upon the dollar cannot fulfil its two main essential functions as a public good: to provide an adequate volume of global liquidity and to favour the resolution of external imbalances. On the contrary, the dollar-based IMS tends to polarize the world by developing a vicious circle which allows for maintaining opposed policy-mixes leading to US dis-saving feeding Emerging Economies excess of savings. The role of the dollar makes possible to sustain opposed macroeconomic imbalances which do support each other: the accumulation by emerging economies of long-term US bonds are combined with artificially low interest rates on these bonds which are themselves make possible thanks to this demand for reserve, while the excess demand for reserves responds partially to the need of protection against external financial instability. This circular causality tends to perpetuate the policies explaining the external disequilibrium with the US economy becoming the *'consumer and borrower of last resort'*.

Although this systemic polarization had played a positive role for financing the extend of globalization and the very fast development of some emerging economies, it leads to several negative geopolitical consequences, each of them endowed with a conflictive potential:

1. a strange coalition of interests between the US debtor and some of its Emerging Economies creditors maintains this perverse generation of imbalances based upon costly policies; the US domestic growth and employment objectives call for ever more external financing for increasing US Keynesian demand policies, which the FED is able to feed indirectly through the spillovers of its own stances; this in turn allows for more net exports by Emerging Economies able to maintain mercantilist trade and exchange-rate policies, leading to more accumulation of excess reserves by these creditors of the US, who buy so more geopolitical lever upon the US administration.
2. a distortion in the net flow of savings, which constitutes a perverse paradox since the capital is not flowing from the advanced economies to less advanced, despite the fact that developing countries have lower levels of capital per worker, *that is* the savings of the less rich economies is absorbed by the consumption of the richest one; this paradox was name the 'Lucas paradox' [1990][9] although it was formulated well before and loudly (in the seventies) by Triffin as a corollary of the Triffin Dilemma.
3. this paradox constitutes so a serious obstacle to the de-carbonization in LDCs and EEs which requires urgently an increase in the flows of capital imports these economies need to increase their investment ratio without compressing further their low consumption level (Ghymers 2021, 2024).

The mentioned "built-in destabilizer" with its global monetary waves creating financial fragilities are combined to these conflictive processes developing counter-productive policies, making the IMS an economically inefficient and incoherent system. Since economists are supposed to promote rational

---

9 Lucas R. (1990), "Why doesn't Capital Flow from Rich to Poor Countries?," *American Economic Review*. 80(2): 92–96.

policies, they have no excuse for postponing actions that could improve a system that is both incoherent and unethical.

2. The first-best option: upgrading the SDR as a multilateral currency issued by the IMF according to technical criteria

This ideal solution for eradicating the Triffin Dilemma with its 'buit-in destabilizer', is technically simple and consists in transforming the IMF into a global central bank, which issues a genuine multilateral currency against national reserves (eligible assets). This means issuing a (n+1)th currency above the «n» national ones for solving the 'redundancy issue' due to the obvious fact than with "n" currencies only n-1 exchange rates and autonomous policies are feasible. The currency which meets the conditions for being demanded as the international reserve by the n-1 others, is condemned to lose its policy autonomy by becoming increasingly a net debtor as far as the n-1 economies consider beneficial to increase their external reserves and to hold them in this currency. This redundancy gives an asymmetric role to the key-reserve currency which generates the so-called *Triffin Dilemma*: in such a system where global liquidity is entirely demand driven, would this economy be able to maintain the capacity (and the size) to answer to the huge global demand for liquid debt in dollar, destined to be held as safe assets for supporting the reversed pyramid of global liquidity? The answer is clearly no, as proved by the shortage of safe assets in dollar that is observable in the structural trend in their decreasing yields and in the pro-cyclical behaviour of private global liquidity provoked by the US monetary policy [Ghymers 2021]. Indeed, the US economy has become relatively too small as a share of the world economy and with respect to the huge demand of dollar safe assets. Indeed, the high development of debt worldwide has continued to be conducted mainly in US dollar and the structural evolution of the global financial markets demands requires a growing proportion of safe assets in dollar. This higher need for dollars is explained by the growing role of the non-bank sector on which transactions need to be backed by collaterals in a much higher proportion than the banking sector. The needed collaterals (asset-backed securitization) are preferably the most liquid safe assets *that is* US T-bills and US certificates of deposits, the higher liquidity of which being due to the character of dominant key-currency of the dollar backed by the Federal reserve. The insufficient supply of these dollar assets is the present expression of the 'old' Triffin Dilemma, a national currency as the dollar cannot cope efficiently the role of international reserve currency for being unable to supply the demanded need for reserves. These structural changes mean paradoxically a stronger need for dollar, but also a worsening of financial fragility since the hyper-development of global liquidity relies upon a shrinking basis of dollar safe assets *that is* imposing higher leverage which increases the systemic risks of the global financial system and implies a decreasing trend in their yields. This growing scarcity of dollar safe assets, visible in their lower yields, explains what we qualified as the new form — and the worsening — of the Triffin Dilemma (Ghymers 2021).

The increasing fragility provoked by the impossibility for the US economy to provide sufficient liquid debt as safe assets for responding to demand from the global financial markets that need to be covered by backed assets, demonstrates the major flaw in the present IMS and the urgent need to be able to agree upon an alternative way to issue sufficient safe assets without increasing the external debt of a national economy or a region, and without depending so much on the monetary stance of a single economy. The most rational solution is undoubtedly to issue a multilateral safe asset, a perfectly liquid asset which is not the debt of a single economy and which is issued according to global needs, under purely technical criteria for stabilizing the global liquidity. The best option is to use the existing tool and legitimate IMF institution for upgrading the SDR into a genuine multilateral currency. On the balance-sheet of the LOLR (the reformed IMF), the issuance of this $(n+1)^{th}$ currency consists in increasing the IMF asset-side by buying national reserve-assets to national central banks paid in new SDR by increasing the IMF liability-side as the counterpart of the purchased national assets (Ghymers 2022).

3. Three common objections to the first best option of a single multilateral reserve currency

Unfortunately, this perfect solution, despite intense debates and numerous attempts, has remained unachievable by lack of political consensus at the multilateral level. The present geopolitical deterioration with the multiplication of international conflicts and the trend towards a weakening of multilateralism, makes even stronger the blockade, re-enforcing a dangerous status quo.

A first objection comes from the argument of the loss of sovereignty represented by the transfer of reserves from each national central bank to a supranational institution. Since the national reserves are exchanged for more stable multilateral reserve there is no loss of national power. National monetary policy and exchange-rate regime remain entirely unaffected by the creation of a genuine multilateral currency. As regards the possible divergences in the assessment that an individual central bank could have about the IMF global monetary stance, this central bank remains free to act on its own monetary base, with impacts on the flexible exchange-rates of this currency. So, the internalization of possible impacts from global liquidity changes are ensured. Furthermore, the move from national key-currencies — out of control by the other central banks — to a collegial management of global liquidity constitutes a systemic improvement which actually increases the sovereignty of the national central banks, by internalizing the spillovers generated by the issuers of the key-currencies. The losses of sovereignty are thus completely wrong and reflect an illusion coming from a mere emotional slogan for simplistic populism.

The second objection consists in presenting as more realistic and implying less institutional impacts the option of a system of 'multilateral surveillance' *that is* an international coordination of macroeconomic policies, as recommended by the IMF and most policy-makers. Due to the fact that the existing international coordination does not work[10], this formula would mean a strengthening of policy coordination. This would be even more difficult because it would affect directly national rooms for manoeuvre. As expressed, the first best option of moving to a multilateral reserve currency, not only does not impose any constraint on national policies, but on the contrary, it even would restore more symmetry and room for manoeuvre to national policies.

The third one is merely the necessary approval by the US political authorities because the changes in the IMF statuses implied by the creation of a multilateral currency issued by the IMF, require joining 85% of the votes

---

[10] Clearly demonstrated by the G7 attempts in the eighties with the Louvre Agreements for example, but many other cases show the contradiction between sovereignty and coordination, even in the case of the Euro-area.

while the US alone has a voting weight of 17%. The international role of the dollar being felt as a strategic and financial advantage for the US economy, this belief constitutes the real obstacle.

Already at the end of the fifties, Triffin (1961)[11] developed the idea that reforming directly at multilateral level (IMF) was illusory either by coordination or systemic change, "by lack of close contacts, understanding and mutual trust between too different countries» while «a decentralization will remain necessary for organizing in realistic way an efficient international administration [...and...] I believe that it is within this framework that it is most feasible and most necessary today to initiate the fundamental reforms that I propose"

Therefore, alternatives proposals towards a monetary multi-polar monetary system responds to this blockade and are favoured by the current international evolutions. This emerging of new monetary arrangements should urgently need to be assessed.

4. The deep error of the proposals for a currency competition for reaching a multi-polar monetary system

In an IMS based on key-currencies, the relative diminution of the weight of the US economy and the rapid geographic extension of economic development, makes obvious the idea of a monetary multi-polarity, ensuring coherence with the current multi-polar real economy. In conjunction with this pure logical argument, the legitimate idea of reducing the asymmetrical impacts of the dollar has been strengthened by the geopolitical events since 2014. In consequence of the Russian aggression wars, the dollar was 'weaponized' and, in reaction, the «Global South» claim for more independence from the Western North. The US unilateral sanctions, the extraterritoriality rules applied by the US to the use of the dollar, and the dollar exchange-rate risks, justify a beginning of drop in the market share of the dollar, mainly in the exchange-reserves (more than 10% in 2023 with respect to the beginning

11 Triffin R., « Grandeur et décadence de l'étalon-or », *Stato Sociale*, n°10, Turin, p. 827-838. (our translation from French). This argument for starting at regional level was already expressed in 1949 for proposing the EPU at the OEEC.

of the 2000s) and in trade invoicing. However, it cannot yet be qualified of 'de-dollarization' for two reasons: first, the dominance of the monetary role of the dollar and its asymmetrical effect remains visible and strong, second there is still no competitor currency able to join all the characteristic for taking on its role.

Both reasons cannot exclude that the inertias explained by the network externalities and economies of scale maintaining the dollar supremacy would be suddenly erased with the inevitable increase in the relative importance of China, leading to a reshuffling of the IMS towards a monetary three-polar world. But even in this very probable case (which is actually going on), we sustain that it is a naive error to expect as a solution an IMS based upon three (or more) main key-currencies. Such a regime would be inevitably unsustainable for being systemically unstable. Our argument is merely that the legitimate need to put the monetary system in coherence with the real economic weight cannot be done inside the same system of national key-currency. The reason is that the monetary domain is based upon a centripetal force, different from the economic one: both for market dealers and for the stability of any monetary system, a single standard is required. As regards stability, this centralization of the monetary functions allows for an optimal management of global liquidity by adjusting the monetary base made up with a single reserve currency. Therefore, the only way to adjust easily and safely the monetary world in a multi-polar economic world is through the creation of a multilateral reserve currency which becomes the main tool to adjust the global monetary base at the collegial, legitimate, multilateral level: the IMF transforms in LOLR.

Although the geopolitical realities should and will imply also a political and a monetary re-balance, it is a big mistake to translate naively this requirement in terms of currency competition as a way to re-balance the IMS. Currency competition does not solve the Triffin Dilemma and cannot lead to a stable monetary system, neither at national level nor at international one. The belief into a system based upon several competing key-currencies — transposed at national level — would correspond to expect national financial stability with several commercial banks, by being back to asking them to issue in competition their own currency, without any Lender-of-Last-Resort (LOLR) or national central bank. This corresponds to what pretend those who believe that the IMS could work better with several ('m') national key-currencies playing the role of international currencies, rejecting so the need for a single common international currency. The few 'm' key-currencies would compete for issuing the demanded reserves, sharing as global debtors the lost "nth" degree of policy freedom. Except in case of a total coordination among the central banks issuing these key-currencies, this option cannot escape from the Triffin Dilemma. The only two ways to solve this Dilemma is either to suppress policy sovereignty by imposing a perfect coordination, or to create a '(n+1)th' currency managed by a single LOLR above all the "n" national currencies, which does in fact improve national sovereignties.

It is interesting to observe that there is a general belief — especially among central banks and IMF — that coordination should be the best option for being less demanding than to move to a multilateral currency. In fact, the necessary coordination for making manageable a multi-key-currency system would be much more demanding in terms of abandon of sovereignty than it would be the case with the multilateral single key-currency which, not only does not impose any coordination and any loss of sovereignty, but even restored sovereignty through the internalization of the spillovers once the key-currencies face external constraint and exchange-rate risks. The conclusion is that — paradoxically — the more realistic way to eradicate the fundamental flaw in a key-currency system is also the most legitimate and most logical one: a genuine multilateral currency issued by a multilateral central bank.

Money must be based upon a universal standard, either by a hegemonic power or by a consensual international convention and multilateral institutions. Past experiences as well as inner logics of money make clear that currency competition could only be destabilizing (Kareken J. & Wallace, N. [1981][12]. A monetary system cannot work efficiently with competing alternative tools, all the more that the reserve currencies are closer substitutes. Without formal agreement on a single standard, any news affecting the *moneyness* (liquidity) among competing currencies will imply massive substitutions against the less liquid ones. These substitutions would affect seriously the ability of the central banks to regulate their own liquidity, with damaging consequences for Global Liquidity (GL) provoked by their impact

12 Kareken J. and Wallace N. (1981), "On the indeterminacy of equilibrium exchange rates", *The Quarterly Journal of Economics*, 96(2), pp. 207-222. See also the early work of Ragnar Nurkse (1941) Fahri E., Maggiori M. (2018)

on the global monetary basis. Furthermore, for operational reason, the daily business of dealers could not work by managing simultaneously competing standard in their intra-day fast operations.

Currency competition means exchange-rate instability, generating difficulties to control national liquidities, leading to higher instability of private global liquidity, creating negative impacts on real economies and additional demands for trade protectionism and populism. To control these negative effects would demand an unrealistic degree of international cooperation.

5. The present trend towards regional or strategic payments arrangements

In the present geopolitical context, there appear reactive pressures for some forms of regional monetary areas. This evolution results from the conjunction of growing uncertainties as a result of the weaponization of the dollar which is incompatible with a universal monetary standard, and also of the impacts of exchange rate and capital flow volatility, especially those from the spillovers from macroeconomic policy of the US. At these two factors, the spectacular progress in electronic payments provides a key-facilitator in the initiatives to implement new easy arrangements to use local currencies for cross-border payments as a way to lessen countries' dependence on the dollar for regional trade and investment transactions. In this security strategy, China has taken the lead, in line with its official policy to promote the international use of the RMB, with its Cross border Interbank Payments System (CIPS) accessible now to 123 countries and coupled to a network of currency swap lines across 40 central banks (Hung Tran 2024[13]). This system offers compatibility with the SWIFT but permits to bypass it, augmenting significantly the RMB share in international payments. In combination with the Chinese leadership in digital payments and the internationalization of its credit/debit cards, this successful strategy has resulted in making the RMB the first currency used in cross border payments with China in a few years.

Other cases are also taking speed, along this increasing reaction to the dollar dependence coupled to the opportunities offered by the new technologies

13 Tran H. (2024), *De-dollarization via local currency cross-border payments: democratization and fragmentation of the global system*, Paper prepared for the Lisbon conference.)

in payments. This the case in the ASEAN region and among the BRICS and its recent extension. In particular, the coming adoption of CBDCs, cutting significantly — and faster than between the dollar and third currencies — the transaction costs between local currencies, should spur the success of regional or ad-hoc groups of countries for currency diversification.

Nevertheless, this probability of a multiplication of successful regional arrangements is not sufficient to imply an automatic de-dollarization. The essential feature of a dominant key-currency does not rely so much on the cross-border transactions but rather on its capacity to become the borrower/ consumer of last resort. The unrealistic aspect of the belief in a trend towards a multi-competing currencies dethroning the dominant dollar, allows for making also clear that nowadays the main determinant for assuming the role of the main reserve currency is the existence of a fast growing stock of high-quality (liquid) debt, to be also the dominant debtor. This implies for dethroning the dollar to be:

- either a new dominant economy able to sustain big current account deficits becoming the *consumer of last resort*, which automatically would imply — by accounting definition — that the other big economies cannot simultaneously do the same for being in surplus of saving,
- or that this new dominant economy would want and be able to attract huge liquid liabilities for transforming them into long-term external assets. In fact, this is the contrary of what emerging economies (like China) have been doing up to now.

Therefore, the dollar could only be dethroned in a key-currency system, when another economy could compete with the US by issuing as much or more high-quality debts in its own currency than what the US uses to do in dollar. Neither the EU nor China or the BRICS seem willing or able to meet all the conditions for playing this role. Furthermore, if this would become the case, the global economy would enter into an uncontrollable world inflation. So, even the weaponization of the dollar could not reverse its dominant monetary role in a reasonable predictable horizon, although geopolitical reasons do justify it.

It is crucial to understand that de-dollarization without the creation of a better safe asset would be either impossible or, worse, a global disaster. It is often forgotten that the dollar system, although imperfect and destabilizing, has used to play a very important positive role[14] due to the counterpart given in accepting to be the debtor/consumer of last resort, but also being providing "insurance services"[15] (Gourinchas & others, 2017). Therefore, this systemic mission should be better fulfilling at multilateral level, eradicating the Triffin dilemma in a legitimate collegial way.

Once again, why to try to satisfy the global need for safe assets only with national debts? The easiest solution is the simplest, the less conflictual, the most legitimate, the less risky for world economy, the more stable, the most able to get rid of spillovers, and the less demanding in terms of sovereignty: the alternative way to provide the demanded safe assets is by issuing debt-at-sight perfectly liquid which would not be the debt of a single economy but the liability of a multilateral institution issued by buying reserve-assets to national central banks. The systemic progress is that the international reserves would be created without generating net debt, exactly as a central bank does not create net national debt but increase liquidity by buying other assets on the money market. For the same principle, a technical management of the global liquidity becomes immediately available by adjusting the global monetary base. Furthermore, a multilateral reserve created from a basket of the main key-currencies would be necessarily more stable than any national key-currency compounding this basket.

Therefore, the present trend towards strategic reactions against the dollar dependence is at a crossing road: either to lead to use monetary competition to pursuit a fragmentation in geopolitical blocks in a zero-sum game due to the amplification of financial destabilization, or to seize the opportunity of the legitimate emerging forces towards a geopolitical rebalancing to develop a positive-sum game by using the multiplication of regional monetary arrangements as a game-changer towards eradicating the defects of the present IMS and improve its efficiency in the global interest.

As shown, the legitimate reaction against the flaws in the present IMS should not derive neither into a wild multi-key-currency system nor in

---

14 Would have been possible the fast success of Emerging Economies, like China, without the dollar system?

15 Gourinchas P. O., Rey H. and Govillot N. (2017), *Exorbitant Privilege and Exorbitant Duty*. IMF Working paper.

protectionist blocks, but should be used as an opportunity to anchor the emerging regional monetary arrangements to a reshuffled multilateral one by betting on the present SDR in order to promote the later use of a superior multilateral standard for rebalancing the IMS and rebuilding an efficient monetary multilateral order based upon a federation of regional monetary systems. As developed in section 7, the best option would be to set up a *decentralization* of the IMF by creating regional monetary funds that decide each their own rules and conditionalities for making a regional clearing of intra-regional payments better than relying on national key-currencies, associated to a regional financing of the intra-region deficits.

The only way to prevent a return to protectionism with a costly fragmentation, and to make possible broader coalition among regions for a sound reform of the IMS, would be to jump directly into the SDR for the cleating of regional payments and their financing, allowing so to benefit from multilateral financing from a stronger bargaining position and strengthening their financial credibility on the globalized markets. This is also the best way to rebuild a multilateral IMF covering and complementing the different regional schemes and funds, as proposed long time ago by Triffin (1961 and before).

Such a new monetary architecture is anyway necessary for making possible the urgently required flows of funds addressing de-carbonization in EEs and LDCs, which should be the very first priority in the interests of all nations

6. A proposal in three basic steps for making macro-monetary regionalism a game-changer of the IMS

6.1. The basic rationality of an ideal efficient reform: an IMF decentralization for channelling monetary regionalism towards a common multilateral reserve currency and safety-net managed by a new representative federal IMF

From a collective point of view, the present IMS is objectively suboptimal, as explained by the Triffin Dilemma which is the result of the lack of a global representative LOLR issuing the optimal volume of safe assets without increasing any national debt. In a fragmented world of competing national sovereignties, the option of a perfect international coordination is excluded by definition. However, creating a multilateral currency is compatible with a multi-polar monetary system based on regional monetary arrangements with no need for explicit coordination, but only to agree upon the creation and the use of this better multilateral safe asset for inter-regional transactions and with the IMF. Despite the superior rationality of this win-win game, a resilient status quo has been impeding any progress, policymakers being trapped in a typical *Prisoner's Dilemma*, which has worsened recently with the present fragmentation and geopolitical conflicts. In order to resolve this political economy obstacle, it is worth to start from what should be the final ideal system. Indeed, in theory, the only rational and efficient solution is a 'subsidiary' one. It consists in channelling the legitimate reaction of the emergence of new regional monetary blocks in the doble dimension of the subsidiarity principle applied to monetary institutional features: firstly, a *monetary decentralization* of some traditional IMF functions (surveillance and safety-net) according to conditionality defined at regional level, but, secondly, with *a simultaneously new re-federalization* of the monetary functions through an upgraded super-IMF acting as Multilateral LOLR for issuing the multilateral super-SDR as its liability which plays the role of super-safe assets used as international reserve and for conditional global safety-net. This super-IMF and its super-SDR should increase their legitimacy and respective credibility, with new rules reflecting progressively the relative weights and quality performance of the different regional arrangements. As for the Euro, the monetary representation of the regions would ideally be organized according to the respective weights of the local (common or not) currencies used for intra and extra-regional operations, according to objective criteria to be agreed. All these different regional arrangements would have access to the new IMF (multilateral) safety-net (merging all the existing multilateral facilities) under multilateral conditionality based upon the objective results of the regional conditionality, but according to a joint-decision of both multilateral and regional funds. As a result, a *competition-cooperation* between the Regional Monetary Funds (RMF) and the super-IMF should appear, the best effective regional conditionality being awarded with higher credibility on financial markets (lower spreads) and, according to objective growth, a progressive increase of its weight in the super-SDR and the voting rights in the super-IMF. This kind of *monitored market incentive* favouring the best adjustment policies would spur the adoption of better governance, improving significantly the rationality and the legitimacy of the new multilateral order.

The potential competition between some performant regional currencies could not generate systemic instability, thanks to the management by the multilateral LOLR and the safe-haven role of the super-SDR attracting deposits from the rest of the world since this multilateral reserve absorbs the relative exchange-rate movements. The expected generalization of CBDCs should make this super-safe asset a digital one — the super e-SDR — becoming so the most competitive one as common reserve for the central banks and as vehicle currency for clearing on exchange-rate markets as well as for the private markets for other international/regional operations. A strong market dynamics would "vote" for converting national currencies into a private super-SDR making inevitable to merge official SDR with the private one. This new standard would be the successor of the present SDR once it would become a genuine complete reserve currency *that is* a perfectly liquid liability of the federal IMF/LOLR, in a similar way of the European changeover from the ECU-basket to the Euro issued by the ECB.

6.2. The Triffin's recipe: regional monetary systems could drive towards a new monetary multilateralism

On one side, any multilateral reform of the IMS remains frozen in an amazing status quo, despite the damaging absence for all the countries of a global LOLR issuing the optimal volume of multilateral safe assets, on the other a consequent reaction for lessening countries' dependence on the dollar is developing as indicates the recent trend towards regional monetary arrangements. Both sides expose to systemic risks: the status quo implies to accept the increasing costs of the worsening of the pro-cyclical bias of the dollar system, the regional monetary arrangements could worsen the fragmentation and lead as explained elsewhere to a devastating currency competition.

A possible solution, following Triffin's ideas (1961), could however emerge from a monetary regionalism which would serve as a game-changer under certain conditions. Indeed, the analysis of the present status quo indicates that this collective irrationality is paradoxically the product of individual rational behaviour from the point of view of competing countries facing a high level of uncertainty as regards their partner behaviours, the economic knowledges on the effective working of the world economy, and about the future. This situation is qualified as a *Prisoner Dilemma* trap provoked by the lack of trusty communication between actors.

Since all policy-makers face the same kind of uncertainties, it is logical to think that this general high degree of uncertainty should reduce proportionally more the chances of success of any big multilateral cooperation initiative than it should be the case at regional or sub-regional levels. It is clear that the difficulties to reach a consensus at the multilateral level are bigger than at the regional level where Despite to cross-border communication and mutual knowledge are better among closer cultures. Indeed, among like-minded countries, the degree of uncertainty about the future behaviours of the members is generally lower and could and should be reduced more easily by institution building, all the more that, in case of facing common threats, regional partners tend to benefit from a faster perception of common regional interests, provoking spontaneous reaction of major cohesion. More interdependencies do exist, are more visible among them, and are easier to incorporate. In addition, they have more potential means and opportunities to create common tools for tackling joint-interests or even for defence or retaliation purposes. These common-sense ideas were the basis upon which Triffin (1957)[16] organized in 1949 the European Payments Unit (EPU) leading to the successful post-war return to convertibility in Europe, contributing significantly to the multilateral order. He also extended his method and proposed regional schemes for Latin America (Triffin 1964b) and Africa (Triffin 1964a). Overall, regional partners own more possibilities and incentives to reduce uncertainty among them than it is the case at the too heterogeneous multilateral level.

The demonstration of the higher easiness of regional monetary cooperation — which was already observed in Europe in 1949 — is again demonstrated by the fast emergence of arrangements to use local currencies for cross-border payments as a way to lessen countries' dependence on the dollar for regional trade, investment transactions and promotion of non-dollar reserve currencies. The same is observed in the enlarged BRICS, as well as in the ASEAN, taking monetary and financial initiatives for strengthening their geopolitical power. These arrangements are essentially motivated by reactions against the asymmetric IMS and constitute a *first step*.

16 Triffin R., *op.cit.*

Although this step could not trigger as such a regime change or an effective de-dollarization of the IMS, regional initiatives could be the catalytic motor of the dynamic process for getting out of the prisoner dilemma at regional level allowing for a beneficial deeper regional integration in the main regions (Africa, Asia, Latin America, and other sub-regions). *This second step* has the potential to launch a genuine macroeconomic cooperation leading to the formation of a series of regional monetary systems with clearing of payments in local currencies and financing regional mechanisms which will spur the real and efficient integration (trade & investment) these regions still miss in various degrees for their sustainable development. As far as this step 2 thanks to macroeconomic cooperation, improves the effective regional integration, the question of the emergence of a regional currency should lead to a *third step*: the creation of regional monetary system, with exchange-rate mechanisms or even with common currency projects. These integrated regions endowed with compatible regional funds and the ability to speak with a single voice will easily be aware of their common interests and increased bargaining power with the Hegemon(s) and the IMF. Therefore, they would engage intense inter-regional dialogues to cooperate and to look for consensual positions, forming coalition for reforming the IMS by moving to the multilateral reserve currency they already have adopted among them.

Three major objections characterize generally the conventional sceptical view about regionalism:

i. the European success story is not exportable because it started from a higher level of real integration and was too context-based in a very favourable growth environment not reproductible now;
ii. the expected dynamic process would be an utopian view, due to the institutional and governance weaknesses which could deviate or exploit regionalism for protectionist appetite or vested interests for postponing the necessary reforms;
iii. the basic process would be too risky for being too long for gathering on time sufficient momentum and power;

On the first objection, although it is true that the European case is not transferable as such to other regions, European experiments illustrate a trial-and-error process that wasted too much time but allowed for finding out pragmatic methods which are universal as they reflect human being behaviours, and not economic or institutional aspects. These methods could be successfully adapted to each region and applied for launching a process to be tailored to the specific needs of each group of countries. A first, very important (forgotten) lesson to draw from the historical experience of the European case, is that this region actually started its integration from a pure monetary cooperation — contrary to the conventional view which uses to present monetary and macroeconomic cooperation as a result of trade integration and a *coronation process*. Indeed, the European Payment Union (EPU) in 1949, filled the vacuum left by the failure of the Sterling's convertibility in 1947 and the insufficient resources of the IMF dollar-denominated borrowing rights for the European members. The macro-monetary stabilization was a precondition for an effective trade integration. This basic principle was easier to fulfil in the 1950s in the fixed exchange-rate regime of Bretton Woods. Today, in a much more instable world, this fundamental law remains even more valid and is the priority.

The European success story demonstrates two essential facts: (i) the decisive contribution that a monetary regional agreement can bring to the multilateral order and (ii) the regional monetary cooperation launched a concrete practice of macroeconomic policy coordination which was the keystone for the post-war recovery and the creation of the European custom union with the European Economic Community (institution-building).

These lessons bring to *the second objection* about governance, which is implicitly based on a Eurocentric view. In the new geopolitical context combined to the still high pressures of globalization, regionalism becomes an effective way for improving governance and making up for the weaknesses of national governance, because this new context has reversed the relative importance of the advantages of regional integration in comparison with the European historic case: the static advantages of preferential trade have become less important than the dynamic advantages of institution-building and of improving the decision-making process. The regional level has the power to compensate for the lack of sufficient checks-and-balances at national level, becoming so an important learning and emulation process for policy-makers. regional dimension is a powerful tool with which to make up for institutional failures, insofar as it provides tangible net gains to national policy makers; these benefits can easily be struck through mutual monitoring of macroeconomic policies at the sub-regional level that focuses on their compatibility and acts as a catalyst for cooperative attitudes among national policy makers as well as for strengthening the institutional underpinnings of economies. In turn, a higher rate of sustainable growth should result. Such a positive process works when it uses both *carrot and stick* to both incentives to be cooperative and deterrent to penalize divergences.

This new reality allows for rejecting *the third objection* about the time necessary to launch a successful integration. Again, this objection reflects a static Eurocentric view, based on the idea that the European slowness should be the necessary model, spending half a century for reaching a partial integration. But precisely, the higher importance of national governance for engaging a monetary cooperation associated with the effective scrutiny of neighbouring partners should trigger and accelerate the dynamic process of regional cooperation. Indeed, integration is neither a linear process nor a static one because it generates tipping points creating a positive-sum game in which the positive outcome increases as the game is repeated and extended, becoming rapidly a cumulative wave acting upon policy-makers incentives and public opinion awareness. This allows for leading to beneficial regional institution-building and the emergence of a macroeconomic regional public good, both improving governance. Such a *cooperation for learning* could spurs the very dynamic process necessary to the creation of macroeconomic regional cooperation. The important lesson is that, because of the endogenous nature of the gains from cooperation (and integration), the more time goes by and the more countries interact (and the more interdependencies emerge), the higher the gain from coordination and the lower the interest in defecting. Furthermore, as explained by Axelrod (1984), "the most promising finding is that, if the rules of cooperation theory are known by the participants in advance, the evolution of cooperation can be speeded up". Hence, given the dynamic dimension of cooperation, the incentives to play cooperatively emerge insofar as cooperation is effective, visible and credible, and they displace the incentives to act non-cooperatively, weakening the national populism.

In addition to these systemic aspects, a new sense of urgency is taking speed under the perception of the global warming threat which require regional actions and financing means. Combined with the new external context of geopolitical threats combined with greater financial instability and the growing power of market sanctions, there is a decisive premium on the quality of national institutions and governance: policy-makers incentives are higher than it used to be in Europe half a century ago. On that time, the geopolitical considerations with the Soviet threat, were already a significant cohesion factor for regional integration in Europe. The same kind of factor is again present in the world but it is combined with new competition pressures, explaining that the speed of change could be much higher than it used to be in the European integration. As a consequence, the political economy principles extracted from the European case have become stronger and universal. This is especially true for the pragmatic ways for breaking the trap of the prisoner dilemma that blocked cooperation when national actors are politically independent of each other but economically interdependent.

The main valid lessons drawn from the European experiments (bad and good) are some basic political economy principles related to how to escape the prisoner dilemma for reaping the benefits of macro-monetary cooperation at regional level.

6.3. The political economy recipe for escaping the prisoner dilemma

The European case and other experiments in Africa and Latin America reveal the solution to the prisoner dilemma (Ghymers C. 2005)[17]:

> emerged from the development of personal contacts among policy makers within a collective effort to monitor each economy from a regional perspective, thereby allowing it to be viewed as a continuous game, which, it was hoped, would enhance the credibility of domestic policies. This multi-faceted approach created specific incentives for individual participants to cooperate at the regional level, thereby creating a positive-sum game in which the positive outcome increased with the iteration of the game. Hence, the prisoner's dilemma was resolved through the dynamics of the game: that players had to meet over a long and undefined period, that they could not escape the consequences their decisions had on fellow participants, that the incentives to defect diminished over time and were commensurate with the strengthening of integration, that players learned more and more about each other, that rewards and sanctions were administered progressively and allowed the balance of benefits and costs to be identified, reducing uncertainty regarding the results

[17] Ghymers C. [2005], *Fostering economic policy coordination in Latin America; the REDIMA approach to escaping the prisoner's dilemma*, ECLAC book n°82, Chile: United Nations.

of cooperation — all these factors implied that the cost of non-cooperation rose rapidly with time, and positive outcomes increased with the iteration of the game.

The detailed recipe to initiate a pragmatic process of macroeconomic co-operation among sovereign policy authorities (the step 2 mentioned above) could be built along these principles:

1. the *prisoner dilemma* relies on a lack of trusted information. Therefore, it is necessary to intensify communication among the parties involved, thereby reducing risks of misunderstandings and uncertainty and building trust. The following recipe proved to be the most efficient:
   - to circumvent the traditional logic of formal international bargaining by *reversing the conventional way international relations* and integration diplomacy has been generally using to work: to start betting upon the technical experts (macroeconomists) by allowing them to create their own network for organizing regular, personal and confidential exchanges of views and information, in order to prepare the pertinent background elements for ulterior political decision meetings.
   - this *two-tier system* engages a positive-sum game in which the beneficial outcome increases as the technical game is repeated, since the participants have to meet in a long process without the possibility to escape the consequences of their analysis, but players learn more and more about each other, their incentive to cooperate fully increases. However this dynamic process works well only if the technical level — which does not take any decision — is based on personal contacts of technicians who enjoy some degree of continuity and autonomy. Thus, the permanent national members must be allowed to act strictly confidentiality (*Chatham rule*) under their own personal professional responsibility, and not as the representatives of their ministers because they don't meet for negotiate, but only prepare (*closed doors*) the information of their respective national authorities.
   - this experimented method permits a fast development of a team spirit, building mutual confidence, collegiality and emulation among participants as they face common issues and constraints. This reduces uncertainty, improve *mutual understanding*, and leads to identifying differences and raising awareness of the common interests shared

by all participants. Participants win motivation and increase their credibility inside their own administration as they provide their ministers with key-inside information. Another advantage of this specific type of network is the greater motivation and continuity of technicians compared with political teams or officials directly linked to the cabinet.

2. *applied to step 2*, the technical group is dedicated:
   · first to monitoring the specific monetary arrangement (step 1) and to issue recommendations to the decision-makers.
   · second, inevitably, this kind of monitoring will soon be obliged to *discuss exchange-rate development*, leading subsequently to examine each policy-mix backing these exchange-rate movements. The key-mechanism for moving from a pure monetary arrangement to a sustainable regional integration is to make the exchange-rate evolution a *matter of common concern* for the region, providing a tangible opportunity to undertake at regional level a technical dialogue (closed doors) on each country's internal policies. This was the pragmatic way which emerged, after many failed alternatives in Europe (thanks to the European Monetary System and its Exchange-Rate Mechanism). This lesson is confirmed by the opposite practices in other regions where a lack of dialogue and cooperation on exchange-rate policies significantly contributes to the failure of regional integration.
   · third, in conformity with the main purpose of these regional monetary arrangements, and as a consequence of the previous dialogue, participants will deal with the possible formula to use local currencies for intra-regional transactions, then about setting a regional clearing among participants, and so on (i) the currency to use for the payments of their intra-regional balances, and (ii) the creation of a Regional Monetary Fund (RMF) for financing intra-regional imbalances and adjustment policies. At this stage, technicians have to discuss what would be the best option: to create their own regional monetary standard (like a regional basket of national currencies) or to opt for a direct multilateralization by using the existing SDR, the cost of which for bundling it from key-currencies is decreasing with the new

technologies. In the first option, the regional monetary reserve must be fully convertible and could appear as a necessary complication with respect to the SDR option. Indeed, the choice of the regional reserve currency conditions also the working of the RMF and its possible relations with other regional schemes as well as with the multilateral institutions and their resources. The best technical formula would probably be what Triffin already proposed repetitively in the fifties and sixties to several regions: national central banks of a region in integration would deposit to the regional fund part of their own reserves, opening the possibility to finance national adjustment under their own conditionalities. The simplest formula is to convert these reserves and all regional financial loans in SDR. This opens also automatically a possibility to discuss with the other RMF and the IMF new formulas of cooperation and coalition.

The step 2 indicates a pragmatic scheme based on dialogue among autonomous actors, creating *mutual trust to escape the Prisoner's Dilemma for participants own interests.* This dialogue is conducted in a way that recognizes that each government legitimately tends to act in its own national interest and the most advantageous for each technical participant. This method makes possible to arrive at a minimum consensus on policies and an acceptance of some basic common rules. In such a process, dialogue stimulates self-discipline by increasing the incentives of both technicians and policy-makers for reaping the benefits of successful integration and for preventing the costs of divergence: participants cooperative attitude is moved by the best interests of each of them to extract benefits from the regional public good, *that is* individual rationality tends to become not opposed to collective rationality, so, the prisoner dilemma vanishes in this process. As already expressed by Triffin (1957)[18]:

> National interests should be made to coincide, through a double mechanism of deterrents and incentives, with the collective interests of the group. Reciprocity and mutual help are the keystones of such a construction (Triffin, 1957).

[18] Triffin R., *op.cit.* p.246

6.4. Creation of several regional monetary systems each endowed with their Regional Monetary Fund (RMF)

Regional monetary integration and economic integration are intertwined and the role of monetary aspects in the integration process is largely debated. Without entering into this «religious war» on the «chicken and egg» origin, it is a pragmatic fact that the present emergence of regional monetary arrangements should help to move to step 2, in which the progress of cooperation and macroeconomic dialogue should make more tangible to policy-makers the national interests they could reap by cooperating. The actions of the incentives/deterrents (through financial markets and national public opinions) will ease a deeper development of monetary and financial cooperation, which in turn eases the economic integration and then should ease too the move to step 3 through an inter-regional dialogue for forging common position. Again, the European trial-and-error process indicates some pragmatic paths which could be applicable elsewhere.

Any monetary arrangement has to decide about the monetary vehicle and financial needs for the working of their clearing houses between local currencies. In step 2, pooling of reserves and financial mechanisms for balance of payments as well as for regional development banks, would be easily converted in SDR using the almost no-transaction costs of the emerging Distributed Ledger Technology (DLT) of block-chain, for bundling or de-bundling SDR from or into key-currencies as well as local ones (Ghymers 2020[19]).

Therefore, an interesting mechanism for the regions trying to achieve their integration, consists in using each Regional Monetary Funds — RMF», as a carrot for spurring the macroeconomic dialogue and accelerating so the coordination of national macroeconomic policies. This was also a fundamental mechanism used by Triffin [1957] in the EPU and was a key-component of his successive plans for the European Community in the fifties and sixties. This kind of regional funds would be used as *solidarity financing* mechanisms that ideally should be *expressed directly in SDR*, which soon will be convertible without almost no costs in any currency. The access to these regional resources would be submitted to conditionalities fixed by the regional authorities,

---

[19] Ghymers C. (2020), *The Emerging Revolution of Digital Currencies: a Technological Opportunity for Rebalancing the International Monetary System*, RTI Paper no. 13, Torino: Centro Studi sul Federalismo.

among which the obligation for each member state to participate to a «*regional monitoring exercise*» of the national policies for being eligible and having a say in the allocation of the resources of this regional fund. This idea was already organized by Triffin for the EPU (1949), and he had been repeatedly promoting it to the European Community since its creation in 1958 up to the European Monetary System. In intra and inter-regional dialogues, the issues of exchange-rate movements, clearing systems, RMF with the choice of monetary reserves, will become key-aspects to be discussed both inside each region and between regions. These exchanges should allow to identify common interests and possible joint-actions.

6.5. The game-changer of the multiplication of regional monetary systems and RMF

A generalization of these RMF leads to imagine the scenario of a significant ownership of effective coordination of national policies, implying a clear improvement in national governances everywhere, giving access to the dynamic process of deepening their respective integration, and benefiting from an added value through a higher credibility and effectiveness of decisions and public actions as a result of this regional coordinated approach. Regional monetary arrangements have so the power to create *regional public goods* generating credibility and incentives for policy-makers respecting the regional conditionalities as far as the effective results of regional monitoring and access to solidarity RMF reduce the risk-premium whereas market sanctions act as deterrent on policies opposed to the regional monitoring recommendations.

Such successful results should produce a convergence between regions, making more attractive an inter-regional dialogue. First, useful exchanges-of-best-practices could produce positive learning cooperation, and, second, on this basis, the search for common interests and actions should lead to specific cooperation between the different RMF. From this dynamic process, coalitions or alliances with potential impacts on the credibility of the respective regional schemes could emerge. In particular, an inter-regional kind of coordination among these regions on specific objectives would strengthen the resilience of each region and overall would increase the weight of the coalition group of these cooperating regions. Rapidly, the interregional dialogue could so look for a consensus on propositions to reform the IMS.

At this point, a systemic negotiation with the IMF, the Hegemon and other countries would appear as an inevitable tipping point in the improvement of the global monetary order for the benefits of all. An additional public good at multilateral level would become the natural target of regional monetary arrangements and would generate a significant advantage for all participants. The most important benefit would be the macro-financial stability by escaping to the Triffin Dilemma and to the risk of damaging currency competition. Also, a combination of the different RMF and safety-nets with the access to multilateral financial resources, would generate a value-added through the complementarity between regional and multilateral funds. This would correspond to an agreement on a decentralization of the IMF missions, while the IMF would play the role of global federal system, able to promote a kind of coordination of the different regional schemes. In the same agreement, the national and regional reserves could opt for the SDR as common reserve currency.

The expected new IMS would result from a pragmatic application of the *subsidiarity principle to the IMS*: on one hand, an effective decentralization of the IMF by mandates given to regional monitoring schemes, conditionalities, and RMF, on the other a re-federalization by making each region to adopt a common multilateral safe asset which will be issue as the liability of an upgrading the IMF into a global LOLR *that is* a genuine global central bank, which will regulate the global liquidity by open-market policy controlling so the global monetary base. This upgraded IMF could provide additional resources to the regional schemes, under conditionalities to bargain with each case, particularly by reshuffling all the existing financing multilateral tools and safety-nets. In case of need for more liquidity or for emergency safety-net needs, the global LOLR will buy eligible reserves to national central banks by issuing the new multilateral safe assets (the new SDR). This liability of the global system is not any-more neither a basket of key-currencies, nor a debt of any economy, its increases (or reductions) do not change the degree of indebtedness of the issuers of national key-currencies, making possible a technical increase or decrease of the global liquidity. In case of an excess of liquidity — the global LOLR will sell national T-bills or bonds to national central banks which pay their purchases with their multilateral safe assets, reducing so the global monetary base and the resulting global liquidity.

The global LOLR operations would be entirely decided collegiately by all the central banks of the IMF members on purely technical criteria, proposed by IMF staff, debated with all the regions, and approved by a qualified majority of central bankers. This aspect is important for preserving central banks independence from the Finance Ministers and would imply to create a Central Bank Board inside the Board of Directors of the new IMF. The existing IMF Board would of course be endowed with the right to question publicly the central bank board decisions and criteria, and to engage open debates worldwide among the economist profession.

Conclusion

The present trend towards strategic reactions against the dollar dependence provides an opportunity to re-build the IMS on a more balanced way. Urgent challenges like the financing of de-carbonization and restoring financial stability will impose anyway to eradicate the Triffin Dilemma which perversely deviate saving flows towards US consumption. However, such a structural adjustment exposes the global economy to serious risks, because de-dollarization implies that the positive roles of the dollar have to be fulfilled not by another key-currency, but at multilateral level. Seizing the cooperation opportunity provides by regional monetary arrangements allows for escaping the dangers of a currency competition among a few national key-currencies which would make worse the flaws of the present IMS based upon a dominant dollar. The recipe for making possible a genuine reform of the IMS is based on overcoming the prisoner's dilemma both at regional and inter-regional levels, thanks to the dynamic process of mutual trust that the regional monetary arrangements provides by creating regional public goods offering benefits to all the cooperative participants, especially by creating RMF. Indeed, regular, autonomous and confidential free exchanges between national technical experts generated by the monitoring of the modalities of these arrangements would create a dynamic process of mutual trust and common views. This dynamic moves also the national authorities making tangible the joint-advantages of their cooperation giving access to RMF, with credibility win visible in the reduction of financial spreads (their respective risk-premium on financial markets), while, on the contrary market sanctions act as deterrent for uncooperative policies. Monetary regional cooperation speeds up their regional integration by making more tangible for public opinions, the national interests to be cooperative, a system of incentives and deterrents being linked to the results of the collegial monitoring through the RMF access. The same recipe is applicable in a second step to an inter-region dialogue which leads to organize joint research for common interests, in particular for gathering weight and speaking with a single voice for re-constructing a multilateral monetary order based on the need for a single multilateral safe asset issued by a LOLR able to control global liquidity. This single safe asset would not any-more be a national debt but a liability on the multilateral system. To initiate this process, an important step would be to use the already existing SDR as the currency in which all regional operations and RMF would be libelled. The new technologies based on the block-chain will eradicate the transactions costs implied by bundling and de-bundling the SDR from and to local currencies.

References

Caballero R., Farhi E., Gourinchas P.O. (2017), "The Safe Assets Shortage Conundrum", *Journal of Economic Perspectives*, Vol. 31, No. 3, Summer 2017.

Ghymers C. (2024), "Fostering the Dynamics of the Bi-regional Summit EU-CELAC for Spurring the Cooperation in Climate Change", in Ribeiro Hoffmann, A., *Climate Change in Regional Perspective*, Cham: Springer, https://link.springer.com/book/10.1007/978-3-031-49329-4

Ghymers C. (2022), *The new form of the Triffin Dilemma and its built-in de-stabilizer: the process of relative shortage of dollar safe assets*, IRELAC policy Working paper 2022/07& RTI working paper.

Ghymers C. (2021), *The systemic instability of ballooning Global Liquidity as a symptom of the worsening of the Triffin Dilemm*a, RTI Paper no. 15, Torino: Centro Studi sul Federalismo.

Ghymers C. (2021), "The Systemic Nature of the Global Crisis and Some Principles for Tackling It", in De Souza G. & others, *Financial Crisis Management and Democracy*, Cham: Springer, https://link.springer.com/book/10.1007/978-3-030-54895-7

Ghymers C. (2020), *The Emerging Revolution of Digital Currencies: a Technological Opportunity for Rebalancing the International Monetary System*, RTI Paper no. 13, Torino: Centro Studi sul Federalismo.

Ghymers C. (2005), *Fostering economic policy coordination in Latin America; the REDIMA approach to escaping the prisoner's dilemma*, ECLAC book n°82, Chile: United Nations.

Ghymers C. (1986), "Réagir à l'emprise du dollar", in M. Aglietta, *L'Ecu et la Vieille Dame*, Paris: Economica, 1986.

Gourinchas P. O., Rey H. and Govillot N. (2017), *Exorbitant Privilege and Exorbitant Duty*. IMF Working paper.

Kareken J. and Wallace N. (1981), "On the indeterminacy of equilibrium exchange rates", *The Quarterly Journal of Economics*, 96(2), pp. 207–222.

Lucas R. (1990), "Why doesn't Capital Flow from Rich to Poor Countries?," *American Economic Review*. 80(2): 92–96.

Rey H. (2013), *Dilemma not Trilemma: The Global Financial Cycle and Monetary Policy Independence*, Kansas City: Federal Reserve Bank of Kansas City Economic Policy Symposium.

Triffin International Foundation (2014), *Using the Special Drawing Rights as a Lever to Reform the International Monetary System*, RTI Paper No. 1, https://www.triffininternational.eu/images/RTI/articles_papers/SDR-WP_Final-Report-May-2014.pdf.

Tran H. (2024), *Dedollarization via local currency cross-border payments: democratization and fragmentation of the global system*, Paper prepared for Lisbon conference.

Triffin R. (1964a), *Report on the possibilities of Establishing a Clearing and Payments Union in Africa*, United Nations Economic and Social Council, E/CN 14/262.

Triffin R. (1964b), "Hacia una organización monetaria latinoamericana", in Wionezek, M. S., *Integración de América Latina*, México: Fondo de Cultura Económica, 224–270.

Triffin R. (1961), "Grandeur et décadence de l'étalon-or", *Stato Sociale*, n°10, Turin, 827–838.

Triffin R. (1959), *The international monetary position of the United States*, Hearing before the Joint Economic Committee of the US Congress, 28 October 1959, Employment, Growth, and Price Levels - Google Books, reprinted in Triffin, R. (1960), *Gold and the Dollar Crisis*, Yale; Yale University Press.

Triffin, R. (1957), *Europe and the Money Muddle*, New Haven: Yale University Press, p. 303.

Shin H. S. (2012), "Global Banking Glut and Loan Risk Premium", *IMF Economic Review*, Vol. 60, No. 2.

The Prospects for Regional Monetary Unions in a Changing Global Context

Jean-Claude Brou

Introduction

The Bretton Woods institutions, namely the International Monetary Fund (IMF) and the World Bank were established in the aftermath of World War II to promote and reinforce multilateralism and international economic cooperation. These institutions were created to ensure financial stability, facilitate global economic reconstruction, and foster sustainable development. However, nearly eight decades later, despite significant progress, the global economy stands at a critical crossroads.

The multiple shocks affecting the world today disproportionately affect developing countries and underline the need to reform the global governance system. These shocks have particularly highlighted the limitations of the current international monetary system in addressing global challenges, underscoring the necessity for comprehensive reform in global governance. The celebration of the 80th anniversary of the Bretton Woods Conference provides a timely opportunity to reflect on the future of multilateralism, especially through the perspective of regional monetary unions.

In the next section, we will discuss the global challenges facing the international monetary system. We will then demonstrate how Monetary Unions can reinforce multilateralism and contribute to better address these new challenges. The third section will present the experience of the West African Economic and Monetary Union (WAEMU), highlighting the factors behind its resilience and economic performance.

1. Global challenges for the International Monetary System

Today, the world faces a myriad of challenges that disproportionately affect developing countries. These include recurring climatic shocks, the lingering effects of the COVID-19 pandemic, impact of geopolitical tensions, and security crises, particularly in regions like the Sahel in West Africa. These crises have highlighted the inadequacies of the current international monetary system in addressing global issues effectively.

One of the most pressing issues is the energy transition. As countries strive to reduce their carbon footprint and transition to renewable energy sources, the financial and technological requirements are immense. Despite some progress made, the current international monetary system has not adequately supported this transition, leading to disparities across regions and exacerbating global inequalities. Indeed, it still faces many difficulties in tackling global challenges and addressing the inefficient allocation of public goods.

Indeed, the effects of climate change pose a significant threat to financial stability. Developing countries, which contribute the least to global emissions, often suffer the most from the consequences of climate change. These include extreme weather events, rising sea levels, and disruptions to agriculture and water supplies. An effective international monetary system should be able to facilitate the flow of resources to these vulnerable regions to help them adapt and mitigate the impacts of climate change.

Food security is another critical issue. The COVID-19 pandemic has, among other, disrupted global supply chains, leading to food shortages and price increases in many parts of the world. The international monetary system needs to support mechanisms that ensure more efficient and climate smart production systems as well as stable and resilient food supply chains. Various trade restrictions on food products need to be banned to allow optimal allocation of resources.

Pandemic management has also highlighted major flaws in the system. There is an urgent need for a more coordinated and supportive international monetary system. The uneven distribution of vaccines and medical supplies during the COVID-19 pandemic has exposed the limitations of the current system. Mechanisms must be put in place to ensure that all countries have equal access to medical treatment as well as adequate resources to manage public health crises.

Security crises, particularly those occurring in the Sahel, have profound humanitarian, economic and social impacts. These crises have a negative impact on private investment. They also lead to significant expenditures on security, diverting resources from essential investments in infrastructure and human development. Security is a public good that needs to be addressed at a global level. Greater support should be provided to countries facing such challenges, helping them to maintain stability and productive investment for long-term development.

In light of these challenges, it is clear that the international monetary system needs to be reformed to better address transnational problems and ensure more balanced and equitable multilateralism. Faced with slow progress in this process and rising geopolitical tensions in a more fragmented world, regional economic and monetary unions can provide alternative solution. The experience of existing Monetary Unions can provide valuable insights into how such systems might be designed and implemented.

2. The Role of Monetary Unions in Multilateralism

Monetary unions can greatly contribute to address current economic fragmentation and revive multilateralism. By their very nature, these unions promote deeper integration among member states. They achieve this by eliminating or substantially reducing economic, monetary, and financial barriers, thereby facilitating an environment conducive to free trade and cross-border payments, as well as financial stability. As such, it promotes economic growth and social development. This, in turn, solidifies the foundations of multilateralism.

The increased cooperation required in a monetary union extends far beyond financial arrangements. It necessitates a close coordination of monetary, economic, and fiscal policies, enabling member countries to respond more effectively to global economic challenges and better distribute the economic and social costs of shocks.

Moreover, the principle of solidarity is of paramount importance to the functioning of monetary unions. This principle is essential to foster a more balanced and equitable multilateralism. The interest of richer countries is linked to the progress of the poorest ones (Shared interest is the key to success). As such, monetary unions provide a suitable framework for addressing global challenges in a more effective way.

The emergence of monetary unions can also help mitigate the polarization of influence around a limited number of countries or blocs, which is a constraint to multilateralism. As cooperation is the essence, monetary unions can contribute to the promotion of a more balanced and inclusive international order.

In a monetary union, the shared vision among member states is reinforced through common policies and institutions. This increased cooperation often extends to other areas, such as security, social policies, and environmental initiatives. Fostering collaboration across these domains allows monetary unions to strengthen the overall regional stability and promote development. Hence, it provides a robust framework for multilateralism that addresses both economic and non-economic challenges.

Monetary unions have undeniable advantages, but they can also involve a number of challenges. Indeed, their sustainability must be based on specific and fundamental principles, the most important ones being the following:

- a strong commitment from members to cooperate to overcome any crisis together. It involves the ability to make consensual decisions for the good of the community.
- a close coordination between monetary policy, fiscal and economic policies, with an independent central bank and the establishment of agreed fiscal rules, enabling countries to respond collectively and more effectively to global economic challenges and crises. This policy synergy is essential to maintain economic stability and to address global turbulences. In case of deviation from the fiscal rules, a clear process of returning to the agreed path must be implemented.
- strong, independent and transparent institutions are essential to carry out the regional agenda and to strengthen public confidence in the Union.

In light of the recent multifaceted crisis that the world has experienced these past few years, a coordinated response between a group of countries with a shared vision and common objectives has proved to be a more effective alternative.

3. The Experience of the West African Economic and Monetary Union (WAEMU)

The West African Economic and Monetary Union (WAEMU), established on May 12, 1962, comprises eight developing countries in West Africa, with a total population of 142 million and a GDP of $199,0 billion in 2023. The union is characterized by a common currency, the CFA Franc, pegged to the euro through a fixed exchange rate, with full convertibility guaranteed by the French Treasury. The currency is issued by a common Central Bank.

WAEMU is also distinguished by its unified banking regulatory and supervisory framework. More specifically, any bank or financial institution can operate across all the eight Member States without applying for new licenses in each country. Banking supervision is carried out by the same entity, the Banking Commission. This regional organization facilitates effective crisis prevention, management, and resolution across member states.

A notable feature of WAEMU is the pooling of foreign exchange reserves, enabling member states to access these resources for balance of payments support and foreign liquidity needs. This mechanism has proven to be particularly valuable in times of crisis.

Additionally, the Monetary Union has established an Economic Union with free movement of people, goods, services, managed by a Regional Institution. This is supported by harmonized tax systems. The establishment of a Common External Tariff (CET) and the harmonization of indirect taxes, such as VAT and excise duties, has further integrated the economies of the region.

WAEMU's unified financial market allows member states to issue bonds and treasury bills on the regional market, in order to mobilize financial resources. This integrated market allows not only governments but also the private sector to access savings from other countries within the Union. Banks, in particular, can easily access excess liquidity from other banks across the Union through the single interbank market. This system has allowed efficient liquidity distribution and significantly fostered investment and economic growth throughout the region.

The common Central Bank for WAEMU (BCEAO) has also initiated important projects to promote financial inclusion and the digitalization of the economy at the regional level. For instance, the development of interoperable digital payment systems across the union aims to enhance financial access and efficiency in the eight countries. Discussions are also underway to explore the prospect for introducing a central bank digital currency, which could further streamline transactions and enhance financial inclusion.

The region also features a development Bank for the eight member countries of WAEMU whose role is to finance projects in various sectors that promote economic integration and development in member states. Additionally, a regional stock exchange market operates as an instrument for financial intermediation among these countries.

Over the past two decades, WAEMU has demonstrated remarkable resilience in the face of various crises. During the COVID-19 pandemic, the union recorded positive economic growth of 1.4% in 2020, while the global economy (-2.7%) and Sub-Saharan countries (-1.7%) were in recession. Also, from 2012 to 2019, economic growth in the union averaged 6.3%, compared to 3.6% for sub-Saharan Africa. This performance and resilience can be attributed to several factors, including the union's strong institutional framework, effective policy coordination and the solidarity among member states.

Since 2021, the union's economic growth has returned to pre-pandemic rates, despite ongoing challenges such as climatic shocks, security crises, and the effects of geopolitical tensions. Economic growth is estimated to reach 5.4% in 2023, after 5.7% in 2022. In 2024, growth is expected to be 6.3%. This robust growth trajectory underscores the effectiveness of the union's policies and institutions in managing crises and fostering development.

Inflation, which peaked at 8.8% in August 2022, has been brought under control and now stands at 2.7% as of January 2024. In comparison, the inflation rate in Sub Saharan Africa is 16.2% in 2023. The achievement of the WAEMU reflects the successful coordination of monetary and fiscal policies to counteract the effects of rising world food and oil prices as well as the post-Covid inflationary pressures.

However, the magnitude of recent shocks has led to significant expenditures and subsidies by governments to mitigate the social consequences of the crises. As a result, the union's debt ratio increased from 43% in 2019 to 52% in 2023. The reliance on the regional financial market to mobilize resources, in the context of tightening international financial conditions, has also led to an increase in domestic interest rates, with treasury bill rates rising from 4,0% in 2019 to 6,1% in 2023.

The experience of WAEMU offers valuable lessons. Four key factors have been critical to the effective functioning and sustainability of the union:

- Monetary Union as a shock absorber for members: the monetary union acts as a buffer against economic shocks, preserving monetary and financial stability and maintaining investor confidence. This stability is crucial for attracting investment and fostering economic growth.
- Coordination of Policies: better coordination of fiscal and monetary policies among member states enhances economic performance and policy effectiveness. Sharing best practices, particularly in national fiscal policies, has been a significant factor in the union's success. The existence of a regional market and fiscal convergence Pact, which sets rules for external and internal debt of member countries, further enhances the effectiveness of monetary policy.
- Principle of Solidarity: the union's solidarity ensures mutual support among member countries during crises, facilitating access to both international and domestic liquidity. This solidarity is essential to maintain stability and address imbalances within the union. For instance, a country experiencing a balance of payment shock can still benefit from the international liquidity of the other member states (pool of foreign exchange) to conduct its economic policy and cover its external payments. The mechanism therefore prevents such countries from defaulting on their external debt, provided actions are taken to correct the imbalance according to the fiscal rule.
- Strong and Independent Regional Institutions: effective functioning of the union relies on strong, transparent, and independent regional institutions capable of managing effects of negative shocks and maintaining policy coherence. These institutions provide a framework for peer surveillance and support, ensuring that member states comply with agreed upon policies and rules.

WAEMU is currently discussing with seven other countries in West Africa to create a larger monetary union within the ECOWAS (Economic Community of West African States) with a combined population of 435 million and a GDP of 686.8 billion US dollars in 2023.

Significant steps have already been achieved in this major regional project, such as the trade liberalization scheme, the establishment of the ECOWAS Monetary Cooperation Program and a multilateral surveillance mechanism for the economic and financial policies of member states. Additionally, a detailed roadmap is being implemented with the objective of creating a single currency and a common Central Bank for ECOWAS in the near future.

Other regions in Africa are also committed to similar processes. These efforts underscore a shared belief among stakeholders that monetary unions have the potential to act as powerful catalysts for stronger multilateral cooperation and economic resilience.

Concluding remarks

In conclusion, the journey towards a more supportive and cooperative global order is challenging but filled with opportunities. Economic integration and solidarity are fostered through regional monetary unions which offer a pathway to a revamped multilateralism. They exemplify how aligning economic policies and pooling resources in a shared vision can collectively build a more prosperous and harmonious future.

As we reflect on the 80th anniversary of the Bretton Woods Conference, it is imperative to consider the role of monetary unions in the construction of a more balanced and resilient international monetary system, capable of addressing the global challenges of the 21st century.

Monetary unions demonstrate the potential of regional integration to enhance financial stability, support economic growth, and promote social and human development. Drawing on the lessons learned from the experiences of WAEMU and others, policymakers can better design frameworks that strengthen cooperation, resilience and shared prosperity in other regions.

Sharing Power in the International Monetary System: A Concrete Step

*Renato G. Flôres Jr.**

"We have been lending long – and even giving funds away – while borrowing short and losing gold"
(From Robert Triffin's Testimony at the Us Congress, October 1959)

The Crisis

Sixty-five years after Triffin's statement above and eighty years after Bretton Woods, the US dollar, the hegemon's currency, faces a crisis of great proportions that shares a few similarities with the one denounced by the Belgo-American economist. To understand it, one should perhaps start by wondering how the US dollar[1] could maintain its universal currency status, even after the 1971 devaluation — predicted around ten years before by Triffin — and the end of the gold standard in 1973.

One of the reasons is the superior military power of the US, uncontested already in 1973 in all non-Soviet world, with boots, navy, aircraft, nuclear warheads and bases spread around the planet, and temporarily reinforced after the fall of the Soviet Union in 1999. This supremacy clearly supports the dollar as the universal currency and directly connects it to a massive and encompassing structure of power.

It is behind the strong opposition of the US to share, even under a multilateral framework, the dollar predominance in several occasions. An emblematic case being the 1975 OPEC members' decision to use International Monetary

---

* Director, FGV IIU International Intelligence Unit, Professor, FGV EPGE Graduate School of Economics. E-mail: renato.flores@fgv.br; I'm indebted to José Luís Cardoso, Christian Ghymers, Fabio Masini, Luís Máximo dos Santos, Anoop Singh, Bernard Snoy and Hung Tran for help, comments and incentive, as well as grateful to the participants in the Lisboa Conference. All ideas are of my sole responsibility and do not involve anybody or anything else.

1 The terms 'US dollar' and 'dollar' are used interchangeably throughout the text.

Fund (IMF)'s Special Drawing Rights (SDR) as a unit of account, jeopardised by Saudi Arabia's opposition. The country enjoys a strong military alliance with the US, hosting bases with substantial ground forces and landed aircraft.

A second one is the enormous complexity of the International Monetary System (IMS). The nowadays System bears a faint resemblance to the one in 1969. The number of agents and possible transactions has grown exponentially, anchored by — many times debatable, in terms of global risk- manifold mathematical developments and formidable, fast computing capacity. Its ever-expanding network, the outgrowth of the interaction among myriad financial institutions, houses and *boutiques* in the Western core, notably in the US, ends up by reinforcing the dollar's predominance.

To many, a change in the current status would seem impossible. However, two key factors have assumed a major dimension.

The US external liabilities and domestic deficit have been spiralling — trillions are the unit of accounting — and dollar assets' holders around the world look with anxiety at their uncontrolled growth. The perverse combination of serious domestic deficits and foreign account increasing liabilities, a situation described in 1959 by Triffin, comes round in a much more disturbing way and, sooner or later, a crisis is inevitable.

Moreover, the hegemon, miscalculating its power, has meddled in too many world affairs and is at present involved, directly or indirectly, in well more than a dozen of violent conflicts around the world, of which around three risks escalating to the nuclear option. An unacceptable danger.

The blind euphoria lasting five to ten years after the fall of the Soviet Union gave way to despair, messy global management and fragmentation. The world has been drowning into an increasing state of flux, together with blunt disrespect for the multilateral institutions and continuous disregard of international law. There is no week when multilateral agreements and decisions or canons of international law are not violated under, most of times, *brute force* arguments and practices.

The hegemon has been abusing its power in several ways. The most recent is the weaponisation of different aspects of international life[2]. It has resorted to an illegal and unbounded use of sanctions of all sorts, hitting the supposed *enemies*, the *friends of the enemies* and *those who transact with the friends*

---

2 See Drezner et al. (2021).

of enemies, in a chain of prohibitions and restrictions whose consequences have not been duly evaluated, besides hurting millions of innocent people. Financial sanctions have reached the unimagined point of sovereign financial assets confiscations, tearing basic rules of the international code of conduct.

Textbooks tell that the universal currency must enjoy more than sufficient liquidity and be safe; it must encompass both qualities in an elusive, immaterial and key one, credibility. The US dollar credibility has staggered, its safety virtues became highly debatable and its liquidity something in the hands of a benevolent god[3]. No lender of last resort nowadays is able to cope with a serious dollar crisis — no need even to be global.

The non-Western core, that is all countries outside the US and the European Union (EU), the Global South[4] in modern terms, lives in a state if not of fear, certainly of great insecurity as regards the hegemon's currency.

In this picture, it is hard to find room to talk about solutions leading to new multilateral formats or enlarging or promoting the classical idea of monetary unions. Endeavours in this area should concentrate in protecting, preserving as much as possible of the frail existing multilateral architecture, coupled with stubborn fighting for the respect of international law: both under severe threat. It is idle to conceive new global institutions and arrangements.

1. Steps to possible solutions

Efforts, within the context of this Conference, should be directed to both inducing and creating concrete realities to push other currencies or mechanisms to substitute the hegemon in select instances of the IMS.

Maybe surprisingly, this may be a way to ease world tensions and lower global uncertainties. The hegemon must be peacefully led to accept sharing power and reducing presence in a set of IMS transactions, what may contribute — eventually and ironically — to his very survival.

It is well known that use of multiple reserve currencies increases and diversifies the quantity of available reserve assets. Alternatives for the dollar

---

3 The reader may choose the god he/she prefers, all are in dire need.

4 Global South is a purposively loose term; its focus is perhaps to call attention that manifold countries outside the US-EU core, even those that one may consider irrevocably tied to it, may someday or somehow strongly diverge from it. Probably all cherish more autonomy from it.

are no novelty. The yen, thanks to the top Japanese banking sector, and the euro, since its creation in 1999, have tried to occupy relevant positions in the System; but they lacked the clout of the hegemon.

In a more rational and encompassing view, others have pledged for such role to be performed by IMF's SDR, Flor (2019); something that continues to be pursued today, Ghymers (2022), anchored on the appealing argument that it is an apolitical, multilateral solution. However, this demands changes in the IMF Articles of Agreement, requires a considerable upgrading of the SDR instrument and (multilateral) measures less feasible and attractive in today's turbulent times. The IMF is too close to the hegemon and too bureaucratic[5] to host in the short to medium run a significant change in the structure of the IMS.

Without denying the vast array of possibilities, a simpler and more direct means is through the trade relations, with payments of the associated flows settled in currencies other than the dollar. They are unavoidable and in itself pose less problems.

The movement could begin in a strong core, irradiate from it to closer associates and from them to countries that trade with them and so on. Considering only the original five BRICS members, with 2022 (UN Comtrade) data, 16 percent of their imports came from the very group, while 18 percent from the US-EU core. As regards exports, the corresponding figures are 12 and 34 percent. This, leaves, starting from these base figures of their intra and extra trade, an additional volume of around 66 percent of their imports and 54 of exports likely in principle to switch to other currencies. The table below summarises the findings.

Table: BRICS countries, combined US-EU shares of their imports and exports, 2022.

	Brazil	India	Russia	China	S. Africa	BRICS
Imports	0.31	0.13	0.31	0.15	0.31	0.18
Exports	0.27	0.34	0.37	0.34	0.33	0.34

Source: Flôres (2024).

5 It is worth reminding that the US holds 16.5 percent of the quotas, easily blocking any substantial decision that requires an 85 percent majority.

Of course, not all countries outside the BRICS and US-EU will adopt another currency in their trade payments, and many, even BRICS members like Brazil, India or China, will keep paying for a sizeable share of their flows in dollars. Careful analysis of trade patterns can however provide educated guesses on the amount of change likely to be expected.

In a quite similar reasoning in a world scale, shares of around 40 percent of world exports and 35 percent of imports may be expected to move away from being settled in US dollars, in a few years[6].

Such a dynamic spillsover to other developments in the realm of the IMS.

The first one is in the composition of international reserves. IMF statistics show that, in 2022, already 3 percent of foreign exchange reserves, considering all its members, were claims in Chinese renminbi (RMB). If one excludes the other three currencies that compose the SDR basket, together with the US dollar, 10 percent of claims were in other currencies. These are due to increase.

At the same time, one is tempted to pose the question on the most likely substitute or group of to emerge. This should remain open and unanswered at this stage.

It seems premature to say that replacement will be fulfilled the by RMB, for instance, as many have been arguing of late. The Russian rouble may gain a wider use in Central Asia, the Brazilian real may enjoy adoption in some transactions in South America and even second league competing currencies, like the euro and the yen might grab some extra shares. Gold may undergo higher demand than the one that is already taking place; it may return to back different financial assets, as the recent Indian gold-denominated bonds. Moreover, many countries — perhaps most in the replacement team — will work with different currencies in their trade payments, as they will continue to entertain import-export relations with the US and, notably for a significant group of African countries, the EU.

Notwithstanding, it is perhaps telling that a recent paper by undisputed representatives of the established order[7], Eichengreen et al. (2022), cogently argues that capital account convertibility is not necessarily a requirement for

---

6 For a careful depiction of the argument in this and the previous paragraphs, supported with tables and detailed figures, see Flôres (2024).

7 The first author is a well-known scholar in international finance and, out of the other four, two are with the Banque de France and one with the European Central Bank.

the RMB acquiring reserve currency status. It is hard not to see a geopolitical sign of the present state of affairs regarding the hegemon's currency. The gist of the argument lies in that a wise combination of four facilities — bilateral currency swaps, offshore clearing banks, panda and dim sum bonds and the expanding Crossborder Interbank Paying System (CIPS), a Chinese platform similar to and compatible with SWIFT[8]— can reduce the direct demand for RMB reserve assets, ensuring liquidity and safety to the currency.

Regional agreements less ambitious than monetary unions may have a role in reducing risks — a factor often forgotten in encompassing innovations. The importance of looser integrations, like ASEAN, and of even looser and non-connected ones, like BRICS+ or the Shanghai Co-operation Organisation must not be underestimated. At their side, multilateral development banks, enhancing something that has been taking place already — in the New Development Bank and in the Asian Infrastructure Development Bank-, may ascribe loans in other currencies. It might be not too far-fetched to speculate that in a little more than five years, even the Inter-American Development Bank, IADB, will adhere to the practice, in its Washington DC headquarters.

These are speculations to be better elaborated. Needless to say, a political momentum lies at the heart of such decisions.

2. Impressionistic cost benefit analysis

The proposal will lead us back to a *restricted version* of a multiple currency scenario, a point much discussed during the last decades[9]. Indeed, a long debate can be traced from Friedrich Hayek's several papers on the theme, either under a national or international perspective, summarised in Hayek (1976), to simple though sophisticated theoretical models where it appears as a solution of an optimisation problem, Fahri and Maggiori (2018)[10].

---

8 Namely Society for Worldwide Interbank Financial Telecommunication, an electronic transfers' platform under Belgian law. See Scott and Zachariadis (2014).

9 Some — like Ghymers (2022), notably in section 5 — seem to firmly reject the multiple currencies scenario today.

10 Passing through discussions by different schools of thought, particularly during the seventies; Mann (1971), Klein (1975, 1976) and Tullock (1975), among others.

It may lead to nuisances, from moderate chaos in the exchange rate market to Nurkse Instability[11], for instance.

A global loss of efficiency is unavoidable but should be framed within the current retreat from globalisation, accompanied by a return of increased fragmentation in specific domains and activities. The hegemon will have its exorbitant privilege reduced. If successful, the spillovers in the IMS will lead to modifications in its realm, like in the shares of the individual payment systems — credit cards included — or in the present distribution of power in the international banking system.

The advantage of the 'trade flows start' is that the process, to a certain point, can be controlled, and its possible damages kept moderately under surveillance. Even the multiple currencies scenario, as emphasized at the top of the section, will be limited.

The important point is that everything must take place within a peaceful mode, in a move that, in the mid to long run, through the power sharing by the hegemon may lower international tensions.

More importantly, any remaining inefficiency in a cost benefit appraisal will be negligible if the weekly irrational loss of human lives and deterioration of basic international standards is reduced, thanks to less tension-fuelled conflict.

No action, or sticking to interesting, abstract formulations, deserves a modern and unfortunate adaptation of Triffin's quote at the beginning of the text. Namely that "we have been lending long on beautiful concepts and ambitious structures, while borrowing short on violent and illegal practices, losing — worst of all — dignity".

References

Drezne D. W., Farrell H. and Newman A. L. (2021), *The Uses and Abuses of Weaponized Interdependence.* Washington: Brookings Institution Press.

Eichengreen B., Macaire C., Mehl A., Monnet E. and Naef A. (2022), *Is capital account convertibility required for the renminbi to acquire reserve currency status?,* Working Paper #892,Paris: Banque de France.

11 See Nurkse (1944), sometimes considered as "the most influential study on the interwar currency period". The book was distributed to the delegates convening to a Bretton Woods preparatory session in Atlantic City, weeks before the famous meeting, and there is a lingering academic debate on how far it influenced the final Agreement.

Fahr E. and Maggiori M. (2018), "A model of the International Monetary System", *Quarterly Journal of Economics*, 133, 295–355.

Flor E. (2019), *SDR: From Bretton Woods to a World Currency*, Brussels: Peter Lang.

Flôres R.G. Jr. (2024), "Replacing the dollar in international payments: a preliminary assessment", Forthcoming in *Contemporary World Economics.*

Ghymers C. (2022), *The new form of the Triffin dilemma and its built-in de-stabilizer: the process of relative shortage of dollar safe assets.* Working Paper: December, Louvain-la-Neuve: Robert Triffin International.

Hayek F.A. (1976), *The Denationalisation of Money.* London: Institute of Economic Affairs.

Klein B. (1976), "Competing monies: comment". *Journal of Money, Credit and Banking*, Vol. VIII, No. 4, 513–19.

Klein B. (1975), "The competitive supply of money", *Journalof Money, Credit and Banking*, Vol. VI, No,4, 423–53.

Mann F.A. (1971), *The Legal Aspects of Money*, Third edition, Oxford: Oxford University Press.

Nurkse R. (1944), *International Currency Experience: Lessons of the Inter-war Period*, Geneva: Series of League of Nations Publications. (reprinted in 1947 by the United Nations)

Scott S. V. and Zachariadis M. (2014), *The Society for Worldwide Interbank Financial Telecommunication (SWIFT): Cooperative Governance for Network Innovation, Standards and Community*, London: Routledge.

Tullock G. (1975), "Competing moneys", *Journal. of Money Credit and Banking*, Vol. VII No. 4, 491–7.

80 Year after, towards a New Green and Fair Bretton Woods

Luiz Awazu Pereira da Silva[*]

Introduction

80 years provides a long enough perspective: we all know that the Bretton Woods system had an essential role for restoring global macro-financial stability in a period of great financing needs for post-WWII reconstruction. It had global acceptance and promoted international collaboration. It was built on an agreement on common rules that created consensus around trust in international payments, financing of controlled current account deficits. Those were needed for rebuilding capital stocks after the destructions of the war and to accelerate the industrial revolution in still largely agrarian societies in Europe. It functioned as a global public good, with a stable international monetary system, adjustment mechanisms, an institutional set-up with the World Bank Group, the International Monetary Fund, or IMF, and later on the World Trade Organization.

Yet, the Bretton Woods System ultimately failed due to several interconnected reasons that culminated in its collapse in the early 1970s. The USA, main guarantor of the system over- extended its US dollar liabilities over the rest of the World, ran excessive balance of payments deficits, and therefore created doubts about the promise of gold convertibility underlying trust in the system. We know all that. But let's not focus on why it failed, but rather on what lessons can it give us today, from its almost three decades of success? That is important because we are facing today a bigger but similar challenge: the need for global macro-financial stability and the need for great amounts of short-term liquidity and long-term financing for the transition to Net Zero. We need a new promising direction and framework.

---

[*] Visiting Professor, University of Tokyo. Deputy General Manager of the Bank for International Settlements (2015- 2023), Deputy Governor of the Central Bank of Brazil (2010-2015), Deputy Finance Minister in charge of international affairs (2004-2006).

It should be acknowledged that a "Green Bretton Woods" idea[1] is not entirely new. I will dwell on some of the existing advocacy pleas but elaborate further on how to operationalize them.

There are many similarities *vis-à-vis* the year 1944. Then, the World was rather bipolar but today's fragmented geo-political landscape is turning into a rising rivalry between the West (*e.g.* the US and its close allies) and the Rest (*e.g.* the so-called Global South with in particular the BRICS countries). World War II was ending, with a great portion of physical and human capital destroyed and in need to be rebuild. New technologies were becoming available and had the potential to pose an existential threat to mankind (*e.g.* nuclear power) or to be a source of beneficial transformation. This duality of scientific progress is present today, with the emergence of fintech, Artificial Intelligence, block chain, DeFi, social networks, etc. and its potential usage for the common good or for confrontation. And like in 1944, rebuilding required enormous financial resources and long-term vision from the victors *vis-à-vis* the needs of all countries including former adversaries during the war. That was the spirit of Bretton Woods, to provide public goods (*e.g.* the idea of an international currency, of long-term loans and institutions forming an international monetary system) put in practice by a Marshall Plan to begin rebuilding Europe.

1. So how should we work towards a more ambitious "New Green and Fair Bretton Woods"?

First, we need to construct a consensus around the following narrative for fighting Climate Change: 1) it requires a global, multilateral, urgent collective action program; it is a global negative externality (I called it the Green Swan[2]), a recognized market failure that no single region, country, actor in society can address alone; and it is urgent to act since our remaining carbon

---

[1] See Aguila N., Haufe, P. and Wullweber J., *The Ecor As Global Money: Towards a Green Bretton Woods System to Finance Sustainable and Just Transformation* (July 6, 2022); Brunnhuber S., *Towards a new, green Bretton Woods: How and why an upgraded financial system will change the world*, February 9, 2024.

[2] Bolton P., Pereira da Silva L. A., Despres M., Samama F., Svartzman R. (2020), *The green swan Central banking and financial stability in the age of climate change*, Basel, Switzerland]: Bank for International Settlements, https://www.bis.org/publ/othp31.pdf

budget is worth only about ten years of our current annual emissions of greenhouse gases; 2) it needs a significant amount of financial resources (*e.g.* the best estimates hover around 2% of global GDP in investment for the transition until 2050 but especially in the next half a decade till 2030); these resources are not simply a countercyclical response to a negative shock; they need to be sufficient to engineer a "Schumpeterian" transformation of the global stock of capital, a radical departure from our carbon-intensive production and consumption practices; 3) it requires helping developing countries that do not have these resources to finance them on a sustainable basis; 4) it would benefit from regional and multilateral agreements to use both existing funding (public and private) but also new innovative sources of global financing (*e.g.* the SDRs, issuances of 'green bonds'); and 5) it can be organized into a global framework whose major pieces have been agreed upon (*e.g.* the principles of the Paris Accord in the COPs, the declarations of the G20) but not enshrined in a new explicit format like the Bretton Woods system in 1944.

Second, we need to put on the table a road map laying out the concrete elements of such a new accord.

Institutional framework: we could use existing institutions: *e.g.* the IMF, the World Bank, the system of regional multilateral development banks or MDBs, the alliance of public banks under the Finance In Common initiative or FICs, the many regional monetary, trade and financial agreements and arrangements among group of countries[3]; the critical feature is that it cannot be blocked by any coalition of sub-groups of countries and depend on the existing system of voting power that is plaguing the current Bretton Woods system; so we can also agree on creating a special fit-for-purpose agency or

[3] The European Monetary Union (EMU), the West African Economic and Monetary Union (WAEMU), the East Caribbean Currency Union (ECCU), the Central American Monetary Council, the Common Monetary Area (CMA) in Southern Africa, the Chiang Mai Initiative Multilateralization (CMIM), the Mercosur, the Bank of the South (Banco del Sur), etc. Regional communities can also be an important vehicle for example the Community of Portuguese Language Countries (CPLP) where 6 African central banks plus Timor and Brazil have met annually with the Banco de Portugal (BdP), especially in 2024 under the Presidency of Brazil in the G20.

institutional framework, a vehicle for channeling resources and guaranteeing their sustainability and value over the medium long term.

Financing: we could use existing resources or existing commitments: *e.g.* those of Official Development Assistance (ODA), of the MDBs, of the private alliances such as the Glasgow Financial Alliance for Net Zero (GFANZ) to begin delivering and implementing existing plans and estimates of green projects, top-down and bottom-up approaches (*e.g.* the Stern Report to the G7, the World Banks Country Climate Development Report (CCDR)); and/or we have to enlarge the scope of resources that can be mobilized to leverage more (*e.g.* international taxation[4], new issuances of SDRs[5], enhance the issuance of green financing and bonds[6]).

2. How would a "New Green and Fair Bretton Woods" work to achieve that?

Third, we need to show how this could become operational. In whatever institutional configuration, the process is straightforward: more green projects making the transition to Net Zero need to be financed in a sustainable way (ensuring flows of funding till projects mature), primarily in poor developing countries where resources are clearly insufficient (*e.g.* developed world is already reducing its emissions and China has, admittedly, enough domestic resources and access to international capital markets). In addition, some poor regions of the world need insurance against extreme weather events and the financing of damage and repairs.

---

4 There are many on-going initiatives using as a new tax base international financial transactions, international shipping and transportation, global wealth of specific individuals and groups, *etc.*

5 In response to the global economic impact of the COVID-19 pandemic, the International Monetary Fund (IMF) approved a historic expansion of Special Drawing Rights (SDRs) in 2021. This allocation, amounting to approximately $650 billion, was the largest in the history of the IMF and was designed to provide liquidity to the global economic system by increasing the foreign exchange reserves of its member countries

6 The Green Bond market has been growing fast; while caution is needed to avoid "green washing", the demand for such instruments corresponds to both regulatory changes and investors needs for diversification away from climate risks.

At their inception, green projects in developing countries are profitable but present a perceived financial risk for investors in addition to a liquidity risk. So, they need both long-term financing availability and short-term money, the very essence of the Bretton Woods logic in post-WWII in Europe and the world.

Therefore, the suggestion to by-pass the present gridlock is twofold:

On the liquidity front: the G7 could re-allocate all or part of their current SDR holdings to poor developing countries that have committed Nationally Determined Contributions (NDCs) objectives with pledges to Net Zero and well-formulated strategies detailed in their Country Climate Development Reports (CCDR). While SDRs are not a currency, they can be used to mobilize hard currency liquidity to launch and pay for the current expenditures of a green project. The regional monetary arrangement Central Banks for countries in each region (Africa, Americas, Asia, Europe) can also contribute to short-term funding. More liquidity can also come from the establishment of regional regulated carbon trading systems. Finally, and in addition, a regular inflow from international taxation mechanisms (on the basis of a *club* logic of *coalition of the willing*, private donations, *etc*) would be brought into the incoming flows of funds.

On the long-term financing front: developing countries' green bond issuances, as well as other climate-risk related financial instruments (*e.g.* CAT bonds) could have a *credit enhancement* feature that would make them *investable* by large asset managers, pension funds and even central banks of developed countries. For that, they need to be at least 'Investment Grade (IG)' and therefore it requires a *guarantor* for future repayments. The guarantor of sub-investment grade (IG) green bonds (sovereign and entities) would provide this *credit-enhancement* for these green bonds to become above IG rating (the higher the better) by issuing a guarantee and/or by using special investment vehicles that can pool these risks and issue its own financial asset to be purchased by investors. Such type of securitization is known and has been used in many cases, including in opaque and non-transparent ways in the run-up to the Global Financial Crisis (GFC) for sub-prime mortgages and other mortgage-backed-securities. But this time, the guarantors have to be the MDB system, the FICs alliance, the old Bretton Woods institutions, etc. Under this type of financial construction, that has to be transparent and part of a new Bretton Woods arrangement, these assets (part of them) can even be invested into the reserves of the G7 central banks and/or by Pooled Investment Funds that they already invest in.

Conclusions

To conclude, a New Green and Fair Bretton Woods is needed to restore a truly multilateral monetary system that deals with the biggest collective action problem that we have for socio-economic and political stability in this 21st century: the existential threat and permanent, irreversible damage that climate change is already causing to all of us. The elements proposed above can of course become more ambitious and broader. One can think of digital green SDRs, of global monetary creation, of making more of our MDBs balance sheets, of using new technologies, digital currencies, AI, debt relief and restructuring for development, new climate insurance policies, disclosure of risks called by thc IFRS, regulatory biding processes, *etc*. For the moment, our global political economy does not allow for such leap forward but we need out-of-the-box financial engineering innovations, private-public partnerships, new green guarantees, more liquidity and long-term loans, grants and funds as a new beginning.

The International Monetary System: Building the SDR as a Reserve Asset

Anoop Singh[*]

"The desirable goal of reforming the international monetary system, therefore, is to create an international reserve currency that is disconnected from individual nations and is able to remain stable in the long run, thus removing the inherent deficiencies caused by using credit-based national currencies."[1]

Conception

The Special Drawing Right (SDR) was created in 1969 and conceived under the Bretton Woods gold exchange standard as an official reserve asset to supplement other sources of reserves. In the IMF's Articles of Agreement, the objective was to make the SDR the principal reserve asset of the international monetary system. The governance rules established that the SDR can be allocated with an 85% weighted majority vote of the IMF's membership.

The SDR was seen as having distinct advantages:

- *as a reserve asset:* it would be the only existing instrument which can be issued without being a direct liability of any single economy; therefore, it could be the most rational channel for providing alternative reserves to central banks that plan to build them up for facing any future crisis,

* Distinguished Fellow, Centre for Social and Economic Progress, New Delhi, Member, 15th Finance Commission of India, and former Western Hemisphere and Asia Pacific Director, International Monetary Fund. This paper has benefitted from previous discussions with Michel Camdessus, former Managing Director of the IMF, and Bernard Snoy, Chairman of Robert Triffin International (RTI).

1 Zhou X. (2009), "Reform the International Monetary System", *Equilibri Rivista per lo sviluppo sostenibile*" 2/2009, pp. 161-166, doi: 10.1406/30179

without implying larger deficits for issuers of national reserve currencies. Furthermore, it is the only existing monetary reserve, which can be issued on the basis of international official procedures. Finally, it is the only one that is accepted by *conventional officials and central bankers* since it has an agreed institutional existence firmly locked in the IMF system.

- *as a store of value*: the SDR is by construction an international standard: as it is defined by definite quantities of the different constituent currencies; a weakening currency loses weight in the basket, while a strengthening one gains weight. The SDR also offers a clear advantage from the standpoint of short-run stability to the extent that its composition is aligned with the relative economic weights of different countries, now including the RMB.
- *as a unit of account:* the SDR has the advantage of being relatively immune to the impact of floating exchange rates; as such it would help reduce the volatility of valuation, in comparison with the use of any single currency. Less volatility of valuation means less necessity to hedge, less impact from financial expectations and, finally, greater market stability. Even though its use would probably increase transaction costs, at least at the start, it could be useful as the invoicing currency in international contracts, especially those related to commodities[2].
- being a claim on its constituting hard currencies (U.S. dollar, euro, renminbi, yen, and British pound), it can supplement central banks reserves and be used in their management of balance of payments deficits and market pressures.
- in summary, SDRs could allow for a more orderly supply of global liquidity, prevent building a global excess of reserves, reduce the asymmetries and

2 The use of the SDR as a unit of account does not require approval by the IMF. The emerging new foreign exchange technologies based on blockchain will likely largely remove such transaction costs.

the deflationary bias of external adjustments and, in principle, resolve the Triffin Dilemma[3].

1. Today's context

As the international monetary system evolved, the Second Amendment of the IMF's Articles of Agreement aimed at making the SDR the "principal asset in the international monetary system"[4]. Nevertheless, its share in reserves has remained small — with the continuing absence of any private market.

This results principally from its limited allocation, as well as the lack of necessary official support that discouraged the private sector from dealing with the additional costs of managing its bond issuance and payments.

Established in 1969, the SDR was allocated twice during its first decade, and then not until 2009, when $250 billion in SDRs was allocated to members of the IMF to help address the global financial crisis. In 2021 another $650 billion in SDRs was allocated to help address the COVID crisis.

Indeed, the use of the SDR has remained limited to rare movements inside the official sector, for amounts that remain insignificant. In particular, SDR operations, in the form of loans or settlement of financial obligations, have been relatively limited, amounting to just about 10% of total SDR transactions.

This cannot be sufficient for a comprehensive reform of the international monetary system (IMS), which should also include the possibility to use the SDR directly in interventions. This would imply extensive private holdings of SDRs and a significant SDR private market.

As mentioned above, interest in the SDR as a unit of account and denomination for financial instruments ("market SDRs" that are settled in currencies) has been periodic — peaking soon after the collapse of the

---

[3] Seen as the dilemma that arises by using a national currency as a global currency—in the case of the U.S. dollar that continues to function as a global currency, the dilemma has been heightened by the rise in the global need for safe and liquid assets and the fall in global confidence in the U.S. dollar.

[4] Article VIII, Section 7.

Bretton Woods par value system — with low overall uptake. Nevertheless, the SDR allocations have now become an important tool of cooperation in international financial crises — most recently, with a general allocation of SDR456.5 billion (equivalent to about US$650 billion) implemented on August 23, 2021 (Figure 1).

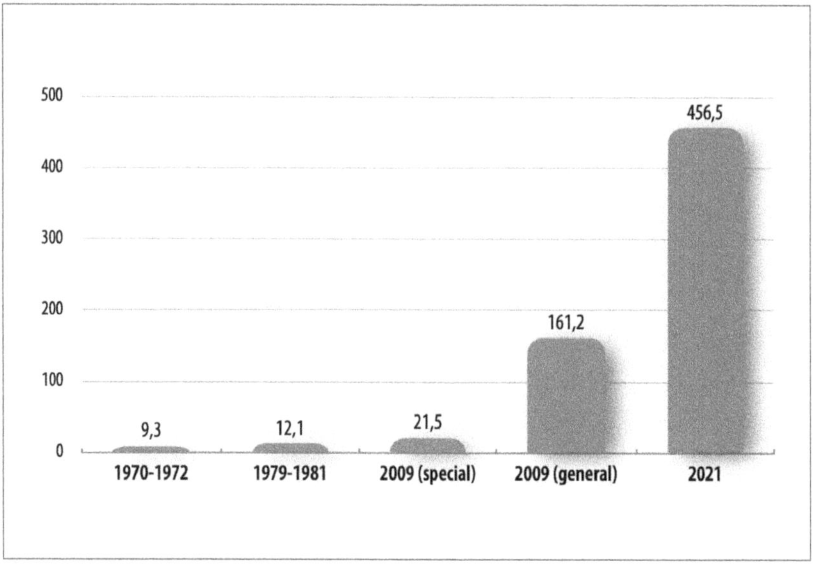

Figure 1. SDR Allocations *(Billions of SDRs)*
Source: IMF Finance Department

Total SDR outstanding are SDR660.7 billion, equivalent to about $943 billion at the U.S. dollar value of the SDR. The SDR's share of foreign currency reserves plus SDR holdings is just 7%, significantly less than the shares of the U.S. dollar and euro (54.6% and 19.6% respectively) but a third more than the Japanese yen's share.

Thus, while some progress has recently been made in using the IMF's SDR, it still falls far short of becoming a key lever to reform the international monetary system. Its use so far can be summarized as follows (Figure 2):

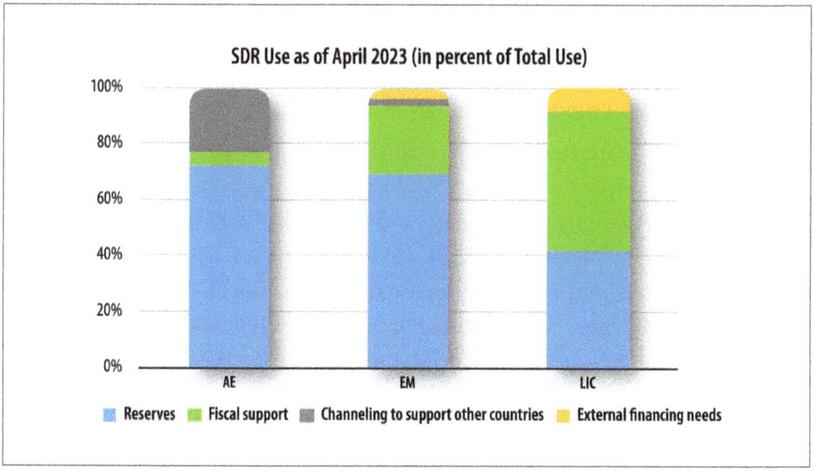

Figure 2. SDR Use

Source: IMF

Briefly, some emerging market and developing economies used their SDRs to improve the composition of financing and repay debt, while others sold foreign exchange to finance ministries in exchange for local currency treasury bonds, thereby boosting foreign exchange liquidity without debt issuance.

2. SDR Reforms

A key and overdue reform is to build much further the role of the IMF's Special Drawing Rights (SDR), that remains still generally underused, and upgrading it over time[5] to become a multilateral currency[6].

There are many steps toward this end. First, to make the SDR as a reserve asset more usable. Then, to consider the extent to which the SDR can acquire the characteristics of other reserve holdings, which have varying degrees of

5 The recognition of the need for this elevation of the SDR has been long recognized from Keynes to Robert Triffin who made clear the need for a true "internationalization" of the foreign exchange component of the world's international reserves (Maes 2021).

6 The RTI has made significant contributions in this regard through the Palais Royal Initiative (2011), and the recommendations of its Working Group on the SDR (2015).

liquidity, rather than limiting itself to its traditional "reserve asset" character. Let's discuss some of the reforms needed.

2.1. Reforms: Fairness in Allocation

The first issue is the fairness of its allocation. In this regard, much more fairness should apply to the status and distribution of the Special Drawing Rights (SDR). As mentioned above, the last SDR allocation, equivalent to US$650 billion was decided in 2021, further to the COVID crisis.

Again, like the preceding allocations, this allocation was distributed in proportion to the quotas of the IMF members, so very generally to countries that need them the least. The ten largest advanced economies hold 55% of quotas, whereas all of the world's 27 low-income countries hold just 3.3%. Of this allocation, almost €150 billion were allocated to the members of the European Union. As no European country is likely to experience balance of payments problems—just like most rich countries– and the eurozone has another very powerful instrument to tackle financial crises (the European Stability Mechanism), SDRs are likely to remain parked in the balance sheets of the Euro System of Central Banks (ESCB).

However, a positive measure related to the 2021 allocation, is that the IMF has invited countries with strong balance of payments positions (including China and some emerging market economies) to give a fraction of their SDRs to the poorest ones through the IMF Trust Funds.[7] This has helped scale up IMF lending to the membership, both through the IMF's Poverty Reduction & Growth Trust (PRGT) and the Resilience & Sustainability Trust (RST)[8]. Overall, the G20 target of re-channelling US$100 billion from economically strong members to vulnerable members has been reached in terms of pledges. Efforts now focus on translating the pledges into contributions and further building the voluntary channelling for the benefit of vulnerable countries.[9]

---

[7] This was in response to the G20 pledge to channel US$100 billion (20% of their SDR allocation) for the benefit of vulnerable members.

[8] The PRGT allows the IMF to provide crucial balance of payments support to deal with external shocks and to support programs that involve debt restructurings. The RST is the first mechanism for the IMF to provide long-term financing to help countries address structural challenges like climate change and pandemic preparedness.

[9] Overall, for PRGT financing to reach significant levels, the resources for ensuring its ability to lend sustainably at near-zero interest rates need to be increased. This

Looking ahead, a change in the system is needed, moving away from allocations in proportion to quota. Among the alternatives, are allocations based on PPP measures of country GDP, and earmarking a proposed percentage (some have suggested 20%) of future allocations for the poorest countries.

2.2. Reforms: IMF Mandate

The mandate of the IMF should explicitly include effective surveillance of capital flows which, in a highly financialized world, have a much greater influence on exchange rates and the macroeconomic situation than fluctuations in current account balances[10]. Toward this, the IMF, together with the BIS and the leading central banks, need to establish a framework for the regular assessment and management of global liquidity, with the objective of preventing financial crises and harmful fragmentation of the global financial system.

SDRs could become an essential tool in this context. By issuing SDRs in the event of a shortage of liquidity or by withdrawing them from circulation in the event of an overabundance, the IMF could play more the role of a global central bank. However, to allow the SDRs to fully play an effective role in the management of global liquidity, steps to broaden the SDR market and develop its role as a global currency need to be taken.

Toward this, the IMF role of lender of last resort should be more explicitly recognized in its Articles of Agreement and its resources potentially available should be significantly increased. This recognition would give countries threatened by aberrant fluctuations in capital movements the assurance of being protected without having to accumulate excessive and poorly productive reserves. More generally, the IMF should be authorized to issue SDRs as needed in a crisis situation and absorb them after the crisis abates.

2.3. Reforms: Building Broader Use

To increase the attractiveness of the SDR, as well as interest in its allocations, there is much more that needs to be done[11]. In particular, the IMF should

---

can easily be done by carefully defined sales of the IMF's gold holdings, as has been previously done without upsetting the global gold market.

10 Comprehensively examined in the RTI's Working Group on Managing Global Liquidity as a Global Public Good (2019).

11 These options are well examined in the RTI's working group report on the SDR.

take the lead in promoting the broader use of SDRs. There are many obvious options that do not entail any change in its reserve asset status[12].

Toward this, the IMF should use the SDR more systematically and visibly in its internal operations, using the SDR as the accounting unit for all items on its balance-sheet, as well as the reference standard in its publications. Thus, the IMF's accounts should be placed on an all-SDR basis — thereby amalgamating the General Resources Account with the SDR account.

Member countries should be encouraged to use the SDR for data release and reports submitted to international institutions. Toward this, China has started using the SDR as a unit in data release of its foreign exchange reserves.

Other international institutions (including the United Nations, the World Bank, as well as the Asian Development Bank, the Asian Infrastructure Investment Bank and other multilateral development banks (MDBs)) should also follow using the SDR as their accounting unit for data dissemination as well as for their lending and borrowing operations.

The next stage in broadening the use of the SDR involves doing more to allow a member country to lend its SDRs without the strings attached that preserve the 'reserve asset' character of the SDR. This is now argued by many as using SDRs to provide new financing to the global development agenda.

Under the proposal made by the multilateral development banks, countries would contribute their SDRs to MDBs in the form of hybrid capital, defined as a financial instrument with perpetual maturity that has both equity and debt properties. This would allow the MDBs to leverage the portion of the hybrid capital that is considered equity (the *equity content*) using their normal leverage ratio. In other words, member countries might be set free to treat SDR holdings the same way they treat their other holdings of reserves, some of which are less liquid than others.

Progress has recently been made in this direction. The IMF has approved the use of SDRs held by participants in the SDR Department in the acquisition of hybrid capital instruments issued by prescribed holders and assessed this as being consistent with the IMF's Articles of Agreement. However, the scope for this use is limited for now, as the approval contains a cumulative cap of

---

[12] Its traditional reserve status derives from its liquidity and its immediate conversion into foreign currencies at face value.

SDR15 billion for SDRs channelled into hybrid capital instruments[13]. While hybrid capital may not be a reserve asset, the proposals do include a "Liquidity Support Agreement" which is meant to guarantee the reserve asset status of the contributed SDRs (Box 1 below).

Box 1: Use of the SDR as Hybrid Capital

1. Whether hybrid capital instruments can be classified as reserves depends on their structure/terms. To count as international reserves, external assets need to (i) be liquid and (ii) be of high quality (i.e., investment grade).
2. On liquidity, the instruments that the AfDB/IDB intend to issue have an encashment mechanism (liquidity support instruments) in which holders promise to acquire hybrid instruments from other holders if these have a balance of payments need. This is modelled after the PRGT and RST, claims on which count as reserves.
3. For the encashment mechanism to be reasonably robust, it needs a minimum number of participants (about 5). This is the main challenge for the AfDB/IDB—finding enough contributors with a strong balance of payments position.
4. On quality, what matter is not the maturity but the likelihood of a loss, which must be very low. In the case of the AfDB/IDB instrument, they have a diversified loan portfolio, credit risk mitigation policies (e.g. exposure limits), preferred creditor status and their ordinary equity as buffer to absorb credit losses before the hybrid capital would be called. Again, this is very similar to PRGT and RST.
5. Rating agencies have already assessed the instruments and rated them close to the AAA status of the AfDB/IDB, which is sufficient.
6. Of course, ultimately each SDR holder will need to assess whether they are willing to invest in these instruments based on their own investment guidelines and legal and regulatory issues etc, but from a statistical perspective these claims could well be classified as reserve assets.
7. Hybrid capital instruments that MDBs can carry are in any case limited by rating agencies (cannot exceed a certain ratio to tier 1). So, these instruments can never resolve all MDB capital problems but SDR15 billion can support about SDR60 billion in MDB credit, which is significant.
8. Finally, the Fund has assessed that channelled SDRs remain reserve assets, implying that the hybrid capital instruments can be counted as reserves.

[13] Important to note that other prescribed SDR operations are not subject to quantitative limits.

2.4. Reforms: Adjusting the Terms of the SDR

The terms of the SDR are summarized in Box 2 below.

Box 2: Existing Terms of the SDR

- The SDR interest rate is determined as a weighted average of the interest rates on short-term financial instruments (3-month government instruments) in the markets of the currencies comprising the SDR basket
- IMF members receive interest on their cumulative SDR holdings and are assessed charges against their cumulative allocation of SDRs. Both interest and charges are assessed at the same rate (the SDR interest rate).
- When IMF members convert their SDR holdings to freely usable currencies or use them in Fund-related operations or in operations authorized by the Fund with other SDR Department participants or prescribed holders, a negative SDR Department position (where the member's SDR holdings are less than cumulative SDR allocations made to the member) may be generated.
- This negative net SDR Department position leads to a net interest expense (which constitute a financial obligation) to the IMF at the SDR interest rate.

Although the SDR interest rate has risen by over 390 basis points since the August 2021 allocation (Figure 3), the SDR should be made more attractive an instrument, and its composition more frequently adjusted to reflect the relative importance of currencies in international financial transactions[14].

This includes raising the interest rate on SDR assets and liabilities, to a broader market rate, thereby reducing distortions in the subsidy effectively associated with SDR use, that may encourage its use but discourages countries from providing foreign exchange in exchange for SDRS. This would rightly sever the link with the remuneration rate on the use of a member's currency in the normal lending operations of the IMF.

---

[14] Presently, it is determined weekly based on a weighted average of interest rates on three-month debt in the money markets of the SDR basket currencies.

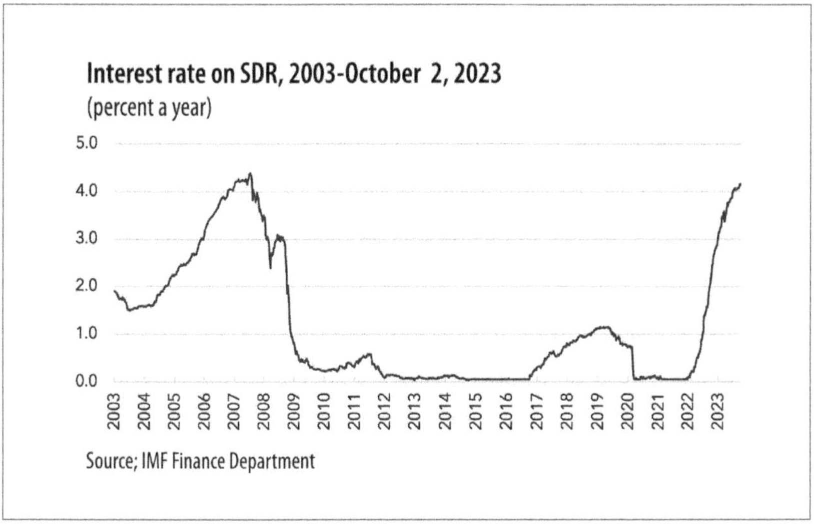

Figure 3. SDR Interest Rate

This reform includes the IMF increasing the number of "freely usable" currencies beyond those (currently five) that are currently included in the SDR basket. This would help build the diversification of reserves internationally, expand the number of currencies provided in exchange for SDRs and to finance borrowing from the IMF. Potentially, this could be part of the strategy of reducing overall reliance on the U.S. dollar. Over time, this would also tend to increase the number of currencies in the SDR basket.

2.5. Reforms: Building SDR Use in Exchange Markets

The IMF's Articles of Agreement state that the SDR is meant to be the *primary reserve asset of the international monetary system*; however, the SDR market is too illiquid for central banks to want to hold SDRs. Hence, the eventual challenge in SDR reform is to move the SDR from being an international reserve asset to becoming an international currency that could be used for interventions in exchange markets. Toward this a private SDR market needs to develop with competitive transaction costs in these markets.

Thus far, SDRs can be held only by the official sector, namely, Fund members and *prescribed holders*[15]. Prescribed holders may acquire, hold and use SDRs in operations with other prescribed holders and participants in the SDR Department.

As part of the process, which needs to be initiated by the private sector, with clear official support, a variety of SDR-denominated financial instruments needs to develop to meet the diverse needs of market participants. This may include SDR-denominated bonds, loans, derivatives, and other structured products that offer exposure to SDRs.

Significant reforms are needed to move in this direction, and the emergence of central bank digital currencies (CBDCs) should open the way for use of the SDR by the private sector, by removing its bundling costs[16]. Among these, is the need to build structures for the functioning of a private SDR market (as was done in helping the private ECU bond market). This includes establishing trading platforms, clearing houses, and settlement systems that can handle SDR transactions efficiently and securely. Such an SDR clearing house would need to be recognized as a prescribed holder of SDRs, as the Bank for International Settlements (BIS) is so recognized.

In summary, for a private SDR market to develop, a link between private and official SDRs needs to be created — effectively allowing private banks to hold SDRs. This will require amending the IMF's Articles of Agreement.

Conclusions

The stock of the world's SDRs is currently valued at about $950 billion, and the vast majority of these remain relatively unused in the balance sheets of advanced economies' central banks and finance ministries. While progress in being made in using the IMF's SDR, it still falls far short of becoming a

---

15 The Fund has so far prescribed 20 official institutions as holders of SDRs, including the Bank for International Settlements (BIS) and the European Central Bank (ECB). Of these, five were approved in 2023, namely the Caribbean Development Bank (CDB), the Development Bank of Latin America (known as Corporacion Andina de Fomento or CAF), the European Bank for Reconstruction and Development (EBRD), the European Investment Bank (EIB), and the Inter-American Development Bank (IADB). Prescribed holders of SDRs do not receive SDR allocations.

16 Carefully explained and examined in the RTI Paper no. 13 on the emerging revolution of the digital currencies.

key lever to reform the international monetary system. Key steps that have periodically been recommended include:

- to build the international public role of the SDR, the IMF's accounts should be placed on an all-SDR basis. This can be done by amalgamating the General Resources Account with the SDR account.
- the SDR should be made more attractive an instrument, and its composition more frequently adjusted to reflect the relative importance of currencies in international financial transactions. This would help build the diversification of reserves internationally.
- toward this a private SDR market is needed. Official support by the public sector (in their financial operations) is needed to build the importance of the private SDR market.
- official support is also necessary to build appropriate structures for the functioning of a private SDR market (as was done in helping the private ECU bond market) and moving toward the multilateral clearing of SDR operations.
- for a private SDR market to develop, a link between private and official SDRs needs to be created — effectively allowing private banks to hold SDRs.
- the IMF should be authorized to issue SDRs as needed in a crisis situation and absorb them after the crisis situation.

With these reforms, it would be appropriate to introduce in the IMF's Articles of Agreement a provision that explicitly recognizes the status of the SDR as an international reserve currency so that it is well understood as a global currency. This would be a major part of the reforms needed to resolve the weaknesses inherent in the present International Monetary System and create a multilateral currency, with the IMF acting more as a central bank.

However, such a fundamental change is not likely in the current geopolitical environment. Nevertheless, there is room to do a lot more to move in this direction, by better using the SDR in the International Monetary System. Indeed, a lot could be done in the domains of official and private SDRs, without having to adjust the IMF's Articles of Agreement. However, for the reforms to be significant, a private SDR market should be strongly encouraged, and, for this, it is necessary that a link be institutionalized between official and private SDRs with a view to allowing central banks to use their official SDRs directly in intervention.

References

Boorman J.T., Icard A. (2011), *Reform of the International Monetary System, The Palais Royal Initiative*, New Delhi: Sage.

Camdessus M., Singh A., and Snoy B. (2023), "Act with Urgency to Reform the International Monetary System", *Mint*, 31 October. https://www.livemint.com/opinion/online-views/act-with-urgency-to-reform-the-international-monetary-system-11698753209408.html.

Cooper R. (2011), *Is SDR Creation Inflationary?*, IMF Policy Papers, Washington: International Monetary Fund.

Eichengreen B. (2021), "This SDR Allocation Must be Different", *Project Syndicate*, September 10, https://www.project-syndicate.org/commentary/how-to-get-new-imf-sdrs-to-poor-countries-by-barry-eichengreen-2021-09

End N., Koosakul J., Tanyeri K. and Tovar C. (2023), *Impact of Special Drawing Rights Allocations on Policy Space*", IMF Working Paper, Washington: International Monetary Fund.

G20 International Financial Architecture Working Group (2023), *Co-Chairs's Note to G20 FMCBG on the Total Global Ambition of US$100 bn of Voluntary Contributions for Countries Most in Need.*

Icard A. and Turner P. (2019), *Managing Global Liquidity as a Global Public Good, A report of an RTI Working Group*, Working Papers 1293, Robert Triffin International.

International Monetary Fund (IMF) (2024), *Use of SDRS in the acquisition of hybrid capital instruments of the prescribed holders*, Washington: International Monetary Fund.

International Monetary Fund (IMF) (2023a), *Geoeconomic Fragmentation and the Future of Multilateralism*, Staff Discussion Note 2023/001, Washington: International Monetary Fund.

International Monetary Fund (IMF) (2023b), *Applications to Become Holders of SDRs*, IMF Board paper, Washington: International Monetary Fund.

International Monetary Fund (IMF) (2023c), *Review of Resource Adequacy of the Poverty Reduction and Growth Trust, Resilience and Sustainability Trust, and Debt Relief Trusts, IMF Board paper*, Washington: International Monetary Fund.

International Monetary Fund (IMF) (2023d), *The Big Funding Squeeze*, IMF Flagship report, Washington: International Monetary Fund.

International Monetary Fund (IMF) (2023e), *2021 Special Drawing Rights Allocation–Ex-post Assessment Report*, Washington: International Monetary Fund.

International Monetary Fund (IMF) (2022), *SDR Tracker*, Washington: International Monetary Fund.

International Monetary Fund (IMF) (2022b), How to Record the Allocations of Special Drawing Rights in Government Finance Statistics, IMF Technical Notes and Manuals, Washington: International Monetary Fund.

International Monetary Fund (IMF) (2022c), *Proposal to Establish a Resilience and Sustainability Trust*, IMF Board paper, Washington: International Monetary Fund.

International Monetary Fund (IMF) (2022d), *World Economic Outlook*, IMF Flagship report, Washington: International Monetary Fund.

International Monetary Fund (IMF) (2021a), *Proposal for a General Allocation of Special Drawing Rights*, IMF Policy Paper, Washington: International Monetary Fund.

International Monetary Fund (IMF) (2021b), *Proposal by the Managing Director of the International Monetary Fund for an Allocation of Special Drawing Rights for the Eleventh Basic Period*, Washington: International Monetary Fund.

International Monetary Fund (IMF) (2021c), *Guidance Note for Fund Staff on the Treatment and Use of SDR Allocations*, Washington: International Monetary Fund.

International Monetary Fund (IMF) (2021d), *Fund Concessional Financial Support for Low-Income Countries–Responding to The Pandemic*, IMF Technical Notes and Manuals, Washington: International Monetary Fund.

International Monetary Fund (IMF) (2018a), *Considerations on the Role of the SDR*, IMF Policy Paper, Washington: International Monetary Fund.

International Monetary Fund (IMF) (2016), *Monetary and Financial Statistics Manual and Compilation Guide (MFSMCG)*, IMF Statistics Handbook, Washington: International Monetary Fund.

International Monetary Fund (IMF) (2014a), *Government Finance Statistics Manual (GFSM)*, IMF Statistics Handbook, Washington: International Monetary Fund.

International Monetary Fund (IMF) (2014b), *External Debt Statistics: Guide for Compilers and Users*, IMF Statistics Handbook, Washington: International Monetary Fund.

International Monetary Fund (IMF) (2009a), *Proposal for a General Allocation of SDRs*, IMF Policy Paper, Washington: International Monetary Fund.

International Monetary Fund (IMF) (2009b), *Guidance Note for Fund Staff on the Treatment and Use of SDR Allocations*, IMF Policy Paper, Washington: International Monetary Fund.

International Monetary Fund (IMF) (2009c), *Balance of Payments and International Investment Position Manual–Sixth Edition (BPM6)*, IMF Policy Paper, Washington: International Monetary Fund.

Ocampo J. A. (2019), *The SDR's Time Has Come*, IMF Finance and Development, Washington: International Monetary Fund.

Snoy B. (2015), *Shifts in Global Financial Governance and China's Financial Reform*, Shanghai, paper presented at a Conference, November 1, mimeo.

Shenai N., End N., Koosakul J. and Said A. (2023), *The Financial Cost of Using Special Drawing Rights: Implications of Higher Interest Rates*, IMF Working Paper, Washington: International Monetary Fund, https://www.imf.org/en/Publications/WP/Issues/2023/09/15/The-Financial-Cost-of-Using-Special-Drawing-Rights-Implications-of-Higher-Interest-Rates-539183.

Triffin International Foundation (2014), *Using the Special Drawing Rights as a Lever to Reform the International Monetary System*, RTI Paper No. 1, https://www.triffininternational.eu/images/RTI/articles_papers/SDR-WP_Final-Report-May-2014.pdf.

Triffin International Foundation (2020), *The Emerging Revolution of Digital Currencies: A Technological Opportunity for Rebalancing the International Monetary System*, RTI Paper No. 13, July; https://www.triffininternational.eu/images/RTI/articles_papers/RTI-CSF_Ghymers_Digital-Currencies-and-IMS_July2020.pdf.

Truman E. M. (2022), *The IMF Should Enhance the Role of SDRs to Strengthen the International Monetary System*, Washington: Peterson Institute for International Economics.

Wolf M. (2021), "A Windfall for Poor Countries is Within Reach," *The Financial Times*, June 1; https://www.ft.com/content/fe826780-c973-476f-b057-7a8aa678ec7b.

Zhou X. (2009), *Reform the international monetary system*. March 23, https://www.bis.org/review/r090402c.pdf

Relaunching Multilateralism through Regional Monetary Unions

Andrew Sheng

I want to thank Michel Camdessus and Bernard Snoy for inviting me to address this important conference reviewing the feasibility of relaunching multilateralism through regional monetary unions. My apologies for not being able to attend in person.

We live in unprecedented, fascinating, and dangerous times. After the global pandemic, rising global warming, massive tech disruption and now war in Ukraine and Gaza, we have been forced us to re-think not only our own personal lives, but also the wellbeing, livelihood and interdependency of our families, community, nation, economy, finance, the global order or disorder and planetary existential conditions.

Eighty years after the creation of the present neoliberal multilateral monetary order in Bretton Woods, the model of global peace through free trade, free flow of capital and ideas has morphed into what Winston Churchill called the Gathering Storm or prelude to war. Our current scientific paradigm of rationality is being challenged by huge emotions that demonize those who disagree with us, with populist cries for "every nation for itself", epitomized by America First or the Indian stance, "we are not on any side, only on our own side". Who is on the side of global survival if we are prepared to go to war over individual or national interests?

The post-Bretton Woods model of stability and peace is moving toward an emergence of systemic disorder out of which a new order may be formed, but in between, the linear, mechanical economic model which was expected to automatically revert to equilibrium has failed us. Larger crises and/or depression have been averted by massive central bank intervention, especially after the 2008 GFC. The old general equilibrium model did not factor in all the externalities of bad finance, pollution, corruption, capture, terrorism, offshoring, money politics and the like that have exploded in populism, nationalism, and the K-economy, where climate disasters and social and digital divide prove that natural or social calamities end up with the rich losing a bit of money, whereas the mass poor and weak pay with their lives.

First, we took the politics out of political economy, then we took the moral out of moral hazard, and worse, we took interest rate as an allocator of scarce resources, moved it to zero and negative and then expect central banks to underwrite everything. As a former central banker said wisely, we have no theory to explain how quantitative easing works. The theory does not lay out an experiment with QE where we do not know what the full consequences are.

What should the post-Bretton Woods monetary order look like? Two disparities haunt the modern world. First, the social divisions and disparities, such as wealth, knowledge and power concentrations are so large that no less than a reset in our thinking and then in delivery of policy promises to the masses is necessary. Second, climate warming is the revenge of Nature, in which human abuses of planetary life and resources are such that we will see more carbon emission, natural disasters and collapses of food, water and energy supplies relative to the rising population. The current excessive consumption funded by excessive debt is ultimately extractive and predatory, with no regenerative capacity to sustainability.

To paraphrase Keynes, we have been trapped by dead professors' mindsets and our elites have failed the coming generations. If the rich nations are aging and will also have huge constraints due to internal disagreements, EMEs have to think for themselves how to break out of their development traps. The monetary order is clearly one area, but so long as the voting rights are controlled by the rich countries, there are huge barriers to change. Unfortunately, as the unipolar order fragments, multipolar order has not yet been formed, so there is unlikely to be a top-down consensus and action plan on what to do. The more realistic solution is more bottom-up through national and regional frameworks, pushing the centre to change.

But first, we need to understand the context of change of the Bretton Woods philosophy, which occurred when America emerged as the victorious hegemon after World War Two, with military, monetary and industrial might, feeling generous and willing to promote and fund free trade, investment, and growth. As the United States incur larger and larger fiscal and trade deficits, with net debt to the world of \$19.8 trillion and gross liability of over \$54.3 trillion at the end of 2023 (BEA data), or 18% and 51% of world GDP respectively. Five percent of world population is consuming not just a rising share of global savings, but also an increasing debt owing to the rest. At high US interest rates, money is moving uphill to rich countries, whereas it should be going towards poor countries.

Second, as the unipolar power feels insecure with the rise of challengers, we have to accept that national security has become a major force in both domestic and international relations. After 2016, everything has become weaponized — finance, technology, trade, investment and supply chains, information and media. One third of the world's population is under some form of sanction, and no individual, firm or nation is safe from sanction that is neither appealable to a neutral court of justice, nor do we see in the short-term any unwinding of this trend.

Third, outside the United States, the rest of the world is still bank and debt dominated, with central banks trying to solve liquidity issues by creating more liabilities that transfer risks to the public. Surely the days of increasing debt to solve debt excess is gone? What is the role of equity markets in the deleveraging of corporate debt, or even sovereign debt? What role can central banks play in development finance in terms of providing equity, rather than more debt, even if it is indirect — injection of funds into sovereign wealth funds or development banks?

Fourth, the rise of Artificial Intelligence, Robotics and Tech-based money has meant that the digital divide is widening disparities between the haves and have-nots. Gold is the only money that has no counter-party risk. If nuclear war destroys the fibre-optic, internet, space satellite and data centre infrastructure, cyber-money that is in the cloud will disappear forever. Is the current digital money system sustainable?

Fifth, with the rich world accusing China of overcapacity with rising protectionism in the form of tariff and non-tariff barriers, is the world facing a structural lack of aggregate demand or excess aggregate supply? So long as EMEs (or the Global South) cannot access funds for consumption with face shortage of long-term funding for infrastructure, healthcare, education, tech transformation, climate change because the rich West consider the credit or geopolitical risks unacceptable, then the existing funding is stuck in excess liquidity that is funding speculation.

We are in the Ancient Mariner's lament of "water, water everywhere and not a drop to drink". So long as the reserve currency central banks refuse to acknowledge their role in global resource allocation (being concerned over their national monetary autonomy, then if neither the multilateral Bretton Woods and development banks institutions and Wall Street are unwilling to recycle EME savings back in terms of long-term investments or aid transfers, then EMEs are trapped. Investment banks, hedge funds and asset managers are now increasingly concentrated, and as long as they recycle the money towards advanced markets, EMEs can't get long-term funds to do the structural Net Zero and social transformations necessary to create planetary and social balance.

Complex Systemic Problems demand Complex Solutions

I fully agree with all the arguments of Bernard Snoy that the present system is unsustainable, and reforms must be made to make SDRs a genuine currency. This is both urgent and important. As identified by Christian Ghymers, the USD pre-eminence as pointed out by Robert Triffin, has become turbo-charged by shadow banking so that any shocks could create hyper-illiquidity situations that require cooperative efforts to deal with. Global cooperation is not forthcoming because as the Ukraine and Gaza wars have shown, technology, information and finance have become weaponized, exposing proxy wars, tragic loss of civilian lives and breakdown of international law and order.

The barriers to reform have never been technical, nor through lack of logic, but due to entrenched vested financial and political interests. There is little political will or national interest for the US to support structural change. Moreover, given US veto in Bretton Woods, no amount of EU and EME pressure would change the status quo without US consent. Until the Ukraine War, the EMEs were hopeful that the Europeans can and will help to make some reforms. However, with the joining of Europe and the United Kingdom in post-Ukraine sanctions on Russia and on the seizure of Central Bank of Afghanistan reserves post-US departure, the Rest of the World is clear that no money is safe from unilateral sanctions on financial assets.

To summarize, the multilateral order is in deep trouble. Many would agree that without QE, the world would be in a 1930s-type depression right now. Since the current multilateral governance framework cannot get agreement on many key issues, including on den or NetZero funding, the EMEs are in deep trouble. Accordingly, there is greater attention towards regional cooperative arrangements.

The Global South re-thinking of global monetary arrangements

After the 1997–98 Asian financial crisis, the Global South began to increase their foreign exchange reserves, cut back on foreign exchange debt, allow more flexibility in their exchange arrangements, and in Asia, pushed for the regional Chiangmai initiatives, which was the expansion of the central bank swap arrangements. However, under the ADB leadership, there was push for long-term bond markets using the *Asiabondsonline* initiative. Whilst this was commendable, there was little appreciation that what was needed was deeper expansion of equity markets to deleverage the corporate sector. Furthermore, without a deeper understanding of the problems of the SME sector, the divide between larger companies and SMEs continued to worsen social inequities.

Nevertheless, Asian economies' prudence saved them from the ravages of the 2008/2009 global financial crisis, which affected the North Atlantic economies more. Reform-wise, the 2009 crisis was wasted without addressing the structural issues of how the financial sector could serve the real sector better. The Basel 3 reforms were pushed through also for the emerging markets, also few of EME banks had engaged in the sophisticated financial engineering and derivative that nearly wiped out some major Western banks.

Thus, in the post-2008 period, the period was not just about wasted opportunity to reform the financial system, it led to a massive increase in domestic debt and credit expansion, particularly after China undertook its reform and reflation RMB4 trillion package that grew its shadow banks, expanded corporate and local government debt that relied on rising real estate prices. As the advanced countries lowered interest rates post-2008, there was asset bubbles with predominance of short term speculation over long term investment and emergence of the liquidity trap. As there still lacked a genuine lender of last resort (LLOR), EME savings were tied up in huge accumulation of reserves, whilst at the same time, the advanced Western banks began to withdraw from lending in EME countries, for fear of credit and foreign exchange risks. All these began to unwind with the increase in interest rates in the advanced markets after 2021.

The post-2008 expansion of non-bank financial institutions (NBFIs or shadow banks) worldwide was essentially regulatory arbitrage away from the highly regulated banking system towards the more lightly regulated areas. Thus, when the Fed began to raise nominal interest rates in 2021 to control inflation, the weaker banks and shadow banks began to show signs of stress. Christian Ghymers is correct in identifying how the increasing role of non-banks is magnifying the pro-cyclical behavior of repo-markets, based on an unstable and too scarce volume of collaterals in dollar safe assets. All these signs of stress, including the non-sustainability of US fiscal and trade deficits, the dominant role of US dollar in global capital markets, all new manifestations of the Triffin dilemma.

Experience of Economic and Monetary Unions in Asia

Let me now assess whether regional monetary unions are successful in general. As IMF economists have reviewed, a "full" monetary union exists when independent nation states adopt a single monetary policy and a common currency, with single external exchange rate policy, as well as absence of all exchange controls. The experience of the Euro system is that even with a unified central bank, there has to be alignment of capital markets, fiscal policies and integration of many political views and practices for the monetary union to work. In contrast, a 'pseudo'-monetary union like the Gulf Cooperation Council is an agreement to maintain fixed exchange rates among the member states, but without explicit integration of economic policy, with separate foreign exchange reserves different central banks and monetary policies. Complete monetary integration is absolute for a single currency nation, and monetary unions are looser institutional arrangements that may come apart for different reasons, one of which is whether there is a single underwriter of risks, liquidity and perhaps solvency.

Much has been written about Asian monetary and trade cooperation. The ASEAN trade integration model is known as variable geometry, in which there is no monetary union but willingness to go towards trade integration. Prior to 1997, most ASEAN currencies were tightly linked to the dollar, because trade was essentially intra-ASEAN and with the advanced markets, especially the United States. One of the key tensions in regional trade and monetary arrangements is that trade between ASEAN and China is rising, relative to that with the United States. This is because China has emerged both as the largest global manufacturing center and trading nation and key hub in the Asian supply chain. Even though the dollar is still the major invoicing, payments and store of value in the East Asian region and global supply chains, the US-China tensions and increasing sanctions mean that many in the Global South and even Chinese businesses are considering some form on non-US dollar arrangements is a necessary hedge.

The specific questions I have been asked to address are: (1) Is the Chiang Mai initiative a success? (2) Is China working to build its own monetary zone, promoting specific standards for payments and financial regulations? (3) Will de-dollarization happen on a grand scale and what does this mean for the future of the international monetary system?

Before I begin, let me say that the recent global tensions in shifting from a unipolar to multipolar system and its somewhat chaotic manifestations reflect the unwillingness of the unipolar power to continue funding global security and stability. In short, it has shifted from being a generous provider of global public goods to become willing to tax or enforce its will through sanctions, namely, sticks instead of carrots in US international relations. On the other hand, contenders in the multipolar system are willing to provide carrots, although it is not clear whether there are sticks contained within these carrots.

Under any monetary arrangements which are essentially about sharing of sovereignty where the single currency is a yardstick, the key power nexus is that one party underwrites or is willing to underwrite or ensure final integrity of the system. Smaller members of the monetary union are unable to absorb such losses, but can do so if the losses are mutualized or burden-shared. The leader is that nation that is willing to absorb more than its share of losses and/or manage the monetary union. If minority members feel that there are more sticks than carrots, the union or even alliance will break down.

Let me now move to the question whether the Chiang Mai initiative is a success? The simple answer is that it was an important wake-up call and rallying point for regional cooperation, but operationally it has never been activated. Central bank swaps give the illusion that smaller central banks can access valuable FX from the larger central banks, notably People's Bank of China or Bank of Japan. However, because the condition is to accept IMF conditionality, the facility has never been used. Because of recent tensions between China and Japan over certain issues, the progress of the Chiangmai Initiative is currently on hold.

The more interesting question is on whether China is working to build its own monetary zone, promoting specific standards for payments and financial regulations?

As far as I am aware, China has never made any claims to making its own monetary zone. The idea that the global currency should be the SDR or non-national currency was proposed in 2009 by the then PBOC Governor Zhou Xiaochuan, when he articulated that: "the desirable goal of reforming the international monetary system, therefore, is to create an international reserve currency that is disconnected from individual nations and is able to remain stable in the long run, thus removing the inherent deficiencies caused by using credit-based national currencies." (Zhou 2009)

The PBOC has issued an RMB internationalization index since 2011 and its own index showed that the US dollar is way ahead at 58%, Euro at 22% and RMB at only 3%. Barry Eichengreen put it right when he pointed out that it took the US 75 years to replace sterling, because in 1870, the US GDP had already matched that of the British empire. Chinese GDP is still two-thirds of that of the US, although in PPP terms and trade terms, China has overtaken the US.

We can now answer the third question, whether de-dollarization will happen on a grand scale and what does this mean for the future of the international monetary system?

Since the arrival of digital or cyber-currencies, we need to re-think the whole global monetary system and its operations. The digital landscape of monetary and financial system is that you can digitally transfer payments or value through distributed ledgers which can be highly encrypted. Therefore, not only is money a means of payment (digitally a token), a unit of account (standard or trusted interoperable digital protocol) and a trusted store of value (embedded in blockchain distributed ledgers, including property registries, data banks and centres that are difficult to hack). Digital currency exists in cyber-space, with no counterparty. This means that it will be problematic if cyberspace becomes inoperable during nuclear war.

The main reason why dollar remains dominant is that not only is it very cheap and efficient to use — it is difficult to dislodge because it is the default currency embedded in key financial infrastructure (trading and clearing systems, with US accounting for 40% of global stock and bond market capitalization, 80% of counterparty FX transaction and 60% of official reserves). The weighted return on equity (ROE) using a 60% equity; 40% bond and cash portfolio since 1980 would reveal that ROE on USD assets outperforms any EURO, Pound Sterling, Japanese Yen and RMB-denominated asset portfolio. The fact that REPOs in USD would be cheaper and more liquid than in other currencies would also mean that the Dollar will remain dominant for a long time to come.

However, if sanctions on the usage or holding of US dollar assets increase, with the risk of confiscation or seizure, then the incentives to use the USD or EURO may decline, leading to alternative systems of transactions and store of value.

The rise of tokenization of everything implies that new forms of payment, clearing and transactions or holding of assets in digital token form can be created, so that users do not have to use USD, Euro, Sterling or Yen. Transactions can be affected through stable-coins. Furthermore, instead of using the current Real Time Gross Settlement (RTGS) system, these new clearing and settlement systems can use Netting, including netting of transaction in local currency but settled in stable-coin. Indeed, the current pilot schemes by Hong Kong Monetary Authority, Bank of Thailand, Central Bank of United Arab Emirates under the aegis of BIS Innovation platform means that such models could happen more quickly than anticipated. Any country sanctioned, or fear of being sanctioned, will move quickly in this direction.

Furthermore, stable-coins can be linked to gold and specific commodities or minerals, which have no counterparty risks, since transfers can be effected by DvP, namely delivery of physical gold against payment by digital stable-coin. The recent rise in the price of gold is an indication that as more central banks buy gold and investors realize that gold is a historically tested hedge against fiat currency inflation (or war), implies that the shift away from fiat currency is happening.

In my humble view, even cyber-currencies are not safe assets in the event of nuclear war, because if the internet and cloud computing crashes as war destroys the digital internet infrastructure of satellites, fiber-optic cables and wireless networks, who will have claim against digital currencies when digital records are destroyed?

Bluntly put, the shift towards de-dollarization has happened but these are triggered by the US sanctions and weaponization of the dollar on the basis of national security and geopolitical concerns. Thus, to the extent that the US realizes that such sanctions ultimately erode the power of the dollar as well as the current IMS (international monetary system), then it can still retain its dominant status by carefully balancing the advantages of using the dollar and its undesirable effects. And so long as the US stock market continues to deliver superior returns relative to non-US stock markets, the ROE on holding USD assets will make the current position hard to dislodge.

Fundamentally, the non-US economies, including Europe, Japan, China and the Global South, will not be able to challenge the dollar unless they deliver superior ROE on their local currency assets, which means major structural reforms at the national financial market level. Given the entrenchment of bank-dominated systems (low ROE) and the shortage of innovative tech companies outside the US and China, it will be a while before any national economies can challenge the US dollar asset market in terms of ROE attractiveness.

Thus, in my view, the US dollar dominance is for the US to lose, and not for the others to take over. What does that mean for the international financial system?

A major reason why the IMS has not responded to global changes is because the US is not incentivized to make any fundamental changes that weakens its *exorbitant privilege*. First, in terms of reform of the voting rights of the IMF, the US share will not change that much over time, giving her a de facto veto power. Any quota reform will affect more the smaller European countries, which are declining in relative GDP terms and would have to cede more voting shares to those with rising GDP, such as India, China and the BRIC countries. Thus, any serious reform of the voting rights of the IMF would depend on political consensus for change within Europe, and so long as these EU proposed reforms fit US interests, there could be some room for change.

Moreover, there is currently little consensus on what direction is the reform for the multilateral system. Given the rising power of the BRIC countries (provided there are no serious disruptions to their growth), there is reluctance to cede more financial clout and development resources by the incumbent majority shareholders of the Bretton Woods institutions. These institutions, including the multilateral development banks (MDBs) have less than $1.5 trillion in total assets, far short of the $3–4 trillion gap just to meet SDG goals. If McKinsey estimates to meet NetZero and narrowing social imbalances are correct at $9.2 trillion annually, then there must be a radical step up in the lending power of the Bretton Woods institutions in several orders of magnitude for EMEs to address climate change and uplift poverty effectively.

Given the fact that the United States is feeling more isolationist and unwilling to promote free trade, whilst more inclined towards industrial policy, it would have to wait for another generation of younger presidents to care more about the IMS. The real reason why reform of the IMS is unlikely in the short-term is that current swing to the right in both the US and Europe means that there will be less willingness to fund countries with views different from the West. Such polarization does not auger well for the IMS.

In conclusion, the current trend towards weaponization of everything, including finance and the multilateral financial and trade system, means that the existing IMS can only realistically be reformed by a global crisis, which will occur either through debt default or war. My own conjecture (not forecast) is that arising from such catastrophe, different types of international or regional cooperation will emerge. This is an area of great research and policy interest.

Thus, even as I commend the efforts of the Robert Triffin Foundation and its work in pushing for the SDR as the rightful candidate for the anchor of the IMS, my own brutal assessment is that the present system will muddle on till it collapses or when there is sufficient pain from depression, war or financial disaster to demand a radical and thorough reform. I am not too hopeful of regional monetary unions, because there is no credible lender of last resort currently in any of the smaller monetary systems. Such willingness to absorb losses is a sovereign decision which existing national governments are unwilling to share with other members without some loss of sovereignty by the other members. This is also an ongoing debate within the Eurozone.

In other words, the IMS is ultimately a geopolitical framework in which there must be a cost or loss-sharing mechanism in the event of crises. The current US-China rivalry is often framed as democracy versus autocracy, but ultimately it is whether the system of governance at the multilateral level can tolerate different systems with different values to act together to preserve the whole. If not, war and conflict is then an outcome that creates a lose-lose situation for all.

War is the ultimate sanction and the destroyer of existing orders. No IMS, digital or otherwise, can survive a nuclear war. Reforms of the existing IMS at the margin are periphery to the core issue of how man can live with man in stable, social understanding of mutual peace and tolerance. Only when there is severe loss, will emotion subside towards rationality. We are not yet on that spectrum of global wisdom, at least at the leadership level.

References

Fasano-Filho U. and Schaechter A. (2003), *Monetary Union Among Member Countries of the Gulf Cooperation Council*, USA: International Monetary Fund. Retrieved Jul 5, 2024, from https://doi.org/10.5089/9781589062191.084.

Zhou X. (2009), "Reform the International Monetary System", *Equilibri, Rivista per lo sviluppo sostenibile*" 2/2009, pp. 161–166, doi: 10.1406/30179

Relaunching Multilateralism through Regional Monetary Unions

Clara Raposo[*]

It is with great pleasure that I address you in this celebration of 80 years past Bretton Woods.

Although, sadly, I should start by expressing Governor Mário Centeno's apologies for not being present tonight, against his will and due to last minute unforeseen circumstances. But he asked me to thank The Lisbon Academy of Sciences and The Robert Triffin International Association, in the persons of their Presidents, José Luís Cardoso and Bernard Snoy, for this initiative and for the inclusion of Banco de Portugal in it, as we mark 80 years of an unparalleled event that changed the global financial architecture.

Governor Centeno asked me also to, on his behalf, warmly welcome all distinguished speakers and guests to this conference and to this dinner.

Dear Guests, let me also greet you all but, especially, our distinguished speakers of today and tomorrow — your insightful interventions add to our knowledge and future conduct.

I would like to start by expressing gratitude to our teams at the Banco de Portugal and the Robert Triffin International who made logistics and everything else work beautifully today.

Thank you, José Luís Cardoso, President of the Academy — of which I am also a proud member (my president), and thank you, Bernard Snoy, President of the Robert Triffin International, for tirelessly working so we can be here tonight. Without you it would have been impossible.

Indeed, Bernard, you are a Child of Bretton Woods, born almost exactly nine months after the 1944 conference.

I, myself, was born in 1971, the year of the so-called "Nixon shock", when the United States "temporarily" suspended the US dollar's convertibility to

* This is the text of the dinner speech that Clara Raposo gave on the occasion of the gala dinner kindly offered by the Banco do Portugal.

gold, with the dollar as a fiat currency — the beginning of the end of the Bretton Woods system.

And the rest is history... Our history.

Aren't we all, somehow, children of Bretton Woods? None of our lives would have been what they are, had the IMF or the World Bank not been created, had multilateralism not been a meaningful term.

The agreement emerging from that conference almost 80 years ago is still a cornerstone of today's international monetary and financial system. Although the exchange rate peg that was the symbol of the Bretton Woods system was abandoned in 1973, the IMF and the World Bank remain pillars of the international economic landscape, providing technical and financial assistance to many countries around the globe. These are examples of successful multilateral cooperation that we ought to appreciate, especially today in the face of an increasingly fragmented world.

The floating exchange rate regime that followed the end of Bretton Woods was seen as a proper mechanism to automatically address macroeconomic imbalances that built up in the late 1960s. For countries with sound institutions and credible monetary and fiscal policies, this regime worked well. But for others, it may have induced the idea that competitive devaluations could be a solution to structural problems limiting economic progress. While this may be a necessary mechanism in certain circumstances, it does not by itself treat the root cause of these problems.

In Portugal, we learned it the hard way. We lived through two deep Balance of Payments crises in the early stages of our democratic regime that required the financial assistance of the IMF in 1977–78 and again in 1983. It was only when we entered the then European Economic Community in 1986 that we decisively conducted important structural reforms that would pave the way to a more prosperous future.

Many other countries faced difficulties in adapting to the floating exchange rate regime. Several faced severe banking crises and more generalised financial crises in the 1980s and 1990s. In this context, regional monetary cooperation may provide synergy gains and impose the necessary discipline for a more successful navigation in the international financial system.

The euro is a great example. I would like to address you tonight in an exercise of memory and recognition of the success story of the first 25 years of the euro. There have been massive challenges over the years, including questions about the euro itself, but each time we found the right answers. Today the euro is the common currency of 20 EU countries, used by around 350 million EU citizens every day.

Since its inception, the European integration project was based on the principle of cooperation between independent States, with the ultimate goal of avoiding another war in Europe. The founding fathers believed that strong cooperation and interdependence would foster welfare and peace — and they were right.

Back then, the question was on what dimension to root the European project and how to operationalize it: either through an intergovernmental perspective or a federalist one. The basic dimension of integration was free trade, which materialized in the creation of a customs union that later expanded to a single market. As regards the operating perspective, a combination of intergovernmentalism and federalism was adopted. This combination, with its virtues and its underlying tensions, persists until today.

The progress of the European integration project was gradual, at different speeds across Member States, and along different dimensions. Saying that the European project evolved gradually is not the same as saying that it evolved slowly. Indeed, the relevant historical time frame is much longer than the individual life expectancy. Therefore, given its starting point and progress until now, the European project evolved quite fast. The different speeds of integration were a consequence of political and, most often, economic circumstances. As for the dimensions of integration, the enlargement to new members — the extensive margin — has cohabited with the deepening of integration amongst members — the intensive margin.

Seven enlargements expanded the EU from six founding countries to 27 members today, plus nine candidate countries. The need to sustain strong cohesion policies and an agile decision process in this large and differentiated set of countries are everyday challenges. As for the deepening of the integration process, the full functioning of the single market — with freedom of circulation of goods, services, capital and citizens — and the close coordination and supervision of macroeconomic policies have made the EU a true economic union.

At a given point in this process the creation of a monetary union was possible. The idea had existed for some time, and the monetary union was the right step to take full advantage of the single market. However, only the fall of the Berlin wall and the debate over German reunification made it possible politically.

The benefits and the requirements of the Economic and Monetary Union (EMU) were widely discussed. On the benefits side: the price stability anchored on an independent central bank with a clear mandate, the removal of exchange rate risk amongst members, the reduction of transaction costs and the greater role for the EU in the global market. On the requirements, the need to minimize inflation and competitiveness differentials amongst members, and the need for fiscal prudence ranked first.

The political window of opportunity to create the euro was not wide. The project was initiated without a fully completed architecture and somewhat partial accession criteria. As usual in the EU, the path itself would lead to completion of the process.

The lack of a system to deal with current account crisis (*i.e.* lack of a real lender of last resort), the absence of common supervision and insolvency mechanisms to deal with banks with a systemic importance, the absence of fiscal federalism traits and totally credible fiscal rules were items in the list of things to be done later. Together with a well-integrated European labour market, these items are part of what the literature identifies as criteria for an optimum currency area.

A strong and rapid convergence of inflation and interest rates allowed for a successful adoption of the euro by eleven Member States in 1999, which were joined by Greece two years later. The physical implementation of the euro in 2002 was met with great enthusiasm of most citizens in a surprisingly smooth process.

The first decade of the euro was also very successful. The payments system worked smoothly, and inflation was stable and broadly in line with the ECB's objective. Inflation and interest rate differentials remained remarkably low and stable. Economic agents in countries like Portugal faced financing costs similar to those of its German counterparts.

However, over this period several macroeconomic imbalances began to emerge. Public and external debt of certain countries, among which Portugal, increased significantly, exposing the monetary union to risks for which it was not fully prepared — as some of the most commonly defined criteria for an optimum currency area were not fulfilled, the ability to deal with asymmetric shocks within the monetary union was limited.

The global financial crisis exposed these vulnerabilities in a dramatic fashion. At first, it implied a strong monetary policy response to ensure that liquidity continued to reach all market segments, in a period of extreme distrust among financial market participants. It also ignited a strong fiscal response to minimise the impact of the financial distress on economic activity.

When financial markets shifted their attention to the large fiscal imbalances that had emerged in some countries, we all soon realised that the mere commitment to the single currency was not sufficient to appease these concerns. This had the flavour of a classic speculative attack on a country under a Balance of Payments crisis, but as it could not be addressed through the foreign exchange rate, the burden shifted elsewhere, directly affecting the sovereign debt markets.

The sovereign debt crisis tested the limits of the European integration, and the euro project was even called into question. To be sure, the EU architecture had not foreseen such dire circumstances. But, in the end, the European project emerged stronger. Several reforms and policies implemented in this period were important to provide a more stable environment and enhance the euro area ability to deal with crisis.

The European Stability Mechanism was created to provide financial and technical assistance to countries threatened by severe financing problems. It has been responsible for providing direct financial support to countries under a macroeconomic adjustment programme (as in the cases of Greece, Ireland, Portugal and Cyprus) or in need of indirect bank recapitalisation (as in Spain). But it also offers other instruments — such as purchases of sovereign bonds in the primary or secondary market, or creation of precautionary credit lines — which broadened governments' alternatives to deal with specific liquidity or solvency issues.

At the same time, the EU institutional framework was strengthened. Fiscal rules were reformed to promote prudent fiscal behaviour, while taking into account the cyclical developments of the economy. Macroeconomic imbalances started to be surveyed on a regular basis to better anticipate possible vulnerabilities. Crucially, the first steps towards a banking union that ensures a level playing field for all banks across the EU were also taken, namely with the creation of the Single Supervisory Mechanism and the Single Resolution Board.

Moreover, it is certainly important to recognise the crucial role played by the ECB in guaranteeing a more stable financial environment. ECB President Mario Draghi's words to ensure the ECB's commitment "to do whatever it takes to preserve the euro" in 2012 — and the ensuing announcement of the Outright Monetary Transactions — still echo in our collective memory. The implementation of other non-conventional policy measures, designed to ensure that inflation expectations remained well-anchored, have also supported economic recovery in the aftermath of the sovereign debt crisis.

The lessons learned during the crisis and the reforms in the architecture of the monetary union were decisive to address the unprecedented shocks that hit Europe over the following years.

Policy support at both the European and national levels was crucial to overcome the health and economic crisis triggered by the pandemic. In the presence of a crisis that affected all member countries and not only some, the EU worked together with member states to protect the health of its citizens by promoting research for treatments and vaccines and to mitigate the socio-economic impact of the pandemic by supporting jobs and businesses. The temporary Support to mitigate Unemployment Risks in an Emergency (SURE) is a tangible example of solidarity during this period. It supported short-time work schemes and similar measures that helped Member States protect employees and the self-employed against the risk of unemployment and loss of income. In addition, an ambitious euro area-wide recovery plan was launched in the form of the NGEU and its centrepiece, the Recovery and Resilience Facility. This plan goes well beyond immediate assistance to recover from the crisis and seeks to promote medium-term growth.

Monetary and fiscal policies worked hand in hand, facilitated by the fact that their objectives were naturally aligned. The ECB reacted swiftly by launching an emergency asset purchase programme to counter resurfacing fragmentation risks. The main novelty of PEPP was the unparalleled flexibility of purchases over time, and across asset classes and jurisdictions. This was crucial to safeguard the monetary policy transmission mechanism and ensure that all sectors of the economy could benefit from supportive financing conditions. In turn, governments deployed large fiscal support that went beyond conventional stimulus. Measures were targeted to save lives, to shield the most vulnerable, protect jobs and support firms' financial situation. All this paved the way for a quick recovery after the pandemic.

As we were re-adjusting to more normal times, a second unparalleled shock hit our economies. Russia's unjustified war against Ukraine was particularly hard on European countries which faced the threat of a deep energy crisis. This hampered the ongoing economic recovery and impacted inflation dynamics. Inflation surged as the rise in energy costs spread throughout the economy, adding to inflationary pressures linked to the re-opening of our economies after the pandemic.

Policy priorities changed. The EU has provided Ukraine with humanitarian, political, financial, and military support. On the economic front, EU member states acted together under the *REPowerEU Plan* to address difficulties and disruptions in the global energy market. This translated into savings of almost 20% of EU energy consumption, doubled the additional deployment of renewable energy, and reduce the EU's dependence on Russian fossil fuels. At the same time, euro area governments cushioned against the economic and social consequences of rising prices.

The ECB reacted to the inflation surge by removing the exceptional level of accommodation that characterised the previous years and moved interest rates to restrictive territory. This contributed to bring inflation down towards the target and to keep inflation expectations anchored. The revision of the ECB's new monetary policy strategy announced in mid-2021 played a key role in this period. By recognizing that financial stability is a precondition for price stability, it enabled the approval of the Transmission Protection Instrument (TPI) in July 2022. The conception of the TPI, which has not been activated, insured against fragmentation risks in a context of rising interest rates and allowed for a smooth normalisation of monetary policy.

Despite headwinds, the euro was more resilient than many people thought possible 25 years ago. This is partly due to its popularity among citizens. Support for the euro increased steadily during the most recent period in sharp contrast with the decline seen after the global financial crisis.

While the theoretical conditions for an optimum currency area may still not be fully satisfied, the euro area is now better equipped to deal with asymmetric shocks. Several missing blocks have been put in place, but some are still to be completed such as the capital markets and banking union and a permanent central fiscal capacity. Absence of progress for a prolonged period means exposure to the disruptive consequences of crises.

To keep the euro together, we also need to make the euro area better equipped to deal with medium-term challenges such as population ageing, the climate change and geo-economic fragmentation. Progress in the integration and development of EU capital markets and banking sector is key to mobilise private investments needed to carry out the green and digital transitions and to enhance EU's productivity and competitiveness. Thus, the capital markets union should advance in tandem with the banking union. This is mainly a job for politicians and governments, but central banks can play a part as well, namely by supporting the development and integration of pan-European financial market infrastructures.

Europe is now better prepared and more united. This offers a fertile ground for our joint efforts to continue.

To conclude, let me share some final thoughts based also on the interventions we heard today, by Vice-Governor Máximo dos Santos, the President of the Academy, the President and Vice-Chair of the Robert Triffin International, and by participants in both panels.

Above all, Peace is what united us in Europe, peace and, more generally, the welfare of our citizens. The lessons we have learned must guide us in the difficult current geopolitical setting.

Despite the fact that there is strong antagonism and polarization in today's world, the Bretton Woods institutions are still core, for the multilateral approach that must be adopted to reach a global solution to the challenges of our time. This we know in Europe.

Last month, in Washington D.C., during the Spring Meetings of the IMF and World Bank Group — and with this Lisbon Conference in mind — the first session I attended was precisely The Bretton Woods Committee's session on *Celebrating 80 Years of Bretton Woods: What's Next?* It was the most packed session of the meeting that I attended. I had been invited, had enrolled, and was lucky to find a little step free where I sat, surrounded by people standing. This shows how Bretton Woods is still a safe harbor to plan new journeys.

We need better dialogue; it must be a different kind of dialogue to reach multilateral solutions.

We are all, somehow, children of Bretton Woods. The time has come to honour its principles and, together, at last, build trust and join forces to jointly solve global problems. For the sake of our children.

SECTION 2

The State of Regional Economic and Monetary Cooperation

Lessons from the Past and Issues for the Future

80 Years After Bretton Woods. Opening Remarks

José Luís Cardoso

Welcome to the Academy of Sciences of Lisbon for the continuation of the conference initiated yesterday at the Bank of Portugal.

I am not a specialist in the topics of this conference, so you can rest assured that I won't be talking about the vicissitudes of the international monetary system over the last 80 years, nor about the fantastic adventures of multilateralism and regional monetary unions over the next 80 years. I would never risk making considerations on a subject that does not fall within my areas of expertise, even when the lessons learnt from yesterday's session may suggest that a basic degree of common sense seems to be sufficient to deal with problems that are, after all, more geopolitical in nature. Yet I trust this is a matter for specialists.

However, through the lenses of an historian of economic ideas, I have always been interested in the outcomes of the Bretton Woods Conference, 80 years ago, especially due to the essential role played by John Maynard Keynes in the organization of the conference and of its several preparatory meetings. (It should be noted, *en passant*, that when travelling to the United States for one of these preparatory meetings, Keynes made a stop in Lisbon which was certainly an inspiration for his strategic conversations…).

We all know that his original proposal, that included the creation of a new global reserve currency called *bancor* and an international clearing union to manage exchange rates, did not materialize successfully. Keynes was a leading element of the United Kingdom delegation, which, however, was unable to go against the proposal of the American delegation, led by Harry Dexter White, who favoured a system centred around the US dollar (the hegemon's currency, as labelled by Renato Flôres Jr. in the paper presented to this conference) as the primary reserve currency, backed by gold.

Anyway, a compromise was eventually reached, resulting in the creation of the International Monetary Fund (IMF) and the World Bank (WB), which were based on some of Keynes' ideas and projects.

The outcome of Bretton Woods notwithstanding, it is nevertheless important to stress the innovative nature and inspired vision of the Keynes Plan, according to which creditor countries were obliged to keep their balance of payments surpluses in international currency (the infamous bancor) and were prohibited from cancelling or converting these surpluses into bancor when they accumulate persistently and beyond the fixed limits.

Thus, the Keynes Plan presented: a) a multilateral compensation mechanism integrated into an international organization, aiming at multilateralising intergovernmental payments; b) an international currency disconnected from any country's money supply; and c) an adjustment process in which creditor countries also had their share of responsibility in keeping the sustainability of the system, so to speak.

It is important to recognise that none of these provisions would be incorporated into the Bretton Woods Agreement, neither was Keynes' proposal that the institutions that came out of it (IMF and WB) should immediately play an active role in granting credit to countries that needed it.

However, the way in which the international monetary and financial system was adapted to the concrete needs of economic reconstruction in the aftermath of the Second World War (the Marshall Plan and the European Payments Union) ended up doing justice to some of Keynes' ideas that could not be achieved at the closing of the Bretton Woods Agreement in July 1944. The collapse of the Bretton Woods system in the early 1970s does not prove that Keynes was right, since we do not know what he would have suggested in order to avoid that collapse.

But we always learn from his inspired, innovative, and powerful ideas. Basically, as regards the creation of institutions that serve as a framework to further economic and financial regulation and, above all, to foster international cooperation needed to promote economic stability and development on a global scale. The very nature of the topics to be discussed in our session today, deal precisely with these issues raised by J.M. Keynes.

When referring to this inspiring perspective, I have particularly in mind the contents of the message conveyed by the founding father of modern economics in Portugal, António Manuel Pinto Barbosa, in a conference held at this Academy in 1977 to celebrate the legacy of Keynes, in which he gave special attention to the role played by Keynes in the preparation of the Bretton Woods Agreement[1]. Pinto Barbosa was a distinguished member of

---

1 Barbosa A. M. P. (1981), "Keynes e o Acordo de Bretton Woods", in *Simpósio de Estudos Keynesianos*, Lisboa: Academia das Ciências de Lisboa, 93-116.

this Academy of Sciences and has also served as Governor of the Bank of Portugal, being lately committed to activities at the Bank of International Settlements in Basel.

Therefore, this reference shows the long-lasting concern of this Academy with the study of Bretton Woods and its aftermath, making this place quite appropriate to the presentations and roundtables included in today's programme.

I wish to express again my deep gratitude for the smooth cooperation between the Academy of Sciences of Lisbon, the Bank of Portugal and the Robert Triffin International for the organization of this conference.

The State of Regional Economic and Monetary Cooperation in Africa: Lessons from the Past and Issues for the Future

Zenaida Maria Lopes Cassama

Introduction

Since their independence, African countries have made economic and monetary cooperation and regional integration part of their strategy for structural transformation. The objectives were to overcome the major obstacles hindering the development of African economies, in particular the small size of the economies, the lack of structural complementarities and the dependence on imports of intermediate goods and finished products.

Economic and monetary cooperation should therefore offer opportunities for market expansion, economies of scale and diversification of the productive base. In this context, several economic cooperation and integration agreements have been concluded, including the Common Market for Eastern and Southern Africa (COMESA), the Southern African Development Community (SADC), the Arab Maghreb Union (AMU) and agreements within the Economic Community of West African States (ECOWAS). These agreements have been supported by the action of several continental organizations and institutions, notably the African Union (AU) and the African Development Bank (ADB), through their mission to promote African unity and the development of the continent.

In the face of globalization and renewed geopolitical uncertainty, there is growing interest in economic and monetary unification in Africa. A number of initiatives have been launched, and it is important to draw useful lessons from them in order to gain a better appreciation of the challenges to be met and the main issues to be taken into consideration in an international context marked by growing uncertainties and various shocks.

In this note, which is only meant to set the table for a discussion, we shall analyze the dynamics of cooperation in Africa, highlighting the main lessons to be learned and the perspectives.

The following section presents the current state of economic and monetary integration in Africa. This will be followed by a discussion of the main lessons and challenges before drawing conclusions.

1. Economic and monetary integration in Africa

1.1. Integration at continental level

The ambition of the continent's highest authorities is to create an African Monetary Union by harmonizing regional monetary zones and setting up an African Central Bank (ACB), an African Monetary Fund (AMF) and the African Investment Bank (AIB). This commitment has resulted in a number of initiatives, including:

- the adoption of the Protocol relating to the African Investment Bank (AIB), which aims to stimulate economic integration and the development of the African Union (AU), through the financing of development projects, in accordance with the objectives of the AU. The initial authorized capital is USD 25 billion;
- the adoption of the Protocol relating to the African Monetary Fund (AMF), with an authorized capital of USD 22.640 billion. This Fund aims to promote macroeconomic stability, inclusive and sustainable economic growth and balanced development on the continent, with a view to facilitating the effective integration of African economies;
- the establishment of the African Continental Free Trade Area (AfCFTA), with a view to accelerating intra-African trade and strengthening Africa's commercial position on the world market. The main aim of the AfCFTA is to liberalize trade in goods and services through the gradual elimination of tariff and non-tariff barriers between participating countries, as well as cooperation in the areas of investment, intellectual property rights and competition policy;
- the adoption of the Programme for Monetary Cooperation in Africa (PCMA), which establishes the convergence criteria and defines the economic measures and timetable leading to the creation of the African Central Bank, with a view to a single African currency, in accordance with the AU's Agenda 2063. To this end, eight (8) Regional Economic Communities (RECs), pillars of the AU, have been recognized to facilitate

regional economic integration between the members of each of the continent's regions.

The performance of the RECs is mixed, particularly in terms of trade integration and macroeconomic convergence:

- intra-regional trade within the continent represents only 15.4% of total trade, compared with 61.7% for the European Union and 23.3% for the Association of Southeast Asian Nations. Among the RECs, intra-regional trade is highest in SADC (21.0%), EAC (11.5%) and ECOWAS (10.7%);
- over the period 2020–2023, the performance of the RECs in terms of macroeconomic convergence has deteriorated compared to 2011–2019.

Despite the maintenance of appreciable economic growth in 2023 (between 2.5% and 5.2%), the main difficulties encountered by the RECs relate to strong inflationary pressures (between 6.8% and 20.9%), a high budget deficit (between 3.6% and 5.1% of GDP) and an increase in the public debt ratio (between 50.4% and 66.7% of GDP).

1.2. Economic and monetary cooperation within ECOWAS

The main objective of the Economic Community of West African States (ECOWAS) is to strengthen cooperation between its Member States, with a view to creating an economic and monetary union, in order to raise the standard of living of the population, through increased development of trade and integration into global value chains. In this context, the exercise of taking stock of this cooperation 49 years after the signing of the ECOWAS Constitutive Treaty in 1975 is a difficult task. Essentially, the results of West African regional integration are mixed. However, concrete actions have been taken, namely: (i) the trade liberalization scheme within the Community characterized by the formation of a customs union, with the adoption of the ECOWAS Common External Tariff (ECOWAS CET), which has been in force since 1 January 2015, with a view to accelerating the trade development process, (ii) the introduction of an ECOWAS biometric identity card, as well as (iii) the implementation of several programmes and infrastructure development in the areas of energy and road transport, in order to promote intra-regional trade and the free movement of people and goods.

Furthermore, in order to speed up the process of integrating the region's economies, the option of monetary integration seems to be favored, although it is a necessary but not sufficient condition. This option mainly led to the implementation of the ECOWAS Monetary Cooperation Programme (EMCP) and the creation of a multilateral surveillance mechanism for the Economic and Financial Policies of Member States.

The results of 37 years of implementation of the CMCP show that the Community is experiencing difficulties in achieving economic and especially monetary integration, despite a regularly renewed determination by the region's political leaders to speed up the process. To this end, a roadmap is being implemented with the aim of creating a single currency and a common ECOWAS Central Bank by 2027. With this in mind, high-level technical exchanges are continuing.

The ECOWAS multilateral surveillance mechanism aims to ensure closer coordination of Member States' economic policies and to support the macroeconomic convergence process. In accordance with the provisions of the Community Pact in force, there has been a deterioration in the macroeconomic performance of Member States in terms of compliance with the convergence criteria, due in particular to the COVID-19 pandemic and the war in Ukraine. In 2023, ECOWAS' economic performance have been marked by inflationary pressures, tighter financing conditions, debt sustainability challenges and exchange rate depreciation, among other factors:

- in 2023, real GDP growth stood at 3.4%, compared to 3.9% in 2022;
- end-of-period inflation increased from 16.9% in 2022 to 20.1% in 2023;
- the budget deficit (including grants) was reduced by 1.8 percentage points, from 6.3% of GDP in 2022 to 4.5% of GDP in 2023;
- the budget deficit financing by Central Bank was estimated at 9.9% of fiscal revenue in 2023, compared to 70.9% in 2022;
- foreign exchange reserves in months of imports stood at 3.7 months in 2023, after 4.5 months in 2022;
- the outstanding public debt is estimated at 55.2% of GDP at the end of December 2023, compared to 49.9% of GDP at the end of December 2022.

In total, no ECOWAS country met all the first-rank criteria in 2023 as in the previous two years (2021 and 2022).

1.3 Monetary and economic integration in the WAEMU

The West African Monetary Union (WAMU) has an exceptional longevity in the history of integration in the world, established in 1962 compared to the European Monetary Union established in 1999. The WAMU, which has been in force since the early years of independence, is made up, among other things, of the signatory states of the relevant treaty, characterized by the recognition of the same monetary unit, the Franc de la Communauté Financière Africaine (FCFA), which is issued by BCEAO. In this way, the monetary integration of countries preceded economic and commercial integration. With a view to adding a broader economic dimension to WAMU, the Union's authorities created WAEMU on 10 January 1994.

The main results of the monetary and economic integration of the WAEMU Member States are outlined below.

1.3.1. Some elements of successful monetary and financial integration of WAEMU Member States

In terms of monetary integration, the Union's success is linked to the credibility and effectiveness of BCEAO. The Central Bank has made a significant contribution to creating a favorable environment for economic and financial exchanges, by safeguarding the internal and external value of the currency. In this respect, the Central Bank has constantly ensured price stability in order to preserve the purchasing power of the currency, which has facilitated the convergence of inflation rates in the Member States. Indeed, the Union's inflation rate has risen from +2.5% in 2002–2010 to +1.2% in 2011–2019 and +4.2% in 2020–2023. The underperformance seen over the latter period is linked to the successive shocks of COVID-19 as well as the conflicts in Ukraine and the Middle East. The measures taken by the Central Bank to normalize monetary policy have made it possible to contain the extent of these shocks to the Union's economies.

In the same vein, BCEAO has worked to continuously strengthen the regulatory and supervisory frameworks for the Union's banking sector by aligning the relevant common standards with international norms. It participated in the establishment of the WAEMU Regional Financial Market in 1996 and in the creation, in 2012, of the regional agency to support the issuance and management of the public securities of the WAEMU States, known as 'UMOA-Titres'. It has also undertaken several initiatives to promote financial inclusion and the digitalization of payments, with a view to developing the financial sector, strengthening economic integration and improving the business environment. These initiatives relate, among other things, to: (i) setting up regional payment infrastructures, consisting of real-time gross settlement systems (STAR-UEMOA) and bulk payment clearing systems (SICA-UEMOA and GIM-UEMOA), (ii) adopting a regulatory framework for payment systems with a specific mechanism for issuing electronic money, (iii) the promotion of access by microfinance institutes to the regional payment system, and (iv) the implementation of the digital financial services interoperability project in the WAEMU.

In view of the above, the results of monetary integration in WAMU are largely positive, supported by monetary and financial stability, which is an essential factor in fostering economic growth.

1.3.2. Elements of successful economic integration within the WAEMU

The economic integration aspect of WAEMU has been marked by a number of successful initiatives:

- the introduction of the WAEMU Common External Tariff (WAEMU CET);
- the adoption of the multilateral surveillance mechanism;
- the establishment of the Common Agricultural Policy;
- the development of a forward-looking vision for the Union up to 2040, with the aim of strengthening the competitiveness of WAEMU economies, while at the same time making them part of a sustainable development dynamic.

In particular, the implementation of the multilateral surveillance mechanism complements the actions taken by the Central Bank to consolidate the stability of the macroeconomic framework. As such, this mechanism should make it possible to preserve the effectiveness of monetary policy and the achievements of monetary integration. It relies on the implementation of the Convergence Pact between Member States to ensure peer surveillance. The purpose of this Pact is to strengthen convergence and macroeconomic stability in the WAEMU, and it defines, among other things, the convergence criteria to be respected by the States parties. Within this framework, better coordination of the common monetary policy and national budgetary policies has enabled the Union to post good macroeconomic performances in terms of growth, inflation, budget deficit, debt and current account deficit over the period 2011–2019. However, the successive shocks mentioned above (COVID-19, the Russo-Ukrainian and Middle East conflicts) have significantly affected the momentum of compliance with the convergence criteria by WAEMU Member States over the period 2020–2023.

Table 1: Main economic indicators for the Sub-Saharan Africa and WAEMU over the period 2011-2023

	2011-2019	2020	2021	2022	2023
Sub-Saharan Africa					
GDP Growth (%)	3,8	-1,6	4,7	4,0	3,3
Inflation (en %)	8,3	10,1	11,0	14,5	15,8
Budget deficit/GDP (in %)	3,3	6,5	5,0	4,4	4,3
Public debt/GDP (in %)	37,7	57,1	56,6	57,1	57,7
WAEMU					
GDP Growth (%)	5,6	1,4	6,1	5,7	5,6
Inflation (en %)	1,2	2,1	3,6	7,4	3,7
Budget deficit/GDP (in %)	2,9	5,6	5,4	6,7	5,1
Public debt/GDP (in %)	34,6	49,6	54,6	57,6	59,6

Sources: BCEAO, FMI (October, 2023)

1.3.3. Guinea-Bissau in the WAEMU

In the specific case of Guinea-Bissau, its integration into the WAEMU from 1997 has enabled it to control inflation, strengthen its financial system with solid banking institutions and promote fiscal consolidation, due to the community harmonized rules. As a result, the country's annual inflation rate has fallen from 52.6% between 1980 and 1997 to 2.6% between 1998 and 2023. The exchange rate of the local currency, which had depreciated steadily in the past, stabilized with the adoption of the FCFA. The country's membership of the WAEMU has also enabled Guinea-Bissau to benefit from the common currency reserve and to break out of the cycles of persistent shortages that often prevented Guinea-Bissau from importing essential products, leading to frequent shortages of these products on the markets. The overall budget deficit has been reduced from 15.2% of GDP in 1996 to 6.6% in 2023. The external current account deficit has also improved, from 21% of GDP in 1996 to 7.7% of GDP in 2023. The resilience of the financial sector has been strengthened by actions taken at regional level.

2. Main lessons and perspectives

The slow pace of economic and monetary integration in the regional communities is due to lack of structural reforms and poor quality of institutions, on the one hand, and endogenous and exogenous shocks, on the other. To this end, the following challenges need to be addressed:
With regard to economic policies:

- boosting regional trade, in order to increase the resilience and stability of the RECs;
- significantly improve performance in achieving macroeconomic convergence including by strengthening multilateral surveillance mechanism;
- harmonization of economic policies: improved coordination of monetary, fiscal and exchange rate policies and structural reforms is essential for obtaining better economic outcomes;
- refocusing the medium-term budgetary strategy, ensuring compliance with fiscal rules and better targeting of public subsidies will boost investors confidence;
- establishing a common framework and regulations to ensure the stability of the monetary and financial system at regional and continental level;
- improving the level of financial integration within the continent;
- statistical harmonization to better guide economic policies.

At the political and institutional level:

- resolving issues relating to overlapping membership within the RECs, in so far as the multiple memberships of African countries require them to meet, for example, several convergence conditions and financial obligations as part of their participation in the regional integration process;
- strengthening the principle of the independence of Central Banks.

For WAEMU economies, the challenges lie in particular in:

- preserving the achievements of monetary and economic integration namely by strengthening coordination between monetary and fiscal policy, to ensure strong and sustained growth;
- actions to help Member States accelerate structural transformation of their economies, taking into account the problems associated with climate change;
- deepening the Common Agricultural Policy, with a view to sustainably meeting the food needs of its populations, while contributing to the economic and social development of its Member States;
- improving the security and business climate.

At a time when regional economic and monetary integration in Africa is facing new challenges and opportunities in a world that is more prone to shocks, the role of international cooperation, particularly the international monetary system, remains crucial for inclusive growth and sustainable development in these regions. This role essentially consists of:

- facilitating capital flows and the stability of financial transactions, and preventing financial crises;
- stimulating the financing that developing countries need for their investments;
- promoting the transfer of low-carbon technologies needed to mitigate climate change and its effects on economic growth;
- contribute to raising the continent's voice within international decision-making bodies, in order to better convey Africa's aspirations.

Whatever the results achieved in the integration process, it remains essential to strengthen economic and monetary cooperation in order to stimulate intra-African trade and enhance economic resilience and monetary stability. The outlook should be consistent with this, with resolute ambitions to create a single currency within ECOWAS. Furthermore, the creation of the African Continental Free Trade Area (AfCFTA) offers real prospects in terms of cooperation. In support of this initiative, the Pan-African Payment and Settlement System (PAPSS) was officially launched on 13 January 2022, with the aim of promoting the efficient and secure circulation of money across African borders, while minimizing risks and contributing to the financial integration within the continent.

Conclusion

Regional economic and monetary integration in Africa faces new challenges and opportunities in a world more prone to shocks. The role of international cooperation, in particular the international monetary system, remains crucial for inclusive growth and sustainable development in these regions.

This role essentially consists of:

- facilitating capital flows and the stability of financial transactions, and preventing financial crises;
- providing the financing that developing countries need for their investments;
- promoting the transfer of low-carbon technologies needed to mitigate climate change and its effects on economic growth;
- contribute to raising the continent's voice in international decision-making bodies, in order to convey Africa's aspirations.

The progress towards a more interconnected and mutually supportive world is marked by challenges, but also by great opportunities. Monetary unions, as manifestations of close economic cooperation and regional solidarity, offer a path towards renewed and strengthened multilateralism. They illustrate how, by joining forces and aligning economic policies, member countries can together build a more prosperous and harmonious future for all.

The Escudo Monetary Zone and Monetary Cooperation in Africa: Lessons from the Past and Issues for the Future

Maria Eugénia Mata

Introduction

The contemporary history of Africa is the history of colonization and decolonization (Hopkins 1973). The Portuguese people encompassed the globe since the 16th century, and the country's colonial holdings made Portugal a pillar of prosperity, which vanished with the independence of Brazil in 1822.

The colonial expansion was a traditional feature of the Portuguese nation's culture (Bethencourt, Ramada Curto, 2007). The colonization in Africa came back anew (Smith 1985). In the 20th century, the defeat of Germany and the Ottoman and Austro-Hungarian empires in the First World War led to considerable adjustments in African colonial control and borders. Portugal preserved the colonial empire in Africa, which the Berlin Conference (1885) had established. As in most colonization systems, the principles for this colonial empire were not wholly different from the past, namely in what respects administration, miscegenation, trade specialization, and monetary integration (Accominotti, Flandreau, Rezzik, and Zumer 2009; Frankema 1999; Mata 2007). It is the purpose of this chapter to examine the virtues of the multipolar monetary regime used between Portugal and the African territories under Portuguese sovereignty, in studying the details on the clearing of financial flows among all the regions in such an integrated system.

1. The Monetary Integration in the Escudo Monetary Zone

Economic integration of colonial territories as a road to prosperity and economic growth was a fundamental blueprint for Portugal. The empire in Africa consisted of three territories, Guinea (36,000 km^2), Angola (1,247,000 km^2), and Mozambique (784,000 km^2), and two Atlantic archipelagos, Cape Verde and S. Tome and Prince. Two Asian territories (Macao and East Timor) were also under Portuguese administration, as vestiges of a previous Portuguese empire. The *escudo* was the common monetary unit in all these regions under Portuguese sovereignty. A multipolar system of multilateral trade with free labour and capital movements based a multipolar monetary and financial system to settle payments, the Portuguese *Escudo* Zone Monetary Union (EZMU).

In adding historical evidence on the flaws of the system resulting from a rebel war for the independence of the colonies, this chapter can illustrate the importance of complicity, political cohesion, trust, and confidence, for the success of regional monetary unions. The EZMU went to an end with decolonization. However, the experience on monetary agreements with three African newly independent countries, reveals the monetary collusion coming from the permanent international cooperation between Portugal and African partners.

2. The Portuguese *Escudo* Monetary Union

Although the monetary unit was the *escudo*, in all the spaces under Portuguese sovereignty, there were different currency circulations, which were purposely issued for each one of the territories (Estêvão 1991; Mseba 2016.). The system had three issuing banks. The Bank of Portugal was the issuing bank for European Portugal. The National Overseas Bank (Banco Nacional Ultramarino BNU) was the issuing bank for the entire colonial empire, since 1864, except for Angola, since the 1920s (Bohannan 1959.). The crises of the 1920s awarded issuing rights to Banco de Angola for this colony. This decade had large impact on pricing of tropical commodities and brought difficulties for banking (Gardener 2015; Maxon 1989). In Angola they led to a financial crisis, and BNU lost its issuing rights in favour of Banco de Angola (Kindleberger 1973).

All local *escudos* were equivalent thanks to the 1:1 parity rule. The Bank of Portugal was the central bank of the EZMU, gathering all the means of international payments (gold and foreign currencies) of this monetary union. Laws from 1962 regulated the entire system in detail. Specialized staff in the central bank accounted for the monthly balances of payments of each one of the members in the EZMU with each one of the other members in the system. Based on them, a clearing system was used to account for the net positions for each of the partners, which were presented as net debt or net credit positions, depending on the existence of deficits or surpluses. To match a net debt position of a territory, the agent of the system used gold and foreign currencies of the reserve account of this territory in Banco de Portugal.[1] At the image of the hegemonic stability provided by macroprudential IMF policy in the Bretton Woods system, there was a Fund for the EZMU to award credit to partners who were struggling in settling payments. This was an important aspect, as it provided lending as a last resort. Automatic loans were awarded according to current needs (and respecting established ceilings), but the concession of special loans beyond these ceilings required detailed justification to the Board of Directors of the Fund.

Despite the economic and financial elegance of rules in monetary unions, such as in the Portuguese EZMU, financial stability in the system required a huge and costly effort by political power — as Kindleberger (1973) recognizes for anyone. A monetary union is mainly a political issue. Geographical distance, rigidities, non-reciprocal relationships, asymmetric shocks, and guerrillas brought significant flaws to the EZMU. All colonies could settle their payments among them. The small colonies had cumulative net positions with mainland Portugal of about zero. They had productive specializations and modest amounts of imports because they had few local elites consuming sophisticated imports from mainland Portugal. On the contrary, Angola and Mozambique had no capacity to settle their payments to mainland Portugal. To face this problem, they turned to automatic loans from the EZMU Fund,[2] and they needed to secure special loans from the Fund, putting pressure on the legal ceilings.[3] Development plans launched multi-layered public works and great infrastructures in these colonies (such as rail and road networks, airports, and dams), which required capital for investment in equipment and technology from Portugal, to be paid in mainland escudos (Mata, Costa and Justino 2017). The result was the accumulation of gold and

1 According to articles 28, 29 and 34 of decree-law 44703 of 17 November 1962.

2 According to articles 29 and 35 of decree-law 44703 of 17 November 1962.

3 *Processo nº 40, Aumento da circulação fiduciária de Moçambique".* PT/CGD/BNU/O1OA/5CG/1-O25. *Caixa Geral dos Depósitos* Historical Archives.

other international means of payments in Mainland Portugal.[4] Moreover, guerrillas for independence in both colonies brought fears on the future of the empire. The desire of locals to transfer profits, dividends, and savings to be safer in mainland Portugal led to increasing lags, because local Exchange Funds needed mainland-Portugal escudos or international means of payments for this purpose. This obliged to long queuing for private transfers into mainland-Portugal, which reached almost a full year of delay. Parallel illegal markets could circumvent the problem but using depreciated exchange rates for the Angolan and Mozambican escudos (Mata, Machado 2017). This was a consequence of the intra-empire rules for payments, which precipitated the decision to reform the system in 1971 to increase the capital of the EZMU Fund for more lending as a last resort (Mata 2022).

Decolonization brought the end of the EZMU because of the Portuguese military defeat in Guinea in 1973. Summing up to the end of the Bretton Woods system and the oil shock difficulties, the April 1974 democratic revolution put an end to the Salazar-Caetano political regime, which had been so much politically committed to overseas integration and decided to decolonize (Mata 2023). The EZMU Fund closed operations in 1980.

Looking at past monetary unions, the historical evidence reveals the short duration of those without political cohesion. This is the case of the 1866–1914 Latin Union experiment.[5] The same happened to the 1875–1914 Scandinavian monetary union (comprising Sweden, and Denmark, with Faroe Islands, Iceland, and Greenland), for example. The successful monetary integration of the USA, the German unification, and the Italian unification are the successful cases related with strengthened political cohesion. Successful currency areas and monetary unions suggest strong political commitment, otherwise monetary integration is unsustainable (Frankel and Rose 1998).

---

4 *Relatório do Banco de Portugal*, 1969, p. 15. This argument was retaken during the negotiations for the independence of the territories by the independence movements, particularly FRELIMO, because of Mozambican migrants' work in South African gold mining.

5 Comprising France, Belgium, Italy, and Switzerland since 1866, Greece since 1868, Romania since 1889, Spain since 1868, Bulgaria, Serbia and Montenegro since 1889

3. The monetary systems of Portuguese speaking countries in post-colonial times

Differently from British and French post-colonial cases, the framing of a new post-colonial escudo zone was impossible (Schenk 2010). In the negotiated independence agreements with Portugal, each one of the Portuguese African colonies declared to want a national currency to stress their political independence and celebrate their national heroes. It took some time before national banknotes were printed, case by case. For a while, the colonial banknotes were in circulation, but with a stamp with the name of the new monetary unit, in the country. Table 1 describes the different cases.

Table 1 The new monetary units and their circulation, in the newly independent countries

Country	Independence date	Monetary unit
Guinea-Bissau	10 Sept 1974	*Peso* since 1976
Mozambique	25 Jun 1975, Lusaka agreements	*Metical* since 1980
Cape Verde	29 Sept 1975, Argel agreements	*Escudo, since* 1977
Angola	11 Nov 1975, Alvor agréments	*Kuanza* since 1976
S. Tome and Prince	29 Sept 1975, Argel agreements	*Dobra* since 1976
Macao	20 Dec 1999 China's Administration	*Pataca,* pegged to HKD
East Timor	A long independence process	USD

The case of East Timor long independence process was somewhat complex. Decolonized East Timor suffered a civil war between two different local parties (FRETILIN and UDT), and FRETILIN unilaterally declared the independence on 28 Nov 1975. Indonesian military forces occupied the territory on 7 Dec 1975. Timor was formally annexed by Indonesia on 17 Jul 1976, and the Indonesian rupia became the local currency. As FRETILIN and UDT organized an armed resistance until 1989, negotiations between Portugal and Indonesia with the support of the United Nations (UN), led to a 1999 agreement for a referendum on annexation[6]. The results against annexation led to a transitory UN's administration, and to the independence on 20 May 2002. The USD was adopted as the local currency (Mata, Valério 2011).

The local headquarters of the colonial issuing banks were transformed into their national banks, which also received all assets, liabilities, equipment, and staff (Mata 2020). The cooperation between Portugal and the newly independent countries began immediately after, thanks to a credit system for trading. An international specialization was at work, as a stimulus to Portuguese sectors of commodities such as textiles, shoes, agricultural and industrial technology, or scholar and scientific books, against tropical productions and Angolan oil (Mata, Nunes and Roldão 2021). Multilayered cooperation also included education and training of banking, military and technical staff, road network improvements, seaports, culture assistance (movies, cinema, and theatre), communications, and oil investment, using the same rules for all the newly independent countries[7]. This cooperation has faced the difficulties of dealing with flexible exchange rates, due to their erratic pattern and volatility worldwide. Credible macroeconomic policies and central bank reserves strained "the credibility of uncoordinated intervention in the foreign-exchange market", in a global perspective (Macedo 1986.). To manage this float in a context of trade interdependences, cooperation has led to monetary peg agreements.

4. Portuguese Monetary agreements with Guinea, Cape Verde, and S. Tome and Prince and their Atlantic meaning

In 1990, a first Monetary Agreement was firmed with Guines-Bissau, the Acordo de Arranjo Monetário (AAM), to peg the *peso* to the Portuguese escudo (Macedo 1987). Beginning to work in 1991, it was supported by a credit line of 1,600 million escudos. Portuguese technical aid from BP was at work

---

6 Portugal. Banco de Portugal. 120-002-003 Coop. Bilateral com PALOP e Timor-Leste 1999-2000, Timor.

7 Portugal. Bank of Portugal Historical Archives. Pasta Delegação de Luanda, various; Acordos com os PALOPs (textos originais) 1979/1982. Departamento de Estrangeiro. Divisão da Secretaria e Apoio ao Gabinete Técnico; Acordos de Crédito entre o Banco de Portugal e os Bancos Centrais dos PALOPs 1986-88.

since 1991, thanks to Unidade Técnica do Arranjo Monetário (UTAM)[8]. The AAM failed in 1992, because macroeconomic stabilization could not be achieved (Saramago 1993). As Guinea-Bissau is in French-speaking Africa, long negotiations went on from August 1986 to May 1996 with the West African Monetary Union (WAMU) to join the CFA. With a participation of 1/7 of the equity of Banque Centrale des Etats de l'Afrique Occidentale (BCEAO), on 1 January 1998 Guinea-Bissau joined the CFA at the exchange rate of 65 *pesos*= 1 CFA franc (Bourgui 1979; Black 1986).

The second Portuguese monetary agreement was firmed with Cape Verde in 1998 to peg the Cape Verdean *escudo* to the Portuguese *escudo,* at parity (1:1), after a long cooperation experience[9]. As Portugal joined the Euro Zone, the parity was established with the euro and goes on successfully[10]. The third Monetary Agreement was firmed with S. Tome and Prince in 2010 to peg the dobra to the euro, at parity (1:1) based on a credit line of 25 million euros, after a long run cooperation with Portugal[11]. These two last cases of regional monetary integration have been successful until now as instruments for national political sovereignties, meaning Portugal's respectful consideration for the human real world values that led to national independences[12].

International cooperation with all Portuguese-speaking countries in the world was also expressed on July 17, 1996, when a formal community for them (CPLP) was born[13]. One of the members, Brazil, also belongs to the G5 BRICS, with the two emerging new powers (India and China) beyond Russia and South Africa (Robson 1983). Mathematical and computational exercises on the macroeconomic variables of these countries "help to disentangle

8 Portugal. Bank of Portugal Historical Archives.Various; Garrido, Helena, "Palop e banco central reforçam cooperação", *Diário de Notícias*, 30-10-1991.

9 Portugal. Bank of Portugal Historical Archives. 120-002-006 Acordos de Cooperação 1981-82, Acordos de Cooperação com Cabo Verde.

10 Portugal. Banco de Portugal. Bank of Portugal Historical Archives. 120-002-007 Coop. Multilateral. Encontros e Mesas Redondas. 1991/1992 1º e 2º Encontro de Lisboa. Volume ½; 120-002-007 Cooperação Multilateral, Encontros e Mesas Redondas, 1993, 3º Encontro de Lisboa, vol 1/1.

11 Portugal. Banco de Portugal. 120-002-011 Cooperação. Assuntos diversos 1979-1987.

12 Fieszbein 1989, in Portugal. Bank of Portugal Historical Archives. Pasta Acordo de Arranjo Monétario c/ a Guiné-Bissau, 1991 a 1996.

13 Portugal. Bank of Portugal Historical Archives. 120-002-003 Coop. Bilateral c/ PALOP e Timor 2002. Visitas Estagiários Angola, C. Verde e Guiné-Bissau, 2002.

euphoria about globalization by revealing how financially interconnected the world has become in the new millennium, and how difficult it is to say that the 2008-2015 convergence and synchronization is the turning point for de-globalization" (Lopes; Machado; Mata; Huffsto, 2018). Effective surveillance for higher sustainability of economic growth and welfare is urgent and requires national self-interest defense against what Triffin (1991) calls the *built-in destabilizer mechanics*, because "USA imbalances can be seen as calling the cadence to which integrated markets march — progressing from independent strides of individuals to ever greater lock-step of a unit" Triffin (1991). The new-millennium frequent imbalance episodes of macroeconomic disequilibria, instability, and financial markets pro-cyclicality may require new local or global monetary arrangements for collective global action (Ghymers, 2021; Johnson and Swoboda 1973; Braz 1993)[14]. Global power relations have changed thanks to growing international trade, mobility and increasing capital flows in financial markets, based on an increased number of new national economies, namely in Africa (Masini 2021). This is the time for inclusive, rule-based, global monetary adjustments, to face a possible world tragedy. Synchronized cyclicality may reveal a global trap, because a frictional armament race for recovery may mean the absence of effective cooperation, as it happened the interwar period (Kindleberger 1973). As a result, military conflicts and terrorism may continue to spring up, but this is the bloodiest way to solve competition, as historical evidence can prove (Lopes, Machado, Mata, 2016; Machado, Mata, 2015; Macedo, 1987).

Conclusion

Portuguese historical globalization led to long cooperation ties with Portuguese-speaking partners in three continents (Africa, Asia, and America). This community, CPLP, with a regional integration shape in the international monetary system, has strong multilateral relationships with many other European, Asian, African, and American partners. There are common interests to improve endogenous growth dynamics in CPLP members, for their participation at a more balanced multipolar effective global governance, in

[14] Braz (1993), in Bank of Portugal Historical Archives. 120-002-007 Cooperação Multilateral, Encontros e Mesas Redondas, 1993, 3º Encontro de Lisboa, vol 1/1.

the present and the future. Beyond a common language and culture, they all gather at an annual meeting of their central bank governors for a common strategy to promote economic growth sustainability with workable shared competences in regional (Atlantic and Asian) blocks to rely on regional safety nets, facing the current risk mismatch for national monetary policies. Strong ties to the European culture and the European Monetary Union may bring a fair and conspicuous cooperation between the multipolar regional organizations, to which they may belong, and the Euro area (EMU), to face the growing global imbalances of the new millennium, well explained by the Triffin dilemma.

References

Accominotti O., Flandreau M., Rezzik R. and Zumer F. (2010), "Black man's burden, white man's welfare: control, devolution and development in the British Empire, 1880–1914," *European Review of Economic History*, Vol. 14, Issue 1, 47–70.

Allen P. R. and Kenen P. (1980), *Asset markets, Exchange rates and economic integration, a synthesis*, Cambridge: Cambridge University Press.

Banco de Portugal (1969), *Relatório do Banco de Portugal*, p. 15.

Bethencourt F., Ramada Curto D. (eds.) (2007), Portuguese Oceanic Expansion 1400-1800, Cambridge: Cambridge University Press.

Black S. (1986), *Exchange policies for less developed countries in a world of floating rates*, Princeton: Princeton University Press.

Bohannan P. (1959), "The impact of money on an African subsistence economy", *The Journal of Economic History*, Vol. 19, no. 4 (1959): 491–503. http: //www.jstor.org/stable/2115317.

Bourgui A. (1979), *La politique Française de cooperation en Afrique, le cas du Senegal*, Paris: Bibliothéque Africaine et Malgache.

Braga de Machedo J.(1986), "Small countries in Monetary Unions: the choice of Senegal", in Waterby J., Braga de Machedo J., "Trade and financial interdependence under flexible exchange rates: The Pacific Area", *International Finance*,25, 1986: 277–384.

Braga de Machedo J. (1987), "Uniões Monetárias com Micro-Estados: A criação de uma Zona de Escudo com a República da Guiné-Bissau e a República de S. Tomé e Príncipe", Bank of Portugal Historical Archives. Pasta Acordo de Arranjo Monetaario c/ a Guiné-Bissau, 1991 a 1996".

Braz J. M.F. (1993), "Intervenção do Secretário de Estado do Tesouro, no 3º Encontro de Lisboa dos PALOPs, 21-9-1993", Bank of Portugal Historical Archives. 120-002-007 Cooperação Multilateral, Encontros e Mesas Redondas, 1993, 3º Encontro de Lisboa, vol 1/1.

Estêvão J. (1991), *Moneda e sistema monetária colonial*, Lisbon: Escher.

Fieszbein A., "Uma análise entre o Arranjo Monetário entre a República da Portugal e a República da Guiné-Bissau", Washington D.C., Aug 1989, in Portugal. Bank of Portugal Historical Archives. Pasta Acordo de Arranjo Monetaario c/ a Guiné-Bissau, 1991 a 1996.

Frankel and Rose (1998), "The Endogeneity of Optimal Currency Area Criteria", *The Economic Journal*, 108 (449, Jul.), 1009–1025.

Ewout F. and Booth A. (eds)(1999), *Fiscal Capacity and the Colonial State in Asia and Africa, c. 1850-1960*, Cambridge: Cambridge University Press.

Gardener L. (2015), 'The curious incident of the franc in the Gambia: exchange rate instability and imperial monetary systems in the 1920s', *Financial History Review*, 22, 3, 291–314.

Garrido H. (1991), "Palop e banco central reforçam cooperação", *Diário de Notícias*, 30/10/1991.

Gersovitz M. (1987), *The political economy of risk and choice in Senegal*, London: Frank Cass.

Ghymers, C. (2021), "The Systemic Nature of the Global Crisis and Some Principles for Tackling It", In De Souza Guilherm B., Ghymers, C., Griffith-Jones, S., Ribeiro Hoffmann, A. (eds), *Financial Crisis Management and Democracy*, Cham: Springer, https://doi.org/10.1007/978-3-030-54895-7_3

Hopkins A. G. (1973), *An Economic History of West Africa*, New York: Columbia University Press.

Johnson H. and Swoboda A. (1973), *The economics of common currencies*, Harvard: Harvard University Press.

Kindleberger C. (1973), *The World in Depression 1829-39*, Los Angeles: California University Press.

Lopes A.M., Tenreiro Machado J.A., Mata M.E. (2016), "Analysis of global terrorism dynamics by means of entropy and state space portrait," *Nonlinear Dynamics*, Volume 85, Issue 3, 1547–1560 https://doi.org/10.1007/s11071-016-2778-1

Lopes A.M., Tenreiro Machado J.A., Mata M.E. (2018), Huffstot J.S. (2028), "Dynamical Analysis of the Global Business-cycle Synchronization," *PLOS ONE*, 13/ 2, https://doi.org/10.1371/journal.pone.0191491.

Masini F. (2021), *Time for a Next Generation Africa*, Torino: Centro Studi Sul Federalismo, https://www.csfederalismo.it/images/Research_paper/CSF-RP_Next-Generation-Africa_F.Masini_Nov2021.pdf

Mata M.E. (2023), "Reorganizing the Escudo Zone: Portuguese Monetary Policy and Empire-Union in Africa in the 1960s", *African Studies Review* 66, no. 3, 678–97. https://doi.org/10.1017/asr.2022.159.

Mata M.E. (2022) "(Un)Sustainability in a Monetary Union: Main factors in the Escudo Zone Monetary Union", *Essays in Economic and Business History*. Vol. 40, 233–264, https://www.ebhsoc.org/journal/index.php/ebhs/article/view/520.

Mata M.E. (2020) *The Portuguese Escudo Monetary Zone: Its Impact in Colonial and Post-Colonial Africa*, Cham: Springer-Palgrave.

Mata M.E. (2007), "Inter-racial Marriage in the Last Portuguese Colonial Empire", *Journal of Portuguese History*, Vol. 5, no. 1.

Mata M.E., da Costa J.R. and Justino D. (2017), *The Lisbon Stock Exchange in the twentieth century*, Coimbra: Coimbra University Press.

Mata M.E., Tenreiro Machado J.T. (2017) "Entropy Analysis of Monetary Unions", Entropy, 19 (6), 245. doi:10.3390/e19060245.

Mata M.E., Nunes L.C., Roldão M. (2021), "The Portuguese Escudo Area in Africa and Lessons for Monetary Unions ", *Economic History of Developing Regions*, Vol. 36/3, 392-421, https://doi.org/10.1080/20780389.2021.1890579.

Mata M.E., Nuno V. (2011), *The Concise Economic History of Portugal (A comprehensive guide)*, Lisbon: Almedina.

Mseba A. (2016), "Money and autonomy in a settler colony: the politics of monetary regulation in colonial Zimbabwe, 1930s-1965", in Chia Y.H.,

Luckett T. M. and Vause E. (eds) *The cultural history of money and credit: a global perspective*, Lanham: Lexington Books, 133–148.

Maxon R. M. (1989), 'The Kenya currency crisis, 1919-21 and the ierial dilemma', *Journal of Imperial and Commonwealth History*, 17/3, 323–348.

Robson P. (1983), *Integration, Development and Equity,* London: George Unwin.

Saramago, Luís Boletim do Club de Gestores e Empresáros Portugueses (CGEP) de Bissau, 17/2/1993, Ano II, nº 1, Fev 1993, pp. 1, 7. Portugal. Bank of Portugal Historical Archives. Pasta Documentação da UTAM, Trabalhos, 1990 a 1993. Encontros, 1993, 3º Encontro de Lisboa, vol. 1/1.

Schenk C. R. (2010), *The decline of sterling: managing the retreat of an international currency, 1945-1992*, Cambridge: Cambridge University Press.

Smith G. C. (1985), *The third Portuguese empire: a study in economic imperialism* Manchester: Manchester University Press.

Tenreiro Machado J.A., Mata M.E. (2015), "Analysis of World Economic Variables Using Multidimensional Scaling", *PLOS ONE*, 10/3| https://doi.org/10.1371/journal.pone.0121277

The Impact of Geopolitics on Fiscal Policy*

Vitor Gaspar

1. Growing fault lines and (de)globalization

There are growing fault lines in the world. Polarization and fragmentation make headlines news. Nevertheless, the trade-to-GDP ratio has stabilized, after having substantially increased for decades[1]. That indicates the absence of deglobalization at an aggregate level.

Globalization is a relatively novel concept. That suggests that it should be regarded much more as a process than as a state. The frequency of the word "globalization," "integration," and "fragmentation" appearing in online search engines has increased substantially since the 1990s. But the frequency of these mentions has been slowly declining in recent decades. The geopolitical risk index is also not high on a historical basis and is not even close to the level during the two world wars in the last century. The geopolitical uncertainty index shows that levels of uncertainty in the U.S. and the world have been flat in recent years, although levels in China and Germany have increased. This may relate to their status as major exporters.

---

* The paper presents a series of slides the reader can find along the text

1 See "Cold War II? Preserving Economic Cooperation Amid Geoeconomic Fragmentation," Plenary Speech by IMF First Managing Deputy Director Gita Gopinath at 20th World Congress of the International Economic Association, December 11, 2023.

Globalization

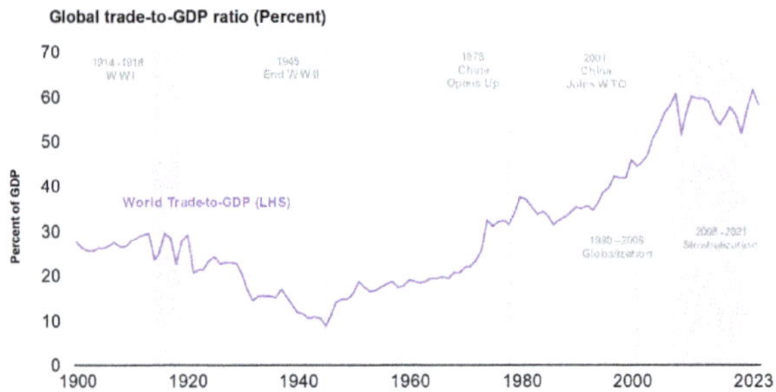

Sources: Cold War II? Preserving Economic Cooperation Amid Geoeconomic Fragmentation. Plenary Speech by IMF First Managing Deputy Director Gita Gopinath at the 20th World Congress of the International Economic Association, Colombia. December 11, 2023

Geopolitical Risk Index

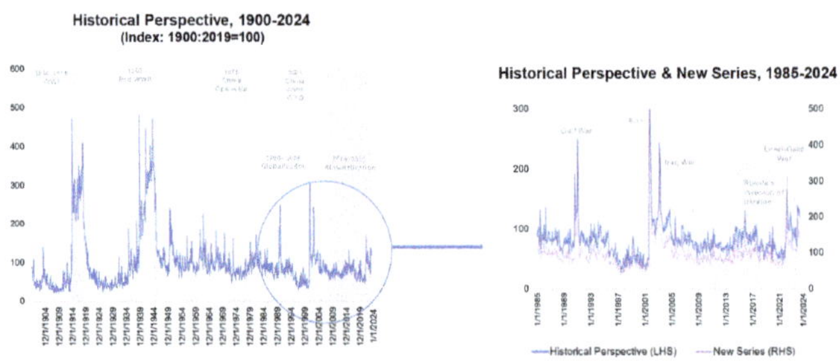

Source: Caldara and Iacoviello (2022). Data downloaded from https://www.matteoiacoviello.com/gpr.htm on March 08, 2024. Latest data point 2/1/2024.

Note: The Historical Index uses 3 newspapers and starts in 1900. The Recent GPR (Index: 1985:2019=100) uses 10 newspapers and starts in 1985.

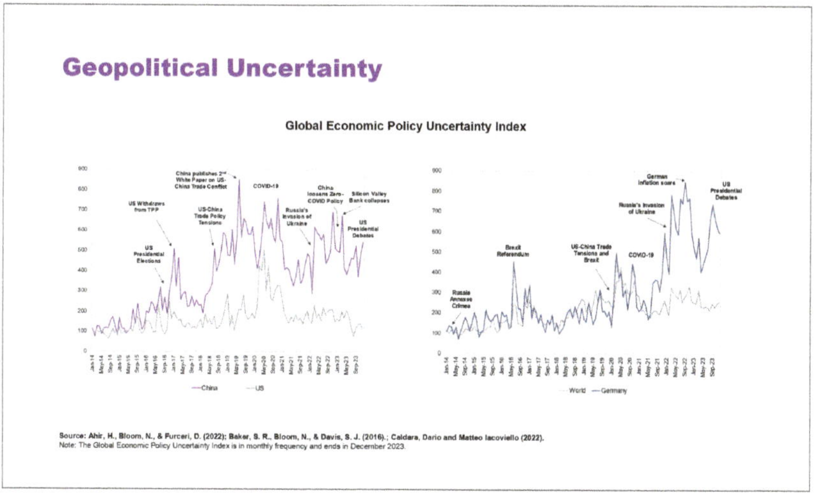

2. Shift in trade patterns and power

Although there is no sign of deglobalization in the aggregate, geopolitics has shifted trade patterns. The U.S. trades more with Vietnam and Mexico, while China trades more with India, Indonesia, Brazil, and Colombia. Indeed, IMF research shows that there is a close correlation between trade intensity and voting patterns at the United Nations. Countries that vote together in the United Nations tend to intensify their trade relations[2].

Looking at the long-run trend, global power has also shifted. The economic share of the European Union has declined and now stands below China. Moreover, the productivity of the four largest economies in the euro area — Germany, Spain, France, and Italy — converged to the level of the U.S. in 1995, but then lagged behind the U.S. afterward, according to research by Isabel Schnabel of the European Central Bank[3]. Similarly, IT-related capital stock in Europe stands far below the US level. Structural issues with European integration could have caused these trends.

---

[2] See "Changing Global Linkages: A New Cold War?," by Gita Gopinath, Pierre-Olivier Gourinchas, Andrea F Presbitero, and Petia Topalova, IMF Working Paper 2024/076.

[3] See "From Laggard to Leader? Closing the Euro Area's Technology Gap," by Isable Schnabel, Inaugural Lecture of the EMU Lab, 16 February 2024.

Meanwhile, there is a strong divergence in the cyclically adjusted primary deficit between the euro area and the U.S. The deficit of the euro area is expected to gradually decline toward zero, while that of the U.S. is projected to stay high even in the medium term. This leads to diverging paths of debt in the two economic areas, with the debt ratio in the U.S. growing much faster than the euro area.

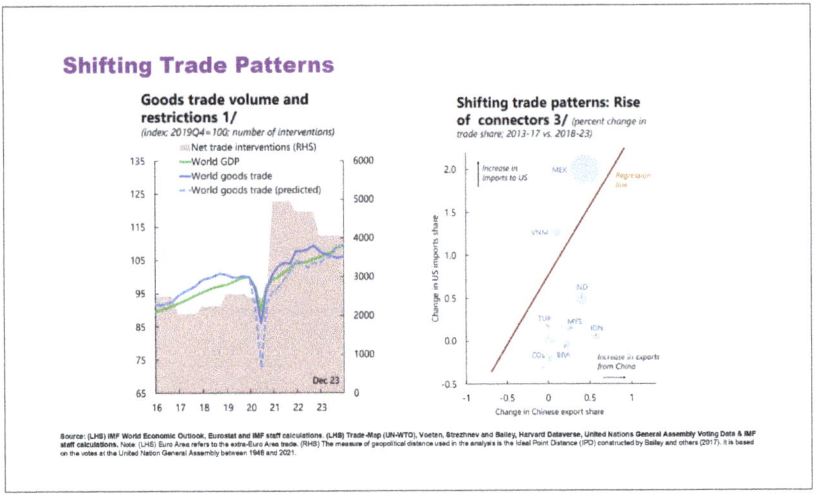

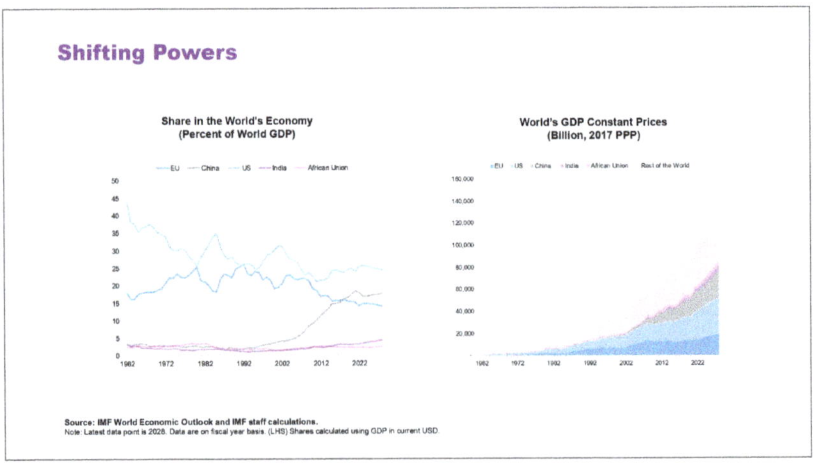

Catching Up Turns Into Falling Behind

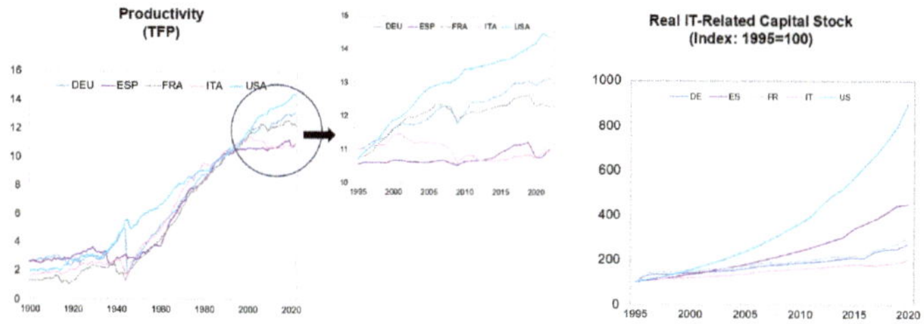

Source: "From laggard to leader? Closing the euro area's technology gap" Inaugural lecture of the EMU Lab by Isabel Schnabel, Member of the Executive Board of the ECB, at the European University Institute

Note: 1) Productivity is TFP ($US 2010 ppp). Real IT Related Capital Stock is the sum of computing equipment and computer software & databases for all NACE industries. See details in: http://www.longtermproductivity.com/about.html 2) Vertical lines indicate 1995, when the European Union was created.

Diverging Trends in Debt and Deficits

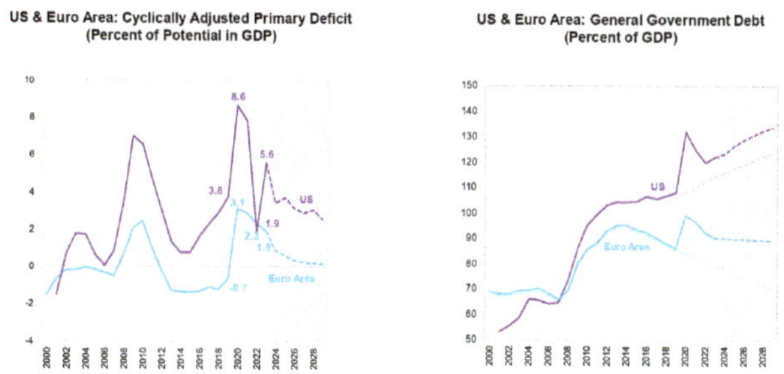

Source: International Monetary Fund World Economic Outlook (WEO April 2024 & January 2020) and IMF staff calculations.

Note: (LHS) –The chart uses April 2024 vintage. (RHS) - The faded lines represent WEO January 2020 vintage which is compared with WEO April 2024 vintage. The dashed lines represent projections. The last data point is 2029.

3. Fiscal policy implications and policy trilemma

What are the fiscal policy implications of the geopolitical tensions we are seeing? As geopolitical tensions intensified over the last few years, a number of countries implemented restrictive measures on trade and direct investment. There is clearly a strong revival of industrial policies, particularly in advanced economies, with Europe announcing the most industrial policy measures in the world. The latest Fiscal Monitor identifies what industrial policies work and what policies do not work. It also makes a very strong case for international cooperation in the area of innovation especially related to climate change.

Therefore, geopolitics has considerable implications for fiscal policy. Amid rising geopolitical tensions, governments are facing an even more difficult policy trilemma.

First, there are strong calls for public spending. Some of the calls come from industrial policies, reflecting a surge in economic nationalism. Spending pressures on defense are also increasing as a direct result of geopolitical tensions. Our estimates show that overall spending pressure amounts to 7 percent of GDP for advanced economies and almost 9 percent of GDP for emerging markets[4].

Second, there is strong political resistance to taxation. Third, there are the imperatives of debt sustainability and financial stability. As in all policy trilemmas, policymakers can have two but not all three elements. With high debts and deficits and real interest rates on the rise, caving in to spending pressures, together with binding limits on taxation, threatens to produce ever-rising debts and deficits. That would place countries on an unsustainable debt path. But even at shorter horizons, Treasuries may face challenging financing conditions or even disorderly markets. The risks of fiscal unsustainability and financial instability loom large.

Looking at the three vertices of the trilemma, it is clear that something has to give. Everywhere, the choice will be political.

---

4 See " How to Assess Spending Needs of the Sustainable Development Goals: The Third Edition of the IMFSDGCosting Tool," by Piergiorgio M Carapella, Tewodaj Mogues, Julieth C Pico-Mejia, and Mauricio Soto, How-To Note No 2023/005, December 14, 2023

The Rise of Industrial Policy

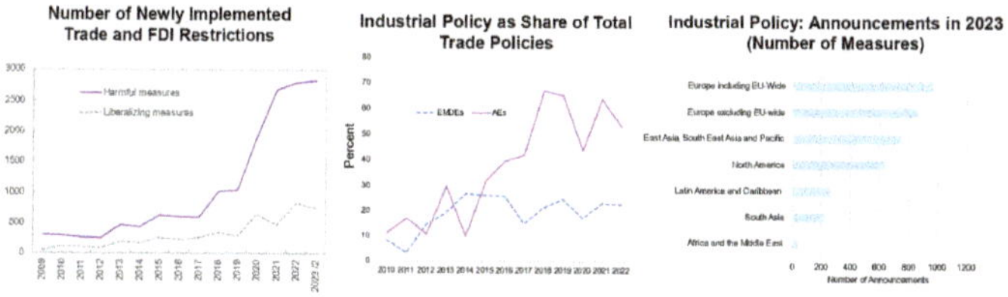

Source: (1) Global Trade Alert. Note: 1/ The number of new policy measures that restrict (harmful) or lieberalize trade or FDI introduced in each year. The metric deso not account fo a measure's intensity. 2/ Cutoff date as of November 22, 2023. (2) Global Trade Alert database, Juhász and others (2022). RHS - Evenett, Jakubik, Martin, and Ruta (2024). (3) GTA NIPO and IMF Estimates.

Policy Trilemma under Rising Geopolitical Tensions

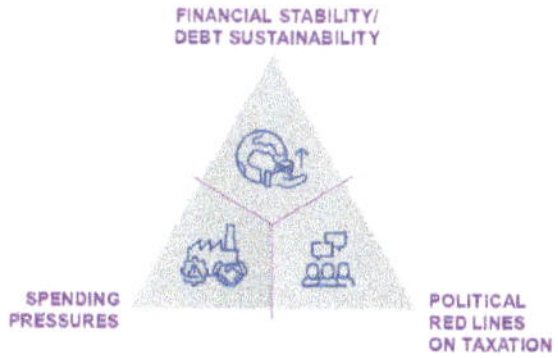

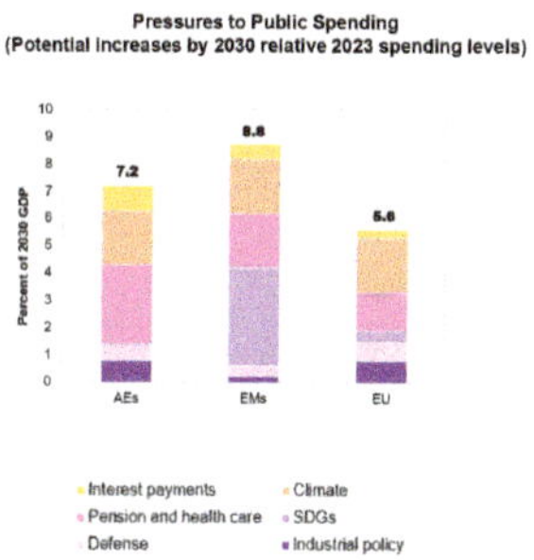

Source: IMF Staff Estimates.
Note: AEs = Advanced Economies, EMs = Emerging Economies, EU= European Union, AU = African Union

Conclusions

What are the recommendations for policymakers? They would be well advised to ensure that:

- spending is effective and efficient.
- revenues keep up with spending.
- fiscal frameworks put emphasis on medium and long-term perspectives and are able to withstand the vagaries of politics.
- fiscal policy is treated as a structural policy that appropriately guides resource allocation and transforms policy priorities into actions.

Building Multilateral and Multi-layered Global Economic Governance: The Role of Regional Integrations

Fabio Masini

Introduction

Most commentators welcomed the bilateral meeting between Xi Jinping and Joe Biden in San Francisco in November 2023 as an important step towards a de-escalation of conflicts worldwide. Yet, I am rather inclined to see the risks of a new global collusive duopoly. From a global perspective, experiencing again a world divided into spheres of influence, under the hegemonic control of two superpowers would be extremely dangerous. Given the increasing need and demand for a few crucial global public goods[1], a new bipolar order would hardly be able to decentralize their provision to fragmented nation-States and/or superpowers, each with its own strategic preferences and incentives.

Increasing economic interdependence worldwide also suggests that fencing off transnational externalities may prove impossible or extremely costly, as we have seen with recent attempts at friend-shoring value chains, and that the internalization of such externalities requires an effective multi-layered system of global governance. The United Nations and its agencies, the economic and financial institutions — such as IMF, WB, WTO, and G20 — all provide venues for talk, but no room for enforceable global decision-making. Consensus building in international fora still means relying on power relations, which are based on the (economic and military) — currently extremely asymmetric — weights of each country and alliance.

1 An increasing academic literature is becoming aware of the global nature of public goods such as: an enforceable and durable peace; the struggle against climate change (both mitigation and prevention measures); universal access to primary resources and fight against poverty (not only in strictly economic terms), implying some forms of wealth redistribution, or at least asymmetric growth; a common strategy against pandemic risks; a stable monetary and financial system that encourages, instead of discouraging, long-term productive investment; regional and trans-regional networks of transport, communication, and energy infrastructures.

In this note, which is only meant to set the table for a discussion, we shall highlight a few steps that might be taken to designing a global multi-layered and multipolar system of monetary and financial relations, stressing the role that regional integration processes may play in the transition towards it.

In the next section we shall briefly describe the emergence of a few historical flaws and attempts at changing the nature and governance of the international monetary system (IMS), and in section two we shall highlight how the issue of economic or monetary integration first (that characterized for many decades the debate on European integration) is mainly a political issue; before briefly illustrating the role of strengthened regional integration processes for multilateralism in two specific contexts: Central and Latin America (sections three) and Africa (section four).

1. The Emergence and Persistence of Historical Flaws in the IMS

The international monetary system traditionally relied on a pivotal currency, be it the roman sestertius, the Florentine forint, the British pound, or the US dollar. Kindleberger (1973) would suggest that this is unavoidable, as providing global financial stability in a highly unstable and conflictual world requires a huge and costly effort that can be borne only by an economic and political superpower.

This approach crucially depends on an underlying assumption, often unexplored: a pathology related to all social sciences that Ulrich Beck called "methodological nationalism" (Beck 2007). This implies that the only legitimate framework to take collective decisions is thought to be the nation-State, be it a continental superpower or a marginalized country at the world periphery. Under this assumption and inherently conflictual framework, international relations can only be stabilized by the most powerful nation, in terms of military capacity and economic strength. Such concept, which realists suggest is a mere description of the (past and) current situation, is becoming an obstacle to the survival of mankind, given the emerging and pressing need to finance and provide the above-mentioned global public goods. A more balanced system of international economic, monetary, and political governance is needed.

An alternative and less conflictual approach to collective decision-making assumes that every individual is a member of concentric and overlapping groups, that require collective choices and should be given deliberative power (Robbins 1937; Sen 2006), thus allowing legitimizing the establishment of a system of shared competences and sovereignty. Such arrangement — that, to be effective, needs a constitutional, enforceable framework — would match the multi-layered dimension of public goods[2] that are necessary for human survival.

Since the end of the Bretton Woods regime in 1971 the dollar, that suspended its convertibility into gold and ceased being *de jure* the pivotal currency in the IMS, acquired a *de facto* hegemony in international payments and reserves under the new floating regime. This resulted in a shift from a *dollar-exchange standard* to a *dollar standard*, which was certainly the outcome of inertial behaviour and lower transaction costs associated with the use of dollars in international payments and reserves, but mostly to the ability of the US government to impose its hegemonic role, well beyond its allies. This reinforced, instead of softening, the narrative of the *exorbitant privilege* and exacerbated the Triffin Dilemma.

History is full of testimonies of attempts made to contrast such asymmetry and establish a more balanced and multilateral system. Such struggle was pursued, for example, with the attempt to boost the role of the SDR, as a multi-currency reserve asset that since its first issue in 1970 has been representing, although with evolving composition and shares, the most relevant economic areas in the world. Soon after the first oil shock in the early 1970s, Saudi Arabia tried to invoice oil in SDR, which at that time included 19 currencies, and the IMF tried to recycle the balance-of-payments surplus of oil-exporting countries towards deficit countries, using SDRs as a potential tool for a supranational, cooperative solution (Spiro 1999). The USA hindered the IMF attempt and set up a bilateral commission to negotiate the continuing

2 Some of them are local in nature (local public transports, utilities, waste and resources management, etc), some other national (social security, health, higher education, etc), some regional (conflict prevention and resolution, military and security management, *etc*), some global (peace, trade guarantees, access to primary resources, pandemic prevention, basic universal education, *etc*).

use of dollar payments for oil against taking responsibility for Saudi Arabia security in the area, which also included a commitment to the stabilization of the Israeli-Palestinian issue (*ibidem*).

During the early 1980s, when the second general allocation of SDRs was just finished and a debate regained momentum for an increasing use of SDRs for development support, the USA even proposed the creation of an alternative global financial infrastructure to reduce the ambitions of the IMF. And when in 1994 the IMF Managing Director Michel Camdessus tried to issue $50billion SDRs to help facing multiple financial threats, the USA (assisted by Germany and with the support of the UK) vetoed him (Camdessus 2014), as they would again veto only a few years later Japan's attempt to tackle the East-Asian financial crisis through the establishment of a regional safety net: the Asian Monetary Fund.

When Kindleberger theorized about hegemonic stability, he merely provided a rationale for the dollar/US dominance, which was a matter of fact. Since the collapse of the bipolar system such hegemony was accompanied and strengthened by the narrative of the *End of History* (Fukuyama 1992), with the USA standing as the representative of the winning liberal democracies. And by an increasing neoliberal turn in US policymaking towards the rest of the world with aggressive capital markets deregulation, that exposed the national strategic assets of most vulnerable countries to market powers, in which US asset managers stood out as dominant market players.

With the emergence of the financial crisis triggered by the subprime mortgage bubble in the USA, followed by an unprecedented credit crunch in the world economy, an unusual cooperative response by the five most important central banks (FED, ECB, PBC, BoJ, and BoE) avoided a major liquidity shortage and the FED played the role of the global lender of last resort through bilateral swap lines (accompanied by the fiscal expansion of the US federal government, who acted as consumer of last resort). The IMF only played an ancillary role issuing $250billion in SDRs in 2009.

In the meanwhile, pressures were mounting for a revision of the international monetary system and regulatory framework, manifestly and increasingly become uncoherent with a weakened monopolistic power of the US in the global economy and geopolitics. Hence the initiatives to revive the process towards a Bretton Woods 2 conference — which had already been circulating in the previous years — aimed at changing the relative weight of each global actor in international institutions, their decision-making process, and ultimately their scope.

In 2009, after Chines CB President Xiaochuan Zhou's (2009) speech, where he cited the Triffin dilemma and pointed at a solution relying on a wider use of a revised SDR, the UN Stiglitz commission made some suggestions that aimed at a more equitable, regulated, and multilateral governance of the IMS. One of such proposals suggested that "the creation of a new global reserve system, with annual emissions of [...] SDRs [...] would help create a more stable global financial system" (Stiglitz 2009, 18).

The macroeconomic rationale behind such proposal had been already made explicit in a 2006 paper in which Greenwald and Stiglitz illustrated how the usual causal relation going from export-led models in most countries to the balance of payments deficit in the US, thus building up global imbalances, should be read in the opposite direction: it was (and still is) reserve accumulation due to the need to face uncertainties (Landau 2014, 120 ff) and the volatility of capital markets that impose, through the need to run current account surpluses, pursuing an export-led model.

The problem, as suggested by Robert Triffin already in 1960, lies in the structure of the IMS: relying on the dollar alone for international reserve accumulation implies global excess saving accumulation that is not always matched by an increasing global demand, resting on the USA to play the consumer of last resort. A problem not only for the world economy, but for the US themselves. As Greenwald and Stiglitz (2010, 329) underlined: "the US is exporting Treasury bills to be held in reserves — partly at the expense of automobiles [...] this means that the government *must* run a fiscal deficit to keep the economy at full employment".

Before the weaponization of the dollar that followed the Russian invasion of Ukraine in February 2021, pressures towards multilateralism in the IMS became increasingly manifest. The acceptance of the Chinese renminbi in the SDR basket in 2016 and the issue of €650billion SDRs in August 2021 were a testimony of this. The debate that preceded and followed such decisions highlighted the growing concern for a potentially powerful instrument, the SDR, relegated only to be parked as a reserve asset in CBs balance sheets, instead of being used as a multiplier for actions devoted to development and/or to the provision of global public goods.

Being issued according to the capital key rule (they are allocated following each country's share in the IMF capital), general allocations of SDRs are not targeted to countries in need of balance of payments relief, nor are they used as a development tool. This prevents the transformation of the IMF into a global financial institution devoted to financing strategic global public goods, nor to playing the role of the lender of last resort, which is usually implemented by the Fed and its bilateral swap agreements. This results in an under-provision of global public goods and in the continuing hegemonic role of the USA in times of severe crises, at least until recently.

These flaws are becoming not only manifest, but also a matter of exploration for alternative institutions to manage the international economy. As Singh (2023) observes, for example: "China's rising role as an international creditor and rescue-lender has been largely developed outside the traditional global financial safety net". And the recent and ongoing discussions among the BRICS+ are meant precisely to show that viable alternatives, although difficult to implement, are not unrealistic. More likely and strategically, they are meant to show that, lacking a radical reform of the current international monetary system, we shall end up with two competitive international strategic, monetary, and financial systems. From the point of view of the global economy, such an evolution should be resisted.

2. Regional integration: moving beyond the *egg-or-hen game*

Regional integrations are key in the transition towards a global multipolar system. Equal dignity of each pole, at least in terms of future perspectives, is crucial for the sustainability of a multipolar system of global governance. This requires strengthening regional integration processes beyond and outside Europe, where regional integration not only has already reached the irreversible establishment of a single currency but is proceeding towards a strengthened regional economic governance and multi-layered economic policy and is exploring some tentative common foreign policy, security and defence, which might eventually lead to something similar to the US economic statehood.

Apart from the South-East Asian countries, where regional integration is rather advanced (ASEAN, CMI, etc) but heavily influenced by Chinese and Japanese strategies, a special focus should be given to Central and Latin America, and to Africa: the two most vulnerable regions from a financial point of view and structural underdevelopment problems. One key obstacle to their regional integration is usually attributed to the old *egg-or-hen game* that started in Europe as early as the late Sixties, with decades-long debates about the opportunity to pursue *economic convergence* or *monetary integration* first. This is particularly true as concerns the two areas under scrutiny, as macroeconomic performances are highly divergent.

This is not only a theoretical issue, as it reflects different strategies to integration and underlying intellectual approaches. In Europe, such debate did not end with the establishment in 1979 of the European Monetary System and impacted on the path towards the single currency since 1989. There are a few lessons that can be drawn from the European experience. The first is that regional monetary integration is a political choice. We can pretend that optimum currency areas criteria are endogenous, as Frankel and Rose (1998) suggested, or that they must be fulfilled ex-ante, but the fact remains that without a strong political commitment, monetary integration is unsustainable. What happened to the euro during the sovereign-debts crisis between 2010 and 2014 stands as a warning. It was the political agreement between France and Germany in June 2012 to allow in July 2012 Mario Draghi, President of the European Central Bank, to be effective with his "whatever it takes".

The second point to be stressed is that no widespread political consensus is needed to anchor such process: a small core of countries is enough to have a centripetal domino effect that will likely involve an increasing number of countries; what is crucial is that the core is strongly politically committed to integration. The third point is that economic governance cannot rely on coordination alone: markets do not only signal but may trigger macroeconomic imbalances. Simple coordination is ineffective if not accompanied by some form of enforceable sovereignty sharing.

Given these premises, it remains true that while imported credibility and macroeconomic stabilization are the most evident *pros* of regional monetary integration, *cons* related to the loss of freedom on exchange rate policy might pose problems of international competitiveness that require costly industrial conversion and greater systemic efficiency. Although such costs are country-specific and should be borne by each country, a regional financial institution (such as an existing or ad-hoc created Multilateral Development

Bank or Fund) or a bilateral agreement with another major global player might help assisting such process with a development plan financed with the issue of bonds denominated in the regional currency or in SDRs on international financial markets.

Now, the central question of this session is what Triffin would propose today to increase the resilience of regional and global financial systems. Although, as a historian of economic thought, I refrain from these kinds of anti-historical traps, I think there are a few directions that might have been suggested by Triffin, such as taking two very concrete initiatives in both Central and Latin America, and Africa.

3. A regional safety net for Latin America

Proposals for regional integration in Central and Latin America are older than the current international organizations established after WWII. The Kemmerer missions in South America in the 1920s provided a few theoretical starting points for discussions about monetary integration in the area. After WWII, the CEPAL provided a venue for studies not only in national development but also in regional integration. Monetary integration was a recurrent concern for Central and Latin American governments, given their vulnerable trade specialization patterns, balance of payment weakness, and financial exposition to foreign and international markets and institutions. The last attempt to revive a public debate on this was made in early 2023 by Argentina and Brazil, that suggested a common parallel currency, the *sur*, should be issued along national ones.

Currently, there are informal talks at the level of Latin America CBs to discuss the potential role and technicalities of such a parallel currency, but its destiny crucially depends on the political will to back and further such proposal. Revitalizing and further strengthening the UNASUR system might provide a venue for further steps in this direction. In any case, integration in the region cannot be thought of as a short-run process: steps should be taken to design a workable integration plan, pending the emergence of a shared political commitment, even among a small number of countries. Once political agreement should emerge (among a few countries, maybe involving also Central America) it might become costly for others to remain outside.

We suggest, though, that an even more simple initiative might be taken in the short run, that Triffin would have forcefully supported. Central and Latin America economies are characterized by financial vulnerabilities that are rooted in flawed historical growth models, often relying on production choices imposed by former colonial powers or by sovereign choices due to predominant corporatist interests. Such vulnerabilities have been recently resulting in undue and skyrocketing accumulation of foreign reserves[3] that have traded off opportunities for domestic investments in productive differentiation, infrastructure strengthening and social protection (key for the resilience of their social systems). All factors that might have reduced political instability (that further reinforces financial instability). It is time to break such vicious circle.

A way to do this is to establish a regional monetary reserve fund, extending and upscaling the current FLAR, pooling 20%-30% of national reserves in gold and foreign assets, as a first line of defence in case of financial crisis. We talk here about a *first line of defence* as we believe that this should be agreed upon with the IMF, in a similar way as the CMI works, towards the establishment of a global multi-layered system of safety nets.

We may imagine that countries may draw up to 30% of their reserve's holdings without conditionality, 30% to 60% with regionally agreed conditionality, and over 60% only if there is already an IMF assistance plan in place, with its conditionality.

This would provide a progressive line of defence that, as in the case of the CMI, might never be needed to start, discouraging short-term speculation.

This step would oblige Central Banks and Treasuries to be more transparent between one another and coordinate their economic policies, without any specific institutional design that might prove premature to face very different and often divergent macroeconomic performances in the area. As suggested by Triffin for Europe since the early 1950s and forcefully again since 1970 (Triffin 1970), such a step would provide the first infrastructure

3 Just to provide some data, Brazil alone has reserves in foreign currencies and gold for around $350k (almost 75k in Peru, around 58k in Colombia, almost 43k in Chile, etc); while the USA has only $250k. Considering Latin and Central America together, their reserves amount to more than $800k.

for monetary cooperation, that might end up in a more structural designing of a regional single monetary system.

4. An EU-Africa Plan for Next Generation

All the existing regional and sub-regional transnational integration infrastructures may play the role of trigger in Africa's regional integration. Here, the obstacles to a common strategy are also paramount but, again, a path might be designed to involve a variable and increasing number of countries, exactly as happened in Europe. Otherwise, the strategy might point at strengthening the political role and institutional weight of the African Continental Free Trade Area (AfCFTA), which might lead to a general monetary arrangement to protect and improve the efficiency of the single market, and possibly a financial safety net to alleviate the potential risks of balance of payments disequilibria.

This solution would have to explore the synergies with the existing sub-regional monetary integration processes already in place: the partly overlapping *West African Economic and Monetary Union* (Benin, Burkina Faso, Côte D'Ivoire, Guinea-Bissau, Mali, Niger, Senegal, and Togo) and *West African Monetary Zone* (Gambia, Ghana, Guinea, Liberia, Nigeria, Sierra Leone, Burkina Faso); East Africa's Kenya, Tanzania, and Uganda *East African Community*; *Southern African Development Community* (SADC), with its *Common Monetary Area* (CMA: Lesotho, Namibia, Swaziland, South Africa), under the hegemonic role of the rand and the South African Reserve Bank. A transition period should aim at the establishment of a pan-African monetary integration process both to stabilize exchange rates among its members and to provide an autonomous regional safety net for crisis management. This should be done in accordance and with the help of the IMF, in a two-tiers logic of multilayered financial net.

We believe that a strategic move in Africa might be establishing a strict relationship with the EU, for reasons connected to their reciprocal ties and geographical proximity, which implies the need to internalize a few externalities such as migration flows, trade patterns, transnational strategic cooperation. The primary problems for Africa are to enhance their financial resilience, which brings us back to the point raised for Central and Latin America, and to trigger endogenous growth dynamics. This requires financial resources and political commitment (the latter might turn out to be more difficult to find than the former). The EU could provide such funds.

As underlined in a previous paper (Masini 2024), I suggest the EU should collect the SDRs of the IMF's last issue in 2021, that are being kept in CBs reserves, and mobilize them to finance a massive *Next Generation Africa*, a plan for the endogenous growth and financial resilience of African countries along the time horizon of ten years.

My basic idea was to channel €150billion SDRs to multilateral development banks (the EIB on the EU part and the ADB in Africa), as prescribed holders, and collateralize them to issue €750billion bonds to be used for a jointly designed development plan, targeting six main objectives: energy independence, digital infrastructure, health infrastructure, green transition and climate change, education, and a regional safety net.

This would constrain African countries to agree on common priorities and strategies; and would also strengthen European identity as a global actor, thus contributing to multilateralism.

Concluding Remarks

Genuine multilateralism is the only sustainable alternative to hegemonic stability, which is no longer tenable in the current world framework. The balance of power is rapidly changing and a duopoly, which is the most likely outcome, would make it difficult to face global challenges and provide the increasingly necessary global public goods.

European regional integration took seven decades to build its current architecture, which is still evolving. Such slow path was not a major problem when the whole world was stuck into the bipolar system, with two manifest hegemons. Europe had all the time it needed to adjust its structure to the challenge of a federalization of fully sovereign states. The establishment of a global multipolar system might not enjoy the same privilege of extended time at disposal as Europe experienced. It is time to accelerate on regional integration worldwide, not with the ambition to create regional (autarchic) blocks, that might turn out to be an obstacle to a more stable international order, but as a crucial step in a multi-layered architecture of global economic governance.

Multilateralism requires that regional poles are built and consolidated. The two more pressing challenges highlighted in this note are regional integrations in Central and Latin America and in Africa. Although several paths can be followed to foster regional integration in those two areas, we suggested that two concrete proposals might be politically and economically palatable: a) a regional safety net in Central and Latin America, meant as a first line of defence in case of financial turmoil and as a first step towards a global multi-layered system of safety net and; b) a jointly designed plan for *Next Generation Africa* financed by the EU pooling and leveraging their recent SDRs allocation, designed both to implement a first-line safety net, as in the case of Central and Latin America, and to trigger endogenous growth.

Both may look utopian suggestions. Maybe they are. But pretending to maintain the status quo in the current dramatically unstable economic and political situation may be even more utopian. And conflicts required to adjust the global governance to the emerging new balance of power might be too costly for humankind to afford them.

References

Beck U. (2007), "The Cosmopolitan Condition: Why Methodological Nationalism Fails", *Theory Culture & Society*, 24(7-8), 286–290.

Camdessus M. (2014), We Had a Chance. Thirteen Years at the Helm of the IMF, Los Angeles: SAGE.

Frankel J.A., Rose A.K. (1998), "The Endogeneity of Optimum Currency Area Criteria", Swedish Economic Policy Review, 108(449), 1009–1025.

Fukuyama F. (1992), The End of History and the Last Man, New York: The Free Press.

Greenwald B. and Stiglitz J.E. (2010), "A Modest Proposal for International Monetary Reform", in Griffith-Jones S., Ocampo J.A., Stiglitz J.E. (eds). Time for a Visible Hand: Lessons from the 2008 World Financial Crisis, Oxford: Oxford University Press, 314–344.

Kindleberger C.P. (1973), The World in Depression: 1929-1939, Berkeley: University of California Press.

Landau J.P. (2014), "International lender of last resort: some thoughts for the 21st century", in Re-thinking the lender of last resort. BIS Papers 79, 119–127.

Masini F. (2024), Unlocking the Strategic Potential of the EU's SDRs: a Plan for Next Generation Africa, RTI Papers, n° 17, February, Torino: Centro Studi sul Federalismo.

Robbins L. (1937), Economic Planning and International Order, London: Macmillan.

Sen A. (2006), Identity and Violence. The Illusion of Destiny, New York: Norton & Co.

Singh A. (2023), Reforming the International Monetary System, Policy Centre for the New South, October 11.

Spiro D.E. (1999), The Hidden Hand of American Hegemony. Petrodollar Recycling and International Markets, Ithaca: Cornell University Press.

Stiglitz J.E. (ed) (2009), Report of the Commission of Experts of the President of the United Nations General Assembly on Reforms of the International Monetary and Financial System, New York: United Nations.

Triffin R. (1970), "Il panorama internazionale oggi e domani", in Bonvicini G. (ed). Verso una moneta europea, Bologna: Il Mulino, 41–56.

Zhou X. (2009), Reform the international monetary system. March 23, https: //www.bis.org/review/r090402c.pdf

De-dollarization via Local Currency Cross-Border Payments: Democratization and Fragmentation of the Global Payment System

Hung Tran

Introduction

The Global Financial Crisis in 2008 caused by excesses in the US mortgage and financial markets amidst lax regulation and supervision was followed by unorthodox monetary operations by the US Federal Reserves (the Fed) and the European Central Bank (ECB). These included unprecedented quantitative easing moves and near-zero interest rates to fight the great recession; followed by aggressive tightening to deal with rising inflation. Such drastic monetary measures put significant pressures on many other countries, especially emerging markets (EM); compelling them to maintain interest and exchange rates not appropriate for their economic circumstances. In particular, many of them suffered from the impacts of volatile capital flows triggered by decisions of major central banks. This is essentially a modern version of the Triffin Dilemma (Bordo, McCaukey 2017) according to which US domestic monetary problems affect the supply and price of dollar to the rest of the world as a reserve currency, leading to its surpluses or shortages causing financial instability in other countries. Historically, in the three decades or so after the second world war, US current account deficits provided dollar liquidity to the rest of the world; but persistently large deficits put pressure on the dollar, eventually breaking the Bretton Woods fixed exchange rate regime in 1973. In modern times, impacts of exchange rate and capital flow volatility have given rise to a desire among EM countries to reduce their exposure to spillovers effects of the Fed's policy actions — basically to avoid the modern Triffin Dilemma.

Moreover, the US has stepped up the use of financial sanctions — restricting access to the dollar-based payment and financial system — to serve its foreign policy objectives. Of particular concern to quite a few countries was the G7 decision to freeze the FX reserve assets of the Central Bank of Russia, held at financial institutions in Western jurisdictions, as part of the wide-ranging sanctions against Russia after its invasion of Ukraine in February 2022. These developments have prompted many countries to develop alternative cross-border payment arrangements to lessen their reliance on the dollar–driven by both economic and geopolitical considerations. De-dollarization has found a fertile ground to grow.

The current de-dollarization trend has been based on arrangements to use local currencies for cross-border payments — basically sidestepping the Triffin Dilemma since earlier attempts to find a solution to the Dilemma have not gained traction. The most comprehensive solution–proposed by Robert Triffin himself — is to replace a national currency based reserve system (such as the current dollar based system) with one based on an international reserve unit not pegged to gold or any national currencies, and managed by an international financial institution like the International Monetary Fund (IMF). Indeed, the IMF tried to do this by launching the Special Drawing Rights (SDR) in 1969 to be used as units of account representing claims to freely usable currencies of IMF members. At present there are SDR 660.7 billion ($943 billion) outstanding, boosted by a SDR 440.7 billion ($650 billion) allocation in 2021 (IMF 2024). This is equivalent to about 8% of the current total FX reserves held by the world's central banks.

However, it is important to understand what the SDR is and how it can be used. An allocation of SDRs to member countries increases their assets and liabilities to the IMF by the same amount — so that their actual reserve positions are unchanged with zero net interest payments or receipts. The situation is similar to the IMF as a mutual credit institution granting a pre-approved line of credit to a member. Only when that country activates the credit line, *that is* uses the SDR — either to pay the IMF or to exchange for a hard currency, which is one of the five constituent currencies of the SRD, to make international payments outside of the Fund — that its SDR liability exceeds its SDR asset, and it has to pay interest on the difference. By contrast, the country accepting the SDR for its national currency — like the US exchanging dollars for SDRs — will have its SDR asset exceeding its liability *vis-à-vis* the IMF, earning interest on the difference. The countries issuing the five hard currencies making up the SDR (*i.e.* the US, the Euro area, China, the UK and Japan) have voluntarily agreed to acquire SDRs from other members in exchange for their own currencies, but like the US, they have reserved the right not to do so if such a refusal would be judged to be in their national interests. More importantly, SDR allocation is implemented infrequently, subject to approval by the IMF Board of Governors, resulting from political negotiations and compromises among the major shareholders according to their geopolitical agendas, and not only motivated by the reserve need of the global economy. In other words, contrary to popular belief, a SDR allocation *does not* mean giving countries free reserve assets without conditions nor leaving the country's debt unchanged — as suggested by some economists (Vasic-Lalovic 2022). Moreover the amount of SDR being used has been minuscule compared to the outstanding stock of SDRs. For example, prior to 2021, only SDR 3 billion were activated out of the outstanding stock of SDR 220 billion (Plant 2021).

For all these reasons, the SDR has failed to live up to expectations that it could become the international reserve currency. The current geopolitical rivalry would make international cooperation to find ways to promote the SDR even more difficult to reach. More importantly, geopolitical tension could conceivably lead to a worst-case scenario where the five SDR countries refuse to take the SDRs tendered to them in exchange for their national currencies — rendering the outstanding stock of SRDs worthless. Until now, this has been a theoretical possibility, not worth thinking about — but going forward, such a risk cannot be totally ignored. In short, the SDR will likely stay in its present status as a useful supplement to the dollar-based reserve system, but not its potential alternative.

Another approach has been to develop one or more alternative reserve currencies to lessen the dominant role of the dollar, diversifying the risk of fluctuations in the provision of the reserve currencies. However, experiences of a major regional common currency — the Euro — have shown how difficult that can be. Backed by the Euro Area (EA) which accounts for about 14% of global GDP and trade volume, the Euro has trailed the dollar in the SWIFT-based international payment system — its share has fallen from 45% in 2012 (Johnson and Tanzi 2023) to 21.9% at present while that of the dollar rose from 30% to 47.4% over the same period (SWIFT 2024). Actually, the portion of Euro transactions outside the Euro Area (EA) (with at least one initiating or receiving bank situated outside the EA) is only 43% of the total (Furtuna et al. 2024). Excluding the Euro transactions inside the EA (where the Euro is really a domestic currency thanks to the European Monetary Union), the portion of the Euro in truly international transactions is only

9.4% — or 43% of the reported share of 21.8% (Tran 2024). This puts the Euro at the head of the group of secondary currencies including the British pound sterling (GBP) and RMB, but not as a peer to the dollar, in a position to compete against it.

The dollar is also well ahead of the Euro as the currency of denomination for international financing, consistently accounting for 60% of foreign assets and liabilities of the international banking system (Tombini 2023) and around 59% of global reserves assets (Arslanalp and Simpson-Bell 2021). Both of these trends have benefited from the large and sophisticated US economic and financial systems. These experiences reveal the difficulties facing any currency aspiring to challenge the dollar. In particular, compared to the dollar, the RMB has been disadvantaged by the fact that China has a controlled capital account, underdeveloped financial system and not so liquid capital markets.

Consequently, recent de-dollarization efforts have been de-risking in nature, focusing on practical arrangements to use local currencies to settle cross-border trade and investment transactions among participating countries, mainly on a bilateral basis but having been extended gradually to third countries on a plurilateral basis. The immediate goal of these efforts is not to replace the US dollar in all of its functions, but to develop alternative payment arrangements to lessen countries' dependence on the dollar for bilateral trade and investment transactions. Against the anti spillovers and geopolitical benefits of reducing reliance on the dollar — especially as a vehicle currency in foreign exchange dealings — many countries seem to accept the costs of using local currencies — in terms of diminished efficiency in directly dealing with each other currency — where market participants have to use less liquid local FX, money and hedging markets.

The local currency cross-border payment approach has rested on three key pillars which complement and reinforce each other:

i. participating countries develop national clearing and settlement systems, preferably on a real time gross settlement (RTGS) basis meeting modern global standards (*i.e.* ISO 20022) and link them together (or make them interoperable). In parallel, efforts to build modern depository and securities settlement systems will help develop local capital and money markets. All of these infrastructure improvements will expedite the settlement of cross-border transactions, minimizing the FX exposure risks of participants.

ii. central banks of participating countries extend currency swap lines to each other, largely on a bilateral basis but in a few cases on a plurilateral basis consisting of several like-minded countries. The currency swap lines will provide a foreign currency to a domestic entity (importers or exporters) — intermediated as needed by the respective central banks, reducing the FX availability and counterparty risks.

iii. many countries have made full use of technological advances in payment solutions, including mobile online payments, digital and tokenized forms of payment such as stablecoins or Central Bank Digital Currencies (CBDCs), eWallets and QR code payment systems. Basically, technological advances could provide solutions to the use of local currency in cross-border payments, making it more efficient and less costly than the case at present.

In recent years, progress has been made in all three areas, leveraging efforts made by countries to implement the G20 Roadmap for Enhancing Cross-Border Payments (FSB 2023). Even though not the original intention of the G20 Roadmap, its drive to develop common standards for payment regulations and infrastructures has helped facilitate the use of local currencies for cross-border payments. This can be illustrated by the experiences of China in promoting the international use of the RMB and two important local currency advocates — ASEAN and BRICS.

1. China to promote international uses of the RMB

Since the 2008 Global Financial Crisis, China has implemented a wide range of measures to encourage international uses of the RMB (Amighini and Garcia-Herrero 2023) — while retaining control over the country's capital account transactions. In 2009 China allowed cross-border trade settlements in Shanghai and Guangdong. It then designated Hong Kong, Singapore and London as offshore RMB centers for bank deposits (which have risen to 1.5 trillion yuan — or $207 billion — then stagnating around that level more recently) and clearing of RMB transactions. A dim sum bond market (RMB-denominated bonds issued by foreign corporate and sovereign borrowers) and a smaller panda bond market (RMB-denominated bonds issued by Chinese companies to foreign investors) were launched in Hong Kong — reaching a small outstanding volume of around $65 billion. More meaningfully in terms of giving international investors access to Chinese financial assets, Beijing set up the HK-Shanghai Stock Connect and then the Stock and Bond Connect programs as well as designating Qualified International Institutional Investors allowed to deal in domestic financial assets. As a result, foreign holding of on-shore Chinese bonds has risen to about 3.71 trillion yuan ($553 billion) (Business Times 2024); and 2.8 trillion yuan ($386 billion) of Chinese equities (Bloomberg 2024) at the end of 2023 — both showing declines since 2022.

In 2016, the IMF added the RMB to the SDR basket (with a 12.28% weight as of 2022) besides the dollar, Euro, yen and GBP; and three-month Chinese Treasury bond yields to the basket used to calculate SDR interest rates (IMF 2024).

More recently, China has shifted its approach to better leverage its significant strength as a top trading partner to most countries in the world as well as leading bilateral creditor to many developing countries — especially those participating in its Belt and Road Initiative (BRI) launched in 2013 — to encourage uses of the RMB in trade and investment transactions with itself. This has been reinforced by another two major measures: the establishment of China's Cross-border Interbank Payments System (CIPS) and the PBOC's currency swap lines.

It is important to recognize that China has already led the world in adopting the global standard ISO 20022 for payment systems (Fintech Futures 2020) — something SWIFT has been pushing its members to do to meet the target date of 2025. In 2015 China launched its Cross-border Interbank Payment System (CIPS) combining SWIFT-compatible messaging facilities with clearing and settling cross-border RMB transactions on a real-time gross settlement basis by providing controlled access to the onshore China National Advanced Payment System 2 (CNAPS 2) (Li 2023). CIPS has grown to have 1482 institutional members in 123 countries, able to process 80% of the total cross-border RMB transactions worth 39 trillion yuan ($5.46 trillion) in the first three quarters of 2023. To the extent that a cross-border RMB transaction is entered directly to CIPS and not via SWIFT, the reported share of the RMB in SWIFT-based global payments tends to under-estimate the yuan's true share in cross-border payments.

The PBOC has entered into a series of bilateral currency swap agreements with central banks of about 40 countries — totaling $550 billion (Tran 2023). These currency swap lines have been increasingly used for cross-border payments in local countries — between a counterpart country and China; as well as in providing liquidity support to participating countries in balance of payments crises.

Last but not least, China has extended its dominant global position in mobile digital payments platforms — used by 82% of Chinese adults, covering 80% of daily consumption transactions in China with the annual value of electronic transactions reaching $434 trillion — spearheaded by Alipay and WeChat Pay each with a billion users (Mehta 2023). This has mainly served Chinese travelers overseas and foreign visitors in China but eventually can be available tor foreigners in general. In addition, China's state-owned monopolistic bank card group Union Pay has grown tremendously overseas — its cards are accepted in 181 countries — having overtaken Visa to be the world's most popular provider of debit cards, with 40% market share compared to Visa's 38.8% (Hope A. 2023). There were 625 billion transactions made in 2022 using credit, debit and prepaid cards from the major bank card providers, with debit cards accounting for 63.8% of the total. These payment platforms have greatly facilitated cross-border payments; at present mainly used by international travelers and retail consumers but can be expanded in future.

Finally, the PBOC has been among several leading central banks in developing and testing large scale uses of its CBDC — the eCNY — both domestically and in a cross-border setting (Lipsky and Kumar 2024). It will likely become one of the first countries to issue a digital central bank currency, enjoying first mover's advantages such as playing a key role in developing international technological and regulatory standards for CBDCs.

As a result of these concerted moves, China has been able to settle about half of its cross-border trade and investment transactions in RMB, more than the now second-ranked dollar (China Daily 2023). Moreover, in an IMF study of 125 economies, the median usage of RMB in cross-border payments with China has increased from 0% in 2014 to 20% in 2021 (Perez-Saiz and Zhang 2023). On a multilateral basis, the share of the RMB in international payments via SWIFT has increased from being negligible in 2012 to 4.7% — behind the British pound GBP at 6.6% but ahead of the yen (4.1%) (SWIFT 2024).

The RMB has also joined other smaller currencies (including the GBP, Swiss franc, Canadian dollar and Australian dollar) in moderately increasing their collective share of global reserves assets at the expense of the dollar which fell from 71.2% at the end of 1999 to 59.2% at present (Arslanalp and Simpson-Bell 2021). In fact, the gradual decline of the dollar's share of global reserves assets in favor of a group of relatively minor currencies is consistent with the growing use of local currencies in cross-border payments — which makes the case for central banks to hold a portion of their reserves in each other's currencies to meet transaction demands in addition to bilateral currency swap lines.

Another notable development is that thanks to much lower interest rates on RMB funds compared to those for the dollar or euro in recent years, the RMB has become an important funding currency. In particular, the offshore yuan has become a popular funding currency for emerging market carry trades (Wong and Burgess 2024). The current outstanding volume of RMB-denominated overseas loans extended by Chinese banks is about 160 billion yuan ($22 billion), accounting for about 28% of Chinese international bank loans in all currencies (Amighini and Garcia-Herrero 2023).

In short, China has made noticeable progress in its efforts to promote the international use of the RMB. In particular, it has reduced — though not eliminated — its vulnerability to US financial sanctions by steadily increasing the share of RMB in settling its cross-border trade and investment transactions. China has also become a driving force in promoting uses of local currencies in cross-border payments. Overall, in the view of many analysts, this would not lead the RMB to overtake the dollar but to a multipolar world of key currencies including the dollar, Euro, GBP, RMB and others (Naef et al. 2022).

2. The history of ASEAN

2.1. Overview

When ASEAN was launched in 1967, one of its goals was to promote regional economic and monetary cooperation and integration. While economic integration has deepened, progress in monetary integration has been much more gradual. Its development has been uneven over time and can be identified with three phases.

The first phase gained momentum during the Asian Financial Crisis in 1998–99, with efforts to lessen Asia's vulnerability to future financial crises. The original initiative came from Japan promoting an Asian Monetary Fund — an idea which did not gain traction for various reasons. Eventually a looser form of pooling reserves for mutual liquidity support took shape as the Chiang Mai Initiative (Hui and Matsutani 2023).

The second phase coincided with the rapid growth in world trade after China joined the WTO in 2001. ASEAN countries agreed to liberalize trade and investment rules among themselves to promote a more integrated economic space to foster growth. They've made good progress in this project, posting annual growth rates of more than 5% in the past 10 years on the back of booming foreign trade reaching more than 90% of their combined GDP.

More economic interactions then set the stage for ASEAN countries to turn their attention to make arrangements to use local currencies in the settlement of trade and investment transactions among themselves in an effort to reduce their reliance on the UDS as an invoice and vehicle currency, which exposes them to the fluctuations in capital flows triggered by changes in US interest rates and exchange rates, driven mainly by the Fed's monetary operations.

The evolution of ASEAN economic and monetary integration, its progresses and constraints, can serve to inform similar efforts in other regions; for example, Africa which has recently launched its Continental Free Trade Agreement. Of particular importance is the sequencing of integration steps: ASEAN has preferred to move gradually, prioritizing economic liberalization and integration before attempting tighter monetary integration. As a consequence, there has been less constraints on member countries' fiscal and monetary sovereignty. By contrast, Euro Area members decided to launch a monetary union with a single currency — before reaching sufficient economic convergence among member countries to sustain an optimum currency area (Hafner and Jager 2013) and without a fiscal union to cushion asymmetric shocks — hoping to use the common currency to promote economic convergence among members. This politically driven approach to economic and monetary integration has led to occasional bouts of financial market tension when high levels of public debt of certain members trigger investor concerns about the long-term sustainability of the Euro.

2.2. From Asian Monetary Fund to Chiang Mai Initiative (Multilateralization)

After years of solid growth dubbed "Asian Miracle" by the World Bank, several East and South East Asian countries suffered a major financial crisis in the late 1990s when rising current account deficits forced a devaluation of their currencies having been pegged to dollar, in the process making the significant amount of dollar debt unsustainable — the dollar debt had been built up by capital inflows to those Asian countries looking to arbitrage interest rate differentials given lower dollar rates (IMF Staff 1998). The upheaval caused by the financial and economic crisis prompted authorities in the region to find ways to better protect themselves against the potentially unsettling impacts of changes in capital flows and dollar exchange rates.

At first Japan floated the idea of an Asian Monetary Fund — presumably with the yen playing an important role — to provide more timely and appropriate support for Asian countries. For many reasons, including opposition by the US and IMF and some countries in the region, that idea was quickly abandoned. In its place, ASEAN+3 (China, Japan and South Korea) launched the Chiang Mai Initiative (CMI). Initially, the CMI was developed in 2000 as a series of bilateral currency swaps among the ASEAN+3 countries aiming to supplement existing international financial institutions in providing liquidity support to members in need (ADB 2024). In 2010 members agreed to upgrade and multi-lateralize the CMI to CMI (Multilateralization) (CMIM) with pooled reserves of $120 billion. Then in 2014, the amount of pooled reserves was doubled to $240 billion, an CMIM Precautionary Line was introduced, and the ceiling of members' access to the reserves not linked to an IMF standby agreement increased from 20% to 30%. In 2019, the IMF de-linked portion was raised again to 40%; and members can also use local currencies in addition to the USD. In addition, the ASEAN+3 Macroeconomic Research Office (AMRO) was established to closely monitor economic policy and performance in the region– hopefully giving early warning signals to the authorities in safeguarding economic and financial stability.

2.3. ASEAN economic integration

In 1992 ASEAN leaders mandated the establishment of an ASEAN Free Trade Area. This effort was intensified in 1997 with the adoption of ASEAN

Vision 2020 for a region with free movements of goods, services, investment and skilled labor…to foster equitable and inclusive growth (ASEAN Secretariat 2024). In 2003, the leaders declared the aim of establishing an ASEAN Economic Community (AEC) with the above goals, targeted by 2020 but later accelerated to 2015. That was succeeded by the AEC Blueprint 2025 — aiming for "an integrated, cohesive, competitive, innovative and dynamic" regional economy.

Even though the AEC aspires to the EU-like goals of free movement of goods, services, investment and skilled labor, it has adopted a much more gradual, flexible and practical path. Instead of aiming for a common market, custom union, single market and monetary union, ASEAN has proceeded to develop a series of building blocks without a rigid structure perceived to be constraining sovereign member states — like in the case of the Euro Area. These building blocks include the ASEAN Trade in Goods Agreement (ATIGA), ASEAN Comprehensive Investment Agreement (ACIA), ASEAN Trade in Services Agreement (ATISA), and Mutual Recognition Agreement (MRA) to facilitate movements of professionals and skilled workers (Hew 2023).

In addition, many member countries have signed free trade agreements (FTAs) with major trading countries in Europe and North America and welcomed FDI flows. Many FTAs in Asia were then amalgamated into the Regional Comprehensive Economic Partnership (RCEP) — the largest FTA in terms of population and GDP — bringing together the 10 ASEAN countries with China, Japan, South Korea, Australia and New Zealand (Alejandro 2023). A particular feature of RCEP is the harmonization of rules of origin — a simplified 40% local content requirement which can be certified by any member country and recognized by the rest.

While the AEC has contributed to solid growth of the ASEAN economy in recent decades, the progress on economic integration is more nuanced. The share of intra-ASEAN trade in its total trade has been stagnant at around 21–22% — mainly because member countries host a significant number of FDI companies which use them as bases to manufacture goods for export to the rest of the world (ASEAN Secretariat 2023). However, trade within Emerging East Asia (excluding China) has increased from 3% of its GDP in 2000 to 3.5% in 2020 (Eckardt et al. 2023). The more pronounced integration has occurred within Emerging East Asia including China: internal export within the group increased from 12% of total export in 2000 to 31%

in 2020– reflecting substantial increases in intermediate goods trade. This was mainly due to China whose trade share rose from 1.6% of that region's GDP to 5.4%.

This pattern of economic integration has mixed implications for ASEAN: offering both opportunities (exposure to the economically dynamic Asian region) and vulnerability (increased dependence on China especially on imports of intermediate goods).

3. Practical projects of monetary cooperation

Based on economic progresses, ASEAN launched the Local Currency Transactions (LCT) initiative in 2023 with six countries participating (Indonesia, Malaysia, Thailand, Singapore, the Philippines with Vietnam scheduled to join) (Kominfo 2023). They also adopted a Local Currency Transaction Framework (LCTF) to implement the LCT plan by enhancing policy coordination and developing necessary infrastructure to promote the use of local currencies in bilateral and intra-regional trade and direct investment transactions. These have been practical measures which can be undertaken by member governments, and are useful in themselves to improve the efficiency of national payment systems. Equally importantly, they lay the groundwork for regional integration by being developed on up-to-date common standards (*i.e.* ISO 20022), operating in real time and amenable to being made interoperable.

Firstly, national payment and settlement systems have been developed and/or upgraded on a real time gross settlement basis, conforming to ISO 20022 standards so that those systems can be made interoperable within and without ASEAN (Publication 2023). A modern national payment and settlement system can visibly improve economic efficiency, contributing to growth — and worth developing in any event.

Secondly, national central securities depositories have also been developed on ISO 20022 standards (Asianbondonline 2020). This will promote the development of national bond market as well as help facilitate cross-border investment in regional bond markets which have been under development as parts of the Asian Bond Market Initiative since 2002. The ASEAN bond market has grown to $2.1 trillion or 60% of the region's GDP — with about 65% of the market in government bonds. In addition, efforts have been underway to develop local currency derivatives markets for interest rates and exchange rates contracts to provide hedging instruments to market participants.

Thirdly, authorities have designated Accredited Cross Currency Dealers (ACCD) — intermediary banks in member countries qualified to provide direct quotes of pairs of local currencies and implement the exchange transactions without using the USD as a vehicle currency. The real time gross settlement of cross-border transactions help to limit the exposure risks of the ACCDs.

In this context, the growing series of Bilateral Swap Arrangements (BSAs) either bilaterally or pluri-laterally among member central banks would ensure access to the local currency of the counterparties' country, reducing currency risks of the ACCDs. The BSAs among ASEAN+3 countries have totaled $404 billion.

Fourthly, ASEAN has been scheduled to launch a universal QR code payment system for goods and services by September 2023 — following a series of bilateral and plurilateral agreements. When realized, that would be the first such an arrangement in the world (Yulius 2023). Moreover, Japan has agreed to participate in the ASEAN QR code payment system by 2025 (Nishino 2024). Such arrangements would allow customers and merchants throughout ASEAN to use their e-wallets and QR code payment systems to make payments and receipts in their local currencies effectively and inexpensively anywhere in participating countries. This will help spur travel and business within ASEAN.

Last but not least, member countries have tried to coordinate and harmonize the operational requirements and regulations of their cross-border banking and payment activities to remove impediments to cross-border local currency settlements.

These steps would develop the infrastructure and regulatory environment allowing an efficient execution of cross-border settlements of trade and investment transactions in local currencies at retail and wholesale levels. This would attract non-financial users including consumers, importers and exporters. And the more economic agents make use of it, the more liquid the system becomes, offering even more benefits in a positive feedback loop. At present, the illiquid direct markets for local currencies remain the major obstacle to regular use of local currencies in cross-border settlements.

The key lesson here is the gradual development of regional payment using local currencies based on building interoperable infrastructures, harmonizing payment regulations and launching concrete products to meet the needs of consumers and businesses in the region. At the end of the day, it is they who will determine the viability of the local currency cross-border payment arrangements.

4. The story of BRICS

Since their inception in 2009/10, BRICS' original member (Brazil, Russia, India, China and South Africa) have worked together to develop alternative payment mechanisms and financial institutions, to reduce their dependence on the USD-led financial and payment system, making them vulnerable to US sanctions or threats of sanctions. Progress has been made in three key areas, and will likely be reinvigorated by several new members admitted at the beginning of 2024 — the UAE, Iran, Egypt and Ethiopia, with Saudi Arabia yet to officially confirming its participation. This has been one concrete achievement of the BRICS even though its ability to coordinate policies among member countries — now more difficult with nine-plus instead of five members — to challenge the G7, or the developed world in general, remains to be seen.

First of all, the New Development Bank (NDB) was launched in 2015, capitalized at $100 billion; now with all members of BRICS as well as Bangladesh and Uruguay (reportedly 15 other countries also want to join) (De Mott 2023). One of the NDB objectives is to mobilize funds and make development loans in members' local currencies — aiming to reach 30% of its portfolio in local currencies from 20% at present (Rangongo 2023).

Secondly, the Contingent Reserves Arrangement (CRA) was also launched in 2015 with capital totaling $100 billion from the five original members, and presumably will be augmented with the new members. The CRA is meant to provide timely support to members in balance of payment difficulties, with access equal to the amount they put in for most members except for one-half in the case of China and two-times for South Africa.

Thirdly and more importantly, most member countries have taken steps to develop national interbank payment and settlement system. As mentioned above, China launched its Cross-border interbank payment system (CIPS) in 2015 combining SWIFT-like messaging functions with real-time gross settlement of transactions (like the US CHIPS) — basically providing international cross-border access to CNAPS2– all consistent with ISO 20022. At present, China ranks third in the world in processing real time payment (RTP) transactions (17.6 billion of them in 2022) (Mehta 2023).

India's National Payments Corporation has introduced its Unified Payments Interface (UPI) to settle interbank transactions, mostly in South Asian countries. India is the leader in RTP in the world, having processed 89.5 billion transactions in 2022, accounting for 46% of the global RTP volume (Mehta 2023).

Russia developed its System for the Transfer of Financial Messages (STFM) and the Faster Payment System (FPS) operated by the Central Bank of Russia, which reported that 20 countries have participated in the FPS.

More recently, Brazil has developed its PIX payment system in 2020, operating in Latin America. Brazil comes in second in RTP with 29.2 billion transactions or 15% of the total (Mehta 2023).

Linking the national payment systems together *and* putting in place currency swap arrangements between BRICS central banks, will facilitate the receipts and payments by exporters and importers in their respective local currencies. The most notable progress has been in the bilateral trade between Russia and China where reportedly 95% of the 2023 trade volume of $240 billion has been settled by Russia's ruble and China's yuan — driven by Western sanctions on Russia (Ramos 2023). Similar uses of local currencies to settle bilateral trades have also been reported for other BRICS members as well. Moreover, the RMB has been reported as being used with third countries in smaller scales. For example, Russia has reportedly been able to use the RMB in trades with a range of countries such as Mongolia, the Philippines, Malaysia, the UAE, Thailand, Japan, Tajikistan and Singapore (Ramos 2023).

Basically, the above-mentioned measures are parts of the BRICS Pay System which has been developed to link all national payment systems together, providing the infrastructure to exchange local currencies, making it easier to use local currencies to settle bilateral and eventually plurilateral trades among BRICS members. This will be greatly facilitated if those local currencies would be in tokenized forms such as stable coins or CBDCs.

Conclusions: democratization and fragmentation of the global payment system

De-dollarization has made good progress in recent years and will spread more widely as the use of local currencies in cross-border payments is likely to reach a critical mass. With the technology for doing so becoming widely available, and leading groups like the BRICS-10 in a position to share experiences and technical know-how, the key issue driving increasing uses of local currencies will be the political and policy decision by countries to embrace the de-dollarization trend. Of particular importance is the willingness to coordinate and harmonize payment policies, regulations, infrastructures and market practices. Judging by statements of leaders in various countries in the Global South, this seems to be their intentions. In short, with political will professed by leaders and technical knowhow readily available, further progress in de-dollarization can be expected in the foreseeable future.

Cross-border payments using local currencies have the important advantage of being within the competency of any country acting together with its partner, not subject to the decisions of any major countries. Thus, its growing popularity is democratizing the global payment system, consistent with the aspirations of countries in the Global South.

However, this will lead to a further fragmentation of the international payment landscape, being parts of the overall geopolitically driven fragmentation of the global economy — estimated by the IMF to reduce global GDP by 7 percentage points, a significant cost to the world especially the low-income countries. Basically, at present it is less efficient to use local currencies in cross-border payments largely on a bilateral basis, instead of using a common means of payment multilaterally on a global basis. As mentioned above, the efficiency costs of using local currencies in cross-border payments could be alleviated over time with technological advances in payment solutions. In the meantime, the tradeoffs between efficiency and de-risking in cross-border payments, and in economic transactions in general, will become more tangible and relevant in countries' considerations to de-dollarize.

References

ADB (2024), "Chiang Mai Initiative (Multilateralization)". *ADB Asian Regional Integration Center*

ADB (2023), "Update on Financial Market Infrastructures in ASEAN+3", *ADB Blogs https://dx.doi.org/10.22617/BRF230568-2*

ASEAN Secretariat (2023), *ASEAN Statistical Yearbook 2023*, ASEAN Blogs *https://www.aseanstats.org/wp-content/uploads/2023/12/ASYB-2023-v1.pdf*

Asianbondonline (2020), *Next steps for ASEAN+3 Central Securities Depository and Real Time Gross Settlement Linkages*, http://dx.doi.org/10.22617/TCS200193-2

Amighini A., Garcia-Herrero A. (2023), "Third Time Lucky? China's Push to Internationalize the Renminbi". *Bruegel Policy Brief 20/2023, https://www.bruegel.org/policy-brief/third-time-lucky-chinas-push-internationalise-renminbi*

Arslanalp S. and Simpson-Bell C. (2021), "US dollar share of global foreign exchange reserves dropped to 25 year lows", *IMF Blog*, https://www.imf.org/en/Blogs/Articles/2021/05/05/blog-us-dollar-share-of-global-foreign-exchange-reserves-drops-to-25-year-low

Bloomberg (2024), "Foreign Investors Flee Chinese Shares, long-delayed data shows", *Bloomberg News*, https://www.bloomberg.com/news/articles/2024-02-21/foreign-investors-flee-chinese-shares-long-delayed-data-shows

Bordo M. and McCauley R.N. (2017), "Triffin: Dilemma or Myth?", *BIS Working Papers*, No. 684, https://www.bis.org/publ/work684.htm

Business Times (2024), "Foreign Investors Increased Chinese onshore bond holdings in December", *The Business Times*, https://www.businesstimes.com.sg/international/foreign-investors-increased-their-china-onshore-bond-holdings-december

China Daily (2023), "RMB records rapid growth in cross-border settlements", https://www.chinadaily.com.cn/a/202305/08/WS64586b76a310b6054fad1aa4.html#:~:text=As%20a%20payment%20settlement%20currency,cross%2Dborder%20receipts%20and%20payments.

De Mott F. (2023), "China-based BRICS bank aims to dedollarize debt by expanding local currency lending", *Business Insider*, https://markets.businessinsider.com/news/bonds/china-brics-bank-dedollarization-dollar-dominance-debt-local-currency-lending-2023-8#:~:text=China%2Dbased%20BRICS%20bank%20aims,by%20expanding%20local%20currency%20lending&text=The%20BRICS%20New%20Development%20Bank,will%20be%20in%20local%20tenders.

Fintech Futures (2020), "China leads the way in adoption of ISO 20022 for payments", *Fintech Futures Blog*, https://www.fintechfutures.com/2020/03/china-leads-the-way-in-adoption-of-iso-20022-for-payments/#:~:text=China's%20low%2Dvalue%20real%2Dtime,200%20banks%20using%20the%20system.

Financial Stability Board (FSB) (2023). *G20 Roadmap for Enhancing Cross-Border Payments: Consolidated Progress. Report for 2023*, Basel: Financial Stability Board, https://www.fsb.org/wp-content/uploads/P091023-2.pdf

Hafner K. And Jager J. (2013), "The Optimum Currency Area Theory and the EMU", *Intereconomics* Vol. 48, No. 5, https://www.intereconomics.eu/contents/year/2013/number/5/article/the-optimum-currency-area-theory-and-the-emu.html

Hope A. (2023), "How did Union Pay become the global debit card king?", *The China Project*, https://thechinaproject.com/2023/05/31/how-did-unionpay-become-the-global-debit-card-king/

Hui B. and Matsutani M. (2023), "How the CMIM has evolved as ASEAN+3's self help mechanism", *AMRO Blogs*, https://amro-asia.org/how-the-cmim-has-evolved-as-asean3s-self-help-mechanism/

IMF (2024), "Special Drawing Rights", *IMF Blog*, https://www.imf.org/en/Topics/special-drawing-right#:~:text=The%20SDR%20is%20an%20international,provide%20a%20country%20with%20liquidity.

Kominfo 2023. Regional Payment Connectivity and Local Currency in ASEAN. *ASEAN Indonesia 2023*

Li Y. (2023), "Innovations Bolsters Cross-border Payments", *The Asset, https://www.theasset.com/article/50644/innovation-bolsters-cross-border-payments*

Lipsky J. and Kumar A. (2024), "The Fed is falling behind as other central banks keep ahead on digital currencies", *Atlantic Council New Atlanticist, https://www.atlanticcouncil.org/blogs/new-atlanticist/the-fed-is-falling-behind-as-other-central-banks-leap-ahead-on-digital-currencies/#:~:text=January%2025%2C%202024-,The%20Fed%20is%20falling%20behind%20as%20other,leap%20ahead%20on%20digital%20currencies&text=This%20will%20be%20a%20year,easing%E2%80%94it%20will%20be%20technology.*

Mehta P. (2023), "China's global digital payment dominance: catalysts and future prospects", *CTM File*, https://ctmfile.com/story/chinas-global-digital-payments-dominance-catalysts-and-future-prospects

Naef A. et al (2022), "The Renmimbi's unconventional route to reserve currency status", *CEPR VOXEU Column,* https://cepr.org/voxeu/columns/renminbis-unconventional-route-reserve-currency-status

Perez-Saiz H. and Zhang L. (2023), *Renminbi usage in cross-birder payments: regional patterns and the role of swap lines and offshore clearing banks,* Washington: International Monetary Fund

Plant M. (2021), "How in the World Are We Going to Track the World's SDRs?", *Center for Global Development,* https://www.cgdev.org/blog/how-world-are-we-going-track-worlds-sdrs

Ramos M. (2023), "De-dollarization: 95% of the trade between China and Russia didn't use the US dollar", *Brasil de Fato* https://www.brasildefato.com.br/2023/12/21/de-dollarization-95-of-the-trade-between-china-and-russia-didn-t-use-the-us-dollar#:~:text=Russia%20became%20China's%20main%20trading,in%20transactions%20estimated%20for%202023&text=In%20a%20recent%20visit%20to,the%20two%20countries%20reached%2095%25.

Rangongo T. (2023), "BRICS Bank aims to increase local currency borrowing to 30%", *Bloomberg,* https://www.bloomberg.com/news/articles/2023-08-23/brics-bank-aims-to-increase-local-currency-borrowing-to-30

SWIFT (2024), "RMB Tracker April 2024". *SWIFT https://www.swift.com/*

The Editors (2023), "The high cost of global economic fragmentation", *IMF Blog,* https://www.imf.org/en/Blogs/Articles/2023/08/28/the-high-cost-of-global-economic-fragmentation

Tombini A. (2023), "The impact of international fragmentation and the role of the US dollar". *BIS Speech, https://www.bis.org/speeches/sp231028.htm*

Tran H. (2024), "The Euro's share of international transactions is likely smaller than it looks", *Atlantic Council Econographics,* https://www.atlanticcouncil.org/blogs/econographics/the-euros-share-of-international-transactions-is-likely-smaller-than-it-looks/#:~:text=Over%2Dreporting%20the%20Euro's%20share&text=Consequently%2C%20excluding%20Euro%20transactions%20within,percent%20share%20reported%20by%20SWIFT).

Tran H. (2023), "Understanding the growing use of local currencies in cross-border payments". *Atlantic Council Econographics*, https://www.atlanticcouncil.org/blogs/econographics/understanding-the-growing-use-of-local-currencies-in-cross-border-payments/

Vasic-Lalovic I. (2022), "The Case for more Special Drawing Rights: Rechanneling is no substitute for a new allocation", *Center for Economic and Policy Research*, https://cepr.net/report/the-case-for-more-special-drawing-rights/#:~:text=We%20conclude%20that%20a%20new,to%20borrow%20from%20the%20PRGT.

Wong M. and Burgess M. (2024, 24 March), "China's Yuan Standout Funder for Emerging Market Carry Trade", *Bloomberg* https://www.bloomberg.com/news/articles/2024-03-24/china-s-yuan-a-standout-funder-for-emerging-market-carry-trade

Yulius Y. (2023), *Interoperable QR Code Payment Ecosystem in ASEAN: what it means for the world*, available at BCG.com, https://web-assets.bcg.com/9c/ac/72af6ed244c39123f679ffc899ee/bcg-asean-interoperable-qr-code-payment-ecosystem-in-asean.pdf

Where Do We Go from Here? What Kind of Initiative Would Robert Triffin Promote?

Ousmène Mandeng

Dear Friends, thank you very much to the organizers for the kind invitation to participate in the panel discussion on the past and outlook for the international monetary system and the most interesting question of what Robert Triffin would do in light of the state of the system today. The system as it was envisaged at Bretton Woods 80 years ago, has a rather mixed record. The most problematic one, I believe, is that only very few currencies serve today in international payments producing a high dependency on the so-called key currencies. Herein lies I think the biggest shortcoming that will need to be addressed going forward. I guess it is also what Triffin would lament the most and focus on as the most pressing issue. A new willingness to adopt unconventional approaches often in relation to central bank digital currencies (CBDC) seems to be pointing in the right direction.

Bretton Woods was unique, as is well known, in establishing for the first time a formal international arrangement on exchange rates with an international treaty, the Articles of Agreement of the IMF. Member countries are subject to a series of obligations. Under Article VIII they must abstain from exchange restrictions, multiple exchange practices and discriminatory currency arrangements for current transactions comprising international trade and interest payments.

One of the IMF's main purposes is to establish a multilateral payment system. This rests in essence in: "The Commission, in asking governments to assume the obligation to make their currencies freely convertible, so that *"each country can count on using the proceeds of its exports to any part of the world to pay for imports from any part of the world"*[1]. The elimination of exchange restrictions was seen as a necessary condition therefor. Article VIII

[1] Report of Commission I International Monetary Fund to the Executive Plenary Session 20 July 1944, Department of State (1944)

was accepted by the main European countries by 1961. But despite the fact that most IMF member countries having subsequently accepted Article VIII their currencies continue to play no or only a very limited role in international transactions. Article VIII has proven not to be a sufficient condition for international currency usage.

The IMF early on was concerned that if few currencies are being used in international exchange it could produce unwanted dependencies. At Bretton Woods, in a memorandum to Committee 2 [Operations of the Fund] of Commission 1 about the use of Fund resources of around 12 July 1944 it stated[2]:"The Fund must be in a position to dispose of its franc balances in meeting payments due to France, its guilder balances in meeting payments due to the Netherlands, etc. There is no doubt that the provision can be made in the Fund proposal to facilitate the use of all of the currencies in the Fund in meeting balances of payments."

The currency concentration problem also manifested itself in the adoption of the scarce currency clause of Article VII outlining that insufficient access to and liquidity in a given currency poses a major challenge for meeting international payments obligations. Initial IMF drawings have been heavily tilted towards a small set of currencies. Of total drawings to December 1960, 87 percent were drawn in dollars (Horsefield 1969). Today it is not very different.

The use of few national currencies in international payments was the foundation of Triffin's critique: "The most fundamental deficiency of the present system, and the main danger to future stability, lies in the fact that it leaves the satisfactory development of world monetary liquidity primarily dependent upon an admittingly insufficient supply of new gold and an admittingly dangerous and haphazard expansion in the short-term indebtedness of the key currency countries"(Triffin 1961, 100).

Triffin proposed several ideas, the Triffin plan, as is well known, to address the shortcomings. The plan aimed for the substitution of "IMF balances for [key currencies] national currencies in all member countries' monetary reserves" (Horsefield 1969). Triffin wanted to reduce the use of national

2 Horsefield (ed) (1969): "This heavy concentration of drawings and repurchases on one currency [the dollar] had not been intended by the drafters of the Articles of Agreement, who had expected that the majority of countries would accept the obligations of Article VIII, Sections 2, 3, and 4, at a fairly early stage of the Fund's life, thereby making their currencies acceptable in repurchases once they had been drawn."

currencies as international reserves and allow the IMF to accommodate liquidity needs flexibly driven by countries making deposits at the IMF[3]. While he was concerned with a lack of international reserves, he also wanted to attain greater diversification in the use of currencies[4]. The Triffin plan argued that any loan extended by the IMF would be deposited to the member's deposit account and could be drawn in any currency to put an end to IMF credits being funded mostly by countries, notably the U.S. suffering significant reserves losses (Triffin 1961, 117 and footnote 19).

The persistent use of a narrow set of currencies remains the big unfinished business of the IMF and echoes the original Triffin critique[5]. The IMF today still considers only 5 currencies, the dollar, euro, renminbi, sterling and yen, as freely usable currencies out of about 145 currencies in circulation. It means countries need to conduct operations with the IMF on the basis of those currencies. It shall be considered here as a proxy for the persistent strong asymmetry in the use of currencies in international transactions today. The IMF by relying only on those currencies risks reinforcing this asymmetry.

The narrow set of currencies seems particularly problematic as large emerging markets remain significantly constrained in using their own currencies in international payments. While emerging markets today represent about half of the world's real economy, their currencies play nearly no role in international payments. Although the renminbi is declared a freely usable currency by the IMF, it has not gained meaningful traction in international payments. China has for some time declared that it would like to pursue internationalization of the renminbi. India recently announced that it wants the rupee to have a bigger role internationally.

---

3 See also *e.g.* Robert Triffin (1961, 25 March), *The Times*.

4 See *e.g.* Lutz (1963, 7): "In the Triffin plan the emphasis is clearly not so much on the increase in the borrowing potential of the participating countries as on the creation of more units of international currency [...]."

5 Triffin was critical of the IMF not supporting a multilateral payment system (Triffin 1961, 116): "[...] it should be noted that the Fund Agreement allows members to purchase foreign currencies in exchange for their own currency — *i.e.* in exchange for their own I.O.U.s — but not in exchange for other foreign currencies owned or acquired by them. This means in effect that the Fund could never really fulfil effectively on of the main purposes stated in Article I, Section (iv) of the Agreement, *i.e.* 'to assist in the establishment of a multilateral system of payments in respect of current transactions between members [...] This was a major gap in the Fund Agreement [...]."

To conclude, 80 years on, Triffin's critique remains as valid today as it was then. His plan to convert the IMF de facto into a central bank has not been pursued to this date and seems an unlikely way forward. Triffin would probably still propose to reduce dependence on a narrow set of national currencies to establish greater stability and symmetry in the system[6]. The adoption of IMF Special Drawing Rights (SDRs) in large part in response to Triffin's critique and subsequent amendment of the Articles by which the SDR is meant to become the principal reserve asset, have brought few if any meaningful changes to the system; SDRs will likely need to be subject to considerable changes to increase their relevance in international transactions.

The shifting geopolitics have brought forward greater urgency in pursuing diversification in the international monetary system. CBDC initiated a new fundamental debate about the use of money. New approaches are being tested on how new technologies can facilitate foreign exchange settlement, establish more direct monetary relations and reduce risk in particular in foreign transactions. The political pressure has increased, including and driven by China and large emerging markets but also to an important extent by the Euro Union with its increasing emphasis on open strategic autonomy and the enhanced role of the euro. Recent initiatives like the BIS Innovation Hub CBDC project *mBridge* aim at conducting international payments using local currencies to advance currency diversification.

Achieving greater diversification remains one of the most enduring challenges of the international monetary system. It may be a necessary condition for the integrity of the system itself. The Triffin plan provided critical ideas that do still seem highly relevant today. Going forward some of the those should be put in practice.

Thank you very much for your attention.

---

6 At the time, other plans were proposed notably but not limited to by Robert Roosa of the U.S. Treasury, Suardus Posthuma of the Netherlands Central Bank, Arthur Stamp of IMF Executive Board, Edward Bernstein of the IMF Research Department.

References

Department of State (1944), *United Nations Monetary and Financial Conference Final Act and related documents*. Retrieved from United States Government Printing Office, Washington.

Horsefield J. K. (1969). *The International Monetary Fund 1945-1965, Volume II: Analysis*. Washington: International Monetary Fund.

Lutz F. (1963), *The problem if international liquidity and the multiple-currency standard*. Retrieved from https://ies.princeton.edu/pdf/E41.pdf

Triffin R. (1961, 25 May), Plan for Atlantic monetary organization. *The Time*.

Triffin R. (1961), *Gold and the dollar crisis*, New Haven: Yale University Press.

Bretton Woods in a New World

Marc Uzan

Introduction

Is the notion of Reinventing Bretton Woods conceivable? This simple question brought a multitude of thoughts about the bold objectives of the 45 nations whose representatives gathered at Bretton Woods, New Hampshire in the summer of 1944 to establish a new economic order; about the extent to which these ambitions have been fulfilled; about the many new challenges that have arisen in the world economy since Bretton Woods; and where, in view of these challenges, the international financial system is leading us.

It is certainly true that the international monetary system has changed considerably since Bretton Woods, and in ways that were largely unforeseen in 1944. Instead of a system of fixed exchange rates among major currencies, we now have a mixed system with major currency areas floating but fixed rates among many smaller countries. Where capital controls were once pervasive, we now have global financial markets. From the relatively small group of 35 countries that became the founding members of the International Monetary Fund, membership has expanded to include virtually every economy in the world.

Indeed, with all the complexities and uncertainties that the existing international monetary system presents, Bretton Woods seems to evoke a more orderly and cohesive world, raising the question of whether the international community should not strive toward a *new* Bretton Woods.

1. A new Bretton Woods?

To answer this question, however, one must first consider more fully what Bretton Woods and the IMF, the institution established to oversee the new monetary order, were intended to achieve. Bretton Woods has become almost synonymous with the fixed exchange rate system that prevailed from the time of the IMF's establishment until the abandonment of fixed rates in 1973. However, the visionaries at the Bretton Woods conference had broader objectives in mind. As stated in the IMF's Articles of Agreement, they were striving toward a system that would "promote international monetary cooperation", "facilitate the expansion and balanced growth of international trade," and "contribute thereby to the promotion and maintenance of high levels of employment and real income". They also aimed to "promote exchange stability [...] maintain orderly exchange arrangements among members and [...] avoid competitive exchange depreciation." At the same time, they wanted to "assist in the establishment of a multilateral system of payments in respect of current transactions between members and in the elimination of foreign exchange restrictions which hamper the growth of world trade." As these goals suggest, the purpose of Bretton Woods was above all to establish a more stable and prosperous world economy, and the role of the IMF *would be* to help promote the preconditions for this.

In 1994, the 50th Anniversary of the Bretton Woods Conference provided the opportunity for a thorough review of the functioning of the international monetary system. This took place in an atmosphere of satisfaction and complacency with the general operation of the system. Long gone were the complaints which characterized the 1970s about the monetary anarchy created by the collapse of the par-value regime for exchange rates and the calls for the IMF to regulate world liquidity through its multilateral new currency the SDR.

Indeed, following the wave of deregulation and liberalization, the concept of an international monetary system seemed increasingly inappropriate or even obsolete: if every country kept its house in order, floating exchange rates and free capital movement would cushion national economies while facilitating adjustment of international payment imbalances. Hence there would be no need for institutions to manage "systemic" issues. Very few voices were to be heard complaining about the current non-system and calling for a new Bretton Woods conference to reinvent the monetary system for the new millennium.

By 2004, the 60th anniversary of the institutions, however, the landscape had changed dramatically. The wave of financial crises in emerging markets in the previous decade — Mexico in 1994/95, East Asia in 1997, Russia Brazil in 1998, Argentina in 2001 — had generated growing discontent with the system. This debate, which took place under the label of reform of the *international financial architecture,* passed through various phases. Initial radical thoughts for setting up a global central bank or a world financial authority, were rejected as impractical. Subsequent thinking coalesced around more pragmatic measures designed to help prevent financial crises and to manage those that occurred better.

An important part of the reform was the establishment of comprehensive standards, representing best global practices toward which all countries participating in the global system would strive. At that time, some observers argued that we had re-entered "the old paradigm". Professor Michael Dooley and his colleagues argued that the previous system was never actually destroyed, just put into hibernation. Just as Europe and Japan benefited from fixed exchange rates in the 1950s and '60s, the reasoning went, so Asia was now profiting from the same. The success of China and India in exporting goods and services respectively was certainly built in part on undervalued currencies. Some Asian currencies kept fixed rates, some had a managed float, but all of them continued to accumulate vast amounts of official reserves in US dollars. The insight of Dooley's team was that this was a contract, like Bretton Woods, not the operation of a free market. China had the potential to be a source of strength as well as vulnerability in reinforcing the precarious stability that had returned to the international financial system, and in underpinning the recently interrupted move toward a genuinely global system of open finance.

By 2014 the 70th anniversary of the Bretton Woods conference, pessimism had returned. The global financial system continued to stumble from crisis to crisis. From the great recession of 2009 to the longest financial crisis in history, to the travails of the Eurozone, there was no end in sight. The philosophy of the global financial system seemed to rely on each country managing its own economy in what it perceives to be its own best interest without giving much attention to global consistency. That was the beginning of the age of fragmentation and divergence.

Supporters of 'muddling through' hope that this will lead to a satisfactory outcome for the world, just as, given certain conditions, the actions of individuals who follow their own self-interest leads to a socially efficient outcome. And so far the world has indeed muddled through in this way, without a disaster comparable to the global depression of the 1930s.Yet many observers felt that it would be wrong to accept this for two reasons: first, the output losses from the great financial crisis have been appallingly high;

secondly, there was no guarantee that the next crisis may not be even more severe.

By the turn of 2024, the current times of uncertainty, economic disruptions, environmental emergency, and repeated geopolitical crises have led to a fragmented and changing world, in which the dynamics we had known for several years have now drastically changed as the global environment becomes "more fragmented, more tensed, more on the edge and more under stress". World leaders may not agree on much these days — but many of them share the sentiment that the world is entering a critical decade in the contest for the future international order. Over the last three decades, businesses and governments around the world operated under the assumption that economic and financial globalization would continue apace.

As the international order has come under strain in recent years, however, the concept of deglobalization — the delinking of trade and investment — has increasingly gained traction with households, companies, and governments. National security and geopolitics are supplanting economics in shaping national and international interactions. Central bankers around the world are being called upon to deal with the repercussions of strategic economic relations on macroeconomic variables, inflation dynamics, monetary policy, financial stability and market infrastructures.

In 2024, as a result, whereas the last 70 years were characterized by increasing globalization, free trade, global connectedness, sluggish economic growth, low inflation, failing bond yields, and absence of fiscal policies, we seem to be moving toward a period of decreasing globalization, free trade and less interconnection, aggressively stimulating fiscal policies, increased US growth, higher inflation and rising bond yields.

Is the world today brimming with economic nationalism that could set off a downward economic spiral reminiscent of the 1930s? As suggested by Professor Joe Stiglitz the volume that we published during that time, the way forward is to finish the work of Bretton Woods but new challenges from digital money, climate finance and development are emerging.

2. The new challenges ahead

In recent years the global economy has faced a multitude of new challenges and unprecedented crises: the global pandemic crisis, the climate crisis due a cost-of-living crisis, new geopolitical challenges. All these developments have dramatically increased economic and geopolitical risks and global uncertainty.

For decades, globalization has been the driving force behind unprecedented economic integration and technological advancement on a global scale. This shift towards fragmentation stems from a confluence of factors, including growing inequality, technological disruption, geopolitical tensions, and the uneven distribution of the benefits of globalization.

And indeed, the last 30 years brought decades of global financial crises, economic booms, technological advancements, and geopolitical shifts and we have learned several key lessons for improving the global financial architecture:

1. *resilience and adaptability*: the global financial architecture must be resilient and adaptable to withstand shocks and crises. Flexibility in policy frameworks, institutions, and regulatory mechanisms is essential to respond effectively to emerging challenges and mitigate systemic risks.
2. *coordination and cooperation*: global financial stability requires coordination and cooperation among countries, central banks, international financial institutions, and regulatory bodies. Close collaboration is needed to address cross-border spill-overs, promote policy coherence, and build consensus on common challenges.
3. *inclusivity and sustainability*: the global financial architecture must prioritize inclusivity and sustainability to ensure that the benefits of economic growth are shared equitably, and that development is environmentally sustainable.
4. *innovation and resilience:* innovation plays a crucial role in driving economic growth and enhancing the resilience of the global financial architecture. Embracing technological advancements, such as digital currencies, blockchain technology, and fintech innovations, can improve efficiency, accessibility, and inclusivity in financial markets while also posing new challenges that require careful regulation and oversight.
5. *multilateralism and cooperation* are fundamental principles for building a robust and inclusive global financial architecture. International financial institutions, such as the IMF, World Bank, and regional development banks, play a central role in promoting multilateral cooperation, facilitating dialogue, and providing technical assistance to member states.

Just as in 1944, we face a pressing need for collective action to address the root causes of instability and inequality. However, the solutions we seek must be adapted to the realities of the 21st century. One of the most striking parallels between then and now is the importance of international cooperation. Just as the architects of Bretton Woods recognized the need for coordinated action to rebuild the post-war world, we must recognize the imperative of working together to address the challenges of today.

3. Adapting to the 21st Century Bretton woods in a new world

At the same time, we must acknowledge that the global landscape has evolved since 1944, and our approach to economic governance must evolve with it. The rise of new economic powers, the emergence of digital technologies, and the growing urgency of environmental sustainability all demand innovative thinking and flexible solutions. We cannot simply replicate the Bretton Woods model; we must build upon it, adapting its principles to meet the needs of a rapidly changing world.

Here are the three main challenges to be discuss today.

3.1. Climate Finance.

In the context of the fragmented global economy, one of the most pressing challenges we face is climate change. The impacts of climate change are already being felt around the world, from extreme weather events to rising sea levels and diminishing biodiversity. Addressing this existential threat requires a concerted effort on a global scale, and financing plays a crucial role in enabling the transition to a low-carbon, resilient economy.

Climate finance encompasses a range of financial instruments and mechanisms aimed at mobilizing resources for climate-related projects and initiatives. From public funds to private investments, climate finance channels capital towards renewable energy, energy efficiency, adaptation measures, and sustainable infrastructure. However, despite significant progress in recent years, there remains a substantial gap between the funds needed to address climate change and the resources currently available.

To bridge this gap, we must explore innovative approaches to climate finance, including leveraging public-private partnerships, enhancing the role of multilateral development banks, and incentivizing sustainable investment through regulatory frameworks and financial incentives. By mobilizing capital at scale and directing it towards climate-resilient solutions, we can accelerate the transition to a sustainable future and mitigate the worst impacts of climate change.

3.2. Digital Currencies

Another area of profound transformation in the global economy is the rise of digital currencies and blockchain technology We are witnessing a profound transformation in the international monetary system, driven by the emergence of digital currencies. As Central Bank Digital Currencies (CBDCs) gain traction across the globe, they are reshaping the very foundations of how we conduct financial transactions and interact in the global economy and raise numerous questions:

1. How can we ensure interoperability and compatibility between different CBDC systems to facilitate seamless cross-border transactions?
2. What regulatory frameworks are needed to govern the issuance, distribution, and use of CBDCs in the international arena?
3. How can we address concerns related to privacy, data protection, and cybersecurity in the context of CBDCs?
4. What role will international organizations and multilateral institutions play in coordinating efforts to integrate CBDCs into the international monetary system?

The legacy of the Bretton Woods system, which laid the foundations for the post-war economic order, continues to shape our understanding of international finance. Yet, as we stand on the precipice of a new era marked by unprecedented technological advancements, we must grapple with the complexities and uncertainties that AI presents to the global economic landscape.

The challenges posed by AI are multifaceted and far-reaching, touching upon every aspect of economic governance and policymaking. From labor market disruptions and income inequality to data privacy concerns and algorithmic bias, AI has the potential to reshape the very fabric of our societies and economies in ways that are both profound and unpredictable.

One of the central challenges posed by AI is the impact on employment and the labor market. Automation and machine learning algorithms have the capacity to transform industries and occupations, leading to widespread job displacement and structural unemployment. This poses significant social and economic challenges, as workers grapple with the prospect of retraining and adapting to new forms of employment in a rapidly evolving technological landscape.

Moreover, the rise of AI exacerbates existing inequalities, both within and between countries. Access to AI technologies and the ability to harness their potential is often concentrated among a small elite, widening the gap between the haves and the have-nots. This raises fundamental questions about social justice, economic inclusion, and the distribution of wealth and power in the digital age.

Furthermore, AI introduces new complexities into the realm of economic policymaking, particularly in areas such as regulation, taxation, and international trade. The borderless nature of digital technologies challenges traditional notions of sovereignty and jurisdiction, posing dilemmas for policymakers seeking to balance innovation and consumer protection, competition and collaboration.

In the face of these challenges, it is imperative that we adopt a forward-looking and proactive approach to AI governance. This requires robust regulatory frameworks that safeguard against the negative externalities of AI while fostering innovation and entrepreneurship. It also demands investments in education and skills training to equip workers with the tools they need to thrive in an AI-driven economy.

Moreover, international cooperation and coordination are essential to address the global dimensions of AI governance. Just as the Bretton Woods system laid the groundwork for multilateral cooperation in the post-war era, we must now come together to establish norms, standards, and protocols that ensure the responsible and ethical development and deployment of AI technologies.

3.3. Power Geopolitics

The weaponization of the global economy represents a troubling departure from the principles of cooperation and mutual benefit that have long underpinned international trade and finance. Increasingly, economic tools are being wielded as instruments of coercion and conflict, threatening the stability and integrity of the global economic order.

Brad Setser's work illuminates the multifaceted nature of this phenomenon, highlighting its impact on trade relations, investment flows, and financial markets. From trade tariffs and financial sanctions to currency manipulation and supply chain disruptions, nations are employing economic measures to pursue strategic objectives and assert dominance in the geopolitical arena.

The evolving dynamics between China and the United States have profound implications for the future of the Bretton Woods system and the global economic order. As the world's two largest economies and key players in the international arena, their interactions shape not only the bilateral relationship but also the broader dynamics of global governance, trade, and finance.

1. How will ongoing tensions and potential conflicts between the United States and China affect the stability and viability of the Bretton Woods system, considering the pivotal role these two countries play in the global economy?
2. What strategies can be employed to mitigate the risks posed by diverging economic interests and geopolitical rivalries between the US and China, while upholding the principles and institutions established under the Bretton Woods framework?

Yet, amidst these challenges, there lies an opportunity for principled leadership and collective action. We must reaffirm our commitment to the principles of multilateralism, dialogue, and cooperation as the cornerstone of global economic governance. By adhering to established norms and institutions, we can mitigate the risks of unilateralism and arbitrary decision-making that undermine economic stability and predictability.

Secondly, we must prioritize diplomacy and conflict resolution as the preferred means of addressing differences and promoting cooperation. Dialogue, not coercion, should guide our interactions, fostering mutual understanding and trust among nations.

Thirdly, we must invest in diversification and resilience-building measures to mitigate the vulnerabilities exposed by the weaponization of the global economy. Strengthening supply chains, promoting financial inclusion, and fostering market diversification are essential steps towards building a more robust and resilient global economic architecture.

What's about the European Union? In the ever-evolving landscape of the global economy and finance, Europe finds itself at a pivotal juncture, poised to play a leading role in shaping the future of our interconnected world.

At the heart of Europe's potential lies its commitment to multilateralism and cooperation In a world characterized by increasing fragmentation and uncertainty. With the rise of China as an economic and technological powerhouse, the resurgence of Russia as a regional actor, and the changing role of the United States in international affairs, Europe must navigate a complex geopolitical landscape while safeguarding its interests and values. As a champion of multilateralism, Europe can advocate for a rules-based international order and the strengthening of multilateral institutions. In an era where unilateralism and power politics threaten global stability, Europe's commitment to multilateralism can provide a counterbalance, promoting cooperation and collective action to address global challenges.

Conclusion

In closing, let us remember the spirit of cooperation and vision that guided the delegates of Bretton Woods 80 years ago.

As we navigate the complexities of a fragmented global economy, let us draw inspiration from previous generations and work together to build a more just, sustainable, and prosperous world.

Summing up of the Debate

Bernard Snoy

Day 1: Monday 6 May 2024
Venue: Museu do Din heiro,
Banco de Portugal

Introduction

The conference, which had 58 registered participants, was opened by a warm welcome speech on behalf of Banco de Portugal by Vice Governor Luis Máximo dos Santos. He recalled that his first contact with Robert Triffin's line of thought was at the University of Lisbon School of Law as a student of Professor Paulo de Pitta e Cunha, his great admirer and promoter in Portugal. He praised also the spirit of cooperation that characterized the Bretton Woods system, the innovative nature of the established solutions and the balance between well defined principles and the pragmatism needed for success. While the Bretton Woods international order had undoubtedly contributed to the Glorious Thirty Years (1945–75), the period following the end of the Cold War appeared not to have revealed so much wisdom. Given the failure of major international institutions to reform and to adapt to new players and the increasing rejection of hyper-globalization, perceived as incompatible with national democracy and national sovereignty, it was a good idea to ask whether the impulse towards monetary regionalization could provide an effective response to geo-economic fragmentation and help relaunch a more effective multilateralism.

In his introductory statement, Bernard Snoy, Chairman of RTI, thanked the co-organizers of the conference, Banco de Portugal and the Academia das Ciências de Lisboa, stressing the personal roles of Prof. Clara Raposo, Vice-Governor Banco de Portugal, and of Prof. Jorge Braga de Macedo, Jubilee Professor of Economics at Nova School of Business and Economics, Treasurer of the Academia and former Minister of Finance, who signed the Treaty of Maastricht, for their key role in preparing the conference. He thanked also the Gutt Fund (Free University of Brussels) for its important financial support to the conference He conveyed the message of Michel Camdessus, former

Managing Director of the IMF, on the danger of new financial crises and of global incapacity to address multiple challenges if we failed to reform the IMF, to broaden its mandate and to improve global economic and monetary governance.

Bernard Snoy explained how RTI was trying to perpetuate the intellectual legacy of the late Belgian-American economist Robert Triffin (1911–1993), who enunciated more than 60 years ago what has become known as the Triffin Dilemma (TD), namely: "It is impossible for a national currency used as a world currency to serve properly both the needs of the national economy of the country issuing that currency and the needs of the international economy". The TD had not disappeared with the suspension of the convertibility of the US dollar in 1971, nor with the generalization of floating exchange rates. Its manifestation were manifold: potential loss of trust in the US dollar given the growing US net external liquid debt, the "exorbitant privilege" due to the disappearance of macroeconomic constraints combined the "exorbitant burden of becoming the world's debtor/creditor and consumer of last resort", loss of control on global liquidity (GL), "built-in destabilizing" effect on the macro-economic policies of emerging economies (EE) and developing economies (DE), obliging them to divert a large part of their savings to accumulate unproductive exchange reserves. He referred to comments by Jacques de Larosière, also former Managing Director of the IMF, clearly linking the financial crises of the last decennia to the lack of action on the Triffin Dilemma (TD). Robert Triffin had also spent his life imagining and advocating solutions, in particular through the move to a potential multilateral global reserve system, based on the Special Drawing Rights (SDRs). The SDRs had been created through the second amendment of the IMF statutes but maintained in a marginal role. In 2010, a group of former central bankers, including Michel Camdessus, Alexandre Lamfalussy, Tommaso Padoa Schioppa and Paul Volcker, had re-actualized most of the Robert Triffin ideas under the "Palais Royal Initiative". Their recommendations had not been heeded. Since then, with the pressing need for the ecological transition, the pandemic and the Ukraine war, the process of economic de-globalization and geo-political fragmentation had created an unfavorable context for global reform. As Robert Triffin had done in his life, namely working on regional integration projects when global reform projects were blocked, RTI had proposed the theme of the conference *Relaunching Multilateralism through Regional Monetary Unions*.

Christian Ghymers, Vice Chairman of RTI, complemented the introduction by drawing attention to the fact that, despite new monetary regionalism and de-dollarization, the US dollar was still the key currency of the international monetary system. More specifically:

- the reason for the continued strength of the dollar is the growing scarcity of dollar safe assets necessary as collaterals on wholesale money markets dominated by non-bank financial institutions. The TD appears to-day not only in this scarcity but in the cyclical differentiation between *first best* and *second best* safe assets, with the danger of cyclical runs on the safest assets while the second best could suddenly become illiquid. The resulting pro-cyclicality of global liquidity could generate huge destabilizing flows.
- the present trend to monetary regionalism comes in response to the weaponization of the US dollar and combines an increasing use of local currencies for cross border payments and a strategy of internationalization of the Chinese RMB as reserve and invoicing currency but this does not mean that the international monetary system is de-dollarizing in the sense that other countries would like to compete with the US for being a larger debtor-at-sight, having the capacity to become the borrower/consumer of last resort. In fact, a world with multiple national reserve currencies could be more unstable, reproducing and making worse the flaws of the current international monetary system.
- nevertheless, de-dollarization is ineluctable, among others because only a multilateral currency-based system will be able to finance de-carbonization in EEs and DEs. It will not take place with substitution for other national currencies. But it would be encouraged by the changes that regional monetarism will provoke.

Ghymers envisions a scenario under which Distributed Ledger Technologies (DLT) would make it possible at no cost to create private SDRs and where demand would lead Central Bank Digital Currencies (CBDCs) to merge the official and the private SDR. The IMF would begin to issue SDR safe assets The regional monetary arrangements would encourage a wider use of the SDR as vehicle currency. They would set up Regional Monetary Funds (RMF), denominated in SDRs and fix their own criteria and conditionality for financial support to their regional members. The RMFs would bargain with the IMF, which could award them specific mandates, allowing for a decentralization of some IMF functions. SDR complementary resources could be transferred — under conditions — from the IMF to the RMFs. These RMFs would also use their power to issue their own *communiqués* diffusing technical assessments about members' policies, giving so a possible action tool for financial markets and official creditors (*e.g.* financial spreads) which would also provide a test of their credibility. They would act as a lever for implementing macroeconomic dialogues both inside and outside each region and with other regions as well as with the IMF. The IMF would remain the global Lender of Last Resort (LOLR). Ghymers suggested three reasons why such ideas were less unrealistic than trying to reach direct agreement at the international level for three reasons:

- regional cohesion might rise under external pressure.
- it was easier to reach agreement among like-minded countries; and
- the next crisis might make the absolute necessity of a multilateral LOLR in SDRs, obvious, in addition to the important role of the Federal Reserve System

Session 1:
80 Years after Bretton Woods: Challenges to Multilateralism and the Prospects for Regional Monetary Cooperation

This session was moderated by Professor Clara Raposo, Vice Governor of Banco de Portugal, Professor at the Institute of Economics and Management (ISEG) of the University of Lisbon. She reminded the audience that the Bretton Woods institutions had been the cornerstone of long-term prosperity, facilitated the response to a number of economic and monetary crises and sustained global peace. However, the global family was now facing structural transformation. We needed to see how these institutions could be strengthened and how deeper regional monetary integration could bring a positive contribution for the adjustment to new challenges.

Jean-Claude Kassi-Brou, Governor of the Central Bank of the States of Western Africa (BCEAO), former President of the Economic Commission of the Western African States (ECOWAS), shared the more than 60 years experience of the Western African Monetary Union, which already involved a banking union and a capital markets union, unlike the European Union. Despite a major devaluation in 1994, pegging first to the French franc and later to the euro had allowed more stability while guaranteeing full convertibility. Member States enjoyed a higher growth rate and were more successful in the fight against inflation. It had mitigated the risks of crises, allowing member countries allowing countries to better coordinate fiscal, structural and other economic policies in the context of a monetary union involving solidarity: if a country faced a shock, it had access at a lower cost to both domestic and international liquidity accumulated at the regional level. This required of course a minimum of political consensus. Also, when a balance of payments shock affected simultaneously all the member countries, external resources would be needed to support the monetary union. This was where the Bretton Woods institutions, enhanced to face the new challenges, could better play their role.

Renato G. Flôres Jr., Director, International Intelligence Unit, Fundaçao Getulio Vargas, Professor at the Post-Graduate School of Economics of Rio de Janeiro, started by asserting that no lender of last resort nowadays would be any more able to cope with a serious dollar crisis. The first question was to understand why, despite the Triffin Dilemma, the US dollar could maintain its universal currency status. The first reason was the continuing superior military power of the US; the second was the enormous complexity of the International Monetary System (IMS), with the exponential increase in its number of participants, transactions and networks. However, two factors are undermining the continued dominance of the US dollar:

- the US external liabilities and domestic deficit are spiraling out of control: sooner or later a crisis is inevitable; and
- the US hegemon has been abusing its power, among others through its unbounded use of sanctions of all sorts, and meddled in too many conflicts, while the world is drowning into blunt disrespect for multilateral institutions and disregard of international law; as a result, the US dollar credibility has staggered; its safety virtues are debatable; its liquidity is something "in the hands of a benevolent god".

This led Flôres to a pessimistic assessment: the non-Western core, *that is* all countries outside the US and the European Union (EU), the Global South in modern terns, live in a state, if not of fear, certainly of great insecurity as regards the hegemon's currency. Contrary to RTI, Flôres finds it useless to talk about reforming global institutions and arrangements. In his view, the IMF is too close to the hegemon. He does not see the US agreeing to the changes in the IMF Articles of Agreement required for the upgrading of the SDR. He sees no chance in enlarging or promoting the classical idea of monetary unions. Endeavors should rather concentrate on protecting, preserving as much as possible the frail existing multilateral architecture, coupled with stubborn fight for the respect of international law.

Flôres sees however steps to possible solutions consisting of inducing and creating concrete realities to push other currencies or mechanisms to substitute the hegemon's in select instances of the IMS. The more direct way would be through trade, with payments of the associated financial flows settled in currencies other than the dollar, concentrating on the trade between the BRICS countries and countries other than the US and EU countries. Shares of around 40% of world exports and 35% of imports might be expected to move away within a few years from being settled in US dollars to other currencies such as the RMB, the Russian rouble, the Brazilian real or the currencies of other emerging countries. Flôres quotes a Working Paper of Banque de France by Prof. Barry Eichengreen et al., arguing that capital account convertibility would not be a requirement for the RMB acquiring reserve currency status. The gist of the argument lies in that a wise combination of four facilities — bilateral currency swaps, offshore clearing banks, panda and dim sum bonds and the expanding Cross- border Interbank Paying System (CIPS), a Chinese platform similar to and compatible with SWIFT — can reduce the direct demand for RMB reserve assets, ensuring liquidity and safety to the currency. Flôres sees a risk reducing role in such arrangements for regional agreements, less ambitious than monetary unions (like ASEAN, BRICS+ or Shanghai Co-operation Organization) and for Regional Multilateral Development Banks. He acknowledges that such a restricted version of a multiple currency scenario might involve a global loss of efficiency but asserts that this loss of efficiency might be more than compensated by the lowering of international tensions that would be associated with a more equitable distribution of power in the international banking system.

Ricardo Mourinho Félix, head of the Directorate of International Relations of Banco de Portugal, former Vice-President of the European Investment

Bank and former Deputy Minister of Finance, reminded the audience that, despite their imperfections, the Bretton Woods institutions had, over the last 80 years, facilitated the move of many EEs and DEs out of poverty. But today's challenges were of a different order: demographic winter in developed economies, climate change affecting in very different ways the African and Latin American and Asian countries, mounting tensions leading to massive migrations, geo-economic fragmentation, friendshoring, global uncertainty, *etc.* The challenge now was to devise, at the global and regional levels, the institutions and the incentives for the largest wealth transfer ever, channeling resources where they were needed for the ecological transition. The European Union had a role to play, building not only on its experience of integration but also as a powerhouse in research and green technology: under the Green Pack, the EU had generated four times more patents than China and twice as many as the United States. The EU was, however, not very good at bringing research to the factory. We have to complete the EU Banking and Capital Markets Union. Europe needed both to strengthen its strategic autonomy and to reorient its external relations towards Africa and Latin America.

Through a preregistered video message, Luiz Awazu Pereira da Silva, former Deputy General Manager of the Bank for International Settlements, former Deputy Governor of the Central Bank of Brazil and former Deputy Finance Minister of Brazil in charge of international affairs, stressed the similarities between the challenges at the time of the Bretton Woods conference and the situation to-day: in both cases, there was a need for global macro-financial stability and the need for great amounts of short-term liquidity and long-term financing, then for rebuilding after the war, now for the transition to net-zero. Pereira da Silva detailed a number of steps to work towards a more ambitious New Green and Fair Bretton Woods, including the following suggestions:

- *on the liquidity front*: the G7 members could re-allocate all or part of their current SDR holdings to poor developing countries that have committed Nationally Determined Contributions (NDCs) objectives with pledges to Net Zero and well formulated strategies detailed in their Country Climate Development Report (CCDR). While SDRs were not a currency, they could be used to mobilize hard currency liquidity to launch and pay for the current expenditures of a green project. The regional monetary

arrangements among Central Banks in each region could also contribute to short term funding.
- *on the long-term financing front:* developing countries' green bond issuances, as well as other climate-risk related financial instruments (*e.g.* CAT bonds) could have a "credit enhancement" feature that would make them "investable" by large asset managers, pension funds and even central banks of developed countries. The guarantors would have to be the Multilateral Development Bank (MDB) system, the members of the Glasgow Financial Alliance for Net Zero, the Bretton Woods institutions themselves...

Pereira da Silva concluded by inviting reforms to *out-of-the-box-financial engineering*, including digital green SDRs, global monetary creation, making more out of our MDBs balance sheets, debt relief and restructuring for development, etc.

In the ensuing debate, speakers came back to the issue of the LOLR. Christian Ghymers reiterated that the shortage of safe assets and the issue of LOLR would be solved if the IMF was allowed to issue SDRs as a genuine currency while Hung Tran pointed to the de facto LOLR role played by the Federal Reserve in the Great Financial Crisis. Renato Flôres said that the Global South did not have sufficient trust in the Fed nor in the IMF. There was no sufficient trust either in the European Union, which, five years after its signature had not yet ratified the Mercosur Treaty and could not be relied upon to challenge the hegemonic role of the dollar. There was a deep sense of insecurity in the Global South and a feeling that the hegemon was resorting too systematically to violations of international law, which was a sign of weakness. The purpose was not to replace the dollar by the Renminbi but to reduce somewhat its exorbitant privilege and to allow some emerging countries' currencies to share in the privilege by having their currency used for reserve purposes. On the issue of Regional Monetary Unions, Ricardo Mourinho Félix recognized that few monetary unions, at their inception, complied with the conditions formulated by Robert Mundell for an optimum currency area. Monetary Unions, when created, were, most of the time, very imperfect and had to fight to meet criteria. Their creation was more a question of political will. Jean-Claude Kassi Brou argued that regional integration was a good and necessary step, bringing stability not only to its members but also to the countries in its neighborhood but that the bigger issue was the management of liquidity at the international level.

Session 2: 80 Years after Bretton Woods: In the face of Geo-economic Fragmentation, do Regional Monetary Unions provide an Answer?

This session was chaired by Ambassador Antonio Martins da Cruz, President of the Portugal Section of ELEC, former Minister of Foreign Affairs of Portugal. He reminded the audience that our world was characterized not only by geo-economic but also by geo-political fragmentation. There were 55 conflicts ongoing in the world, hurting 2 billion people. The United Nations could not provide answers to these conflicts as nations could not agree on common principles and double standards applied. Unilateral sanctions, weaponizing the economy, were hurting 55% of the world population. Concerns about the supply chain, with moves towards nearshoring or friendshoring, could have negative effects for the populations. How, in such a context, could regional monetary unions provide an answer? They were perhaps only recreating an horizon of hope.

The first speaker was Hervé Carré, former Director General of Eurostat. He was one of the architects of the European Monetary System and had been Adviser to Professor Jorge Braga de Macedo when he was Minister of Finance of Portugal in 1991–93. In January 1992, the Maastricht treaty was signed, setting up the roadmap to the adoption of a single currency by 1999. Shortly thereafter, in April 1992 the Portuguese authorities decided to fix the escudo within the Exchange Rate Mechanism (ERM) of the EMS and to use the ERM as an instrument to foster convergence, reduce public sector borrowing requirements, reduce public debt and reduce inflation. However, after the years of deregulations marked by the full liberalization of capital movements, the dismantling of exchange control and the absence of any oversight of the banks external position, it was easy for operators to take positions against the currencies they found weak. They would borrow such a currency, convert it immediately into DM and then await for the weekend realignment which would enable them to make a huge profit with a revalued DM. This is the scenario which was repeated in the crises in 1992/93:

- on 16 September 1992, the Pound Sterling and the Italian lira left the ERM after speculative attacks and the Spanish peseta is devalued by 5%;
- on 23 November 1992, the Spanish peseta and the Portuguese escudo were devalued by 6%;
- on 3 January 1993 the UK authorities decide not to rejoin the ERM in 1993;
- on 14 May 1993, the Spanish peseta and Portuguese escudo devalued again by 8 and 6,5%
- on 2 August 1993, after strong attacks, mainly on the French franc, the ERM fluctuation band was widened to 15% and calm was restored on the markets; with realignment made within the fluctuation band, one way bets disappeared.

With calm restored on the market, the Portuguese authorities took the opportunity to launch an international bond issue of one billion US dollars, which was easily sold. This was the market recognition of the fact that Portugal was on track to adopt the single currency according to the Maastricht treaty. The period from August 1993 to the end of 1998 was one of increasing stability in the run-up to EMU, which Portugal joined from the very beginning. In conclusion, Hervé Carré paid a tribute to the quality of Portuguese leadership of the crucial years following the signing of the Maastricht Treaty.

To the question whether the European EMU was a real monetary union and could be a model for similar unions in Africa, Latin-America or Asia, Hervé Carré answered that a lot of work was still needed, and the EMU would remain incomplete as long as the Capital Markets Union was not effective.

The second speaker, Professor Anoop Singh, former Director of the IMF Asian Department and former Member of India's 15th Fiscal Commission, concentrated on the fundamental impasse — the *historic impasse* according to Michel Camdessus — concerning the global safety net 80 years after the creation of the Bretton Woods institutions. Global public debt not only in the US (a first downgrading of the US debt had already occurred two years ago) but also in advanced and emerging countries was at a historic high, above 120% of global GDP. It would not take long for the debt problems of a few emerging countries to spiral further into a global debt crisis. This was happening at a time when we had no global financial safety net, no monitoring of global liquidity and no LOLR. The IMF had the mandate of monitoring current account balances but no mandate over movements in capital accounts. If the mandate of the IMF was broadened to include a constitutional authority over capital accounts, it would need also instruments to manage global liquidity and to become a genuine LOLR such as the capacity to issue SDRs. In fact, the IMF was the only body that was meant to be the LOLR but had not been endowed with the instruments to implement this fundamental role.

Anoop Singh went on to discuss the related issue of governance. We had all witnessed the long delays encountered with the resolution of the sovereign debt crisis of Sri Lanka and of other emerging countries when the principal creditor was not a member of the Paris Club. The debt resolution plan indispensable to have an IMF program was delayed as creditors were not part of the same "game plan". Here again the IMF was lacking the instruments to be the LOLR. Hopes placed in bilateral or regional financial arrangements proved disappointing. Of course, bilateral swaps extended by the Federal Reserve during the COVID crisis had been helpful but when the Indian Reserve Bank had approached the Fed to be part of such arrangements, it had been told that they were intended only for currencies that could offer "safe global assets". The BRICS had tried already in 2014 to establish, next to their MDB, the New Development Bank, a restricted safety net arrangement involving Contingent Reserve Assets (CRAs). When it was tested, it did not work: the last thing the Central Bank of Brazil wanted was to extend a swap to any of the BRICS partners. Singh's conclusion was: we do have an institution, the IMF, designed 80 years ago to be the LOLR, let us make it work.

In a pre-registered video message, Jose-Antonio Ocampo, former Minister of Finance of Colombia, former UN Undersecretary for Economic and Social Affairs, contrasted the network of Multilateral Development Banks, which was covering all developing countries, with the rather "light" group of existing Regional Monetary Arrangements, providing liquidity support, namely

- the European Stability Mechanism, by far the most important one, set up in 2012, in the aftermath of the sovereign debt crisis in the Eurozone.
- the Chiang Mai initiative established in 2000 after the Asian monetary crisis, involving six ASEAN countries as well as China, Japan and South Korea: the original bilateral swap arrangements had been broadened and multi-lateralized.
- the Latin American Reserve Fund (FLAR) created in 1978 during the Latin American debt crisis as a reserve pooling arrangement for the Andean countries. Subsequently, Uruguay, Costa Rica, Paraguay had joined and Chile, which had left it, had rejoined. It was expected that Mexico would

join soon. The FLAR was providing balance of payments financing, liquidity support and debt restructuring financing.

Jose-Antonio Ocampo advocated the development of such regional arrangements as a network that could complement the actions of the IMF. He saw them also as a base from which a broader use of SDRs could be developed.

Professor Andrew Sheng, former Chairman of the Hong Kong Securities and Futures Commission and Chief Adviser to the China Banking Regulatory Commission, Distinguished Fellow of the Asian Global Institute, addressed the audience through a video message, which was accompanied by slides. He explained how the geopolitics of money were "empire driven". The strongest State in the empire could lead the monetary union and enjoyed the exorbitant privilege of currency creation but it had to underwrite the public good while countries in the periphery might be willing to pay the hegemon for security and other public goods via holding its debt. After World War II, the US had been a generous hegemon, underwriting the Marshall Plan and running a deficit so that Europe and Japan could recover. However, as Triffin had shown, such a system led to excessive debt, inflation, social inequality and low productivity. The system had been transformed into what Sheng called the "Wall Street Hedge Fund Model": the dollar reserve currency status was allowing the US to borrow long-term debt with Treasury bonds paying interest rates between 0 and 4% and to reinvest the proceeds with a higher rate of return in emerging market economies. However, the system had led to greater and greater debt accumulation, with global debt reaching $ 235 trillion or 238% of Global GDP (2022) while the G7 countries had a debt exceeding 120% of their GDP and 39 out of 69 Low-income countries were in or near debt distress. The Congressional Budget Office was estimating that the US debt would grow to 148% of GDP by 2048.

On the conditions of success of a monetary union, such as the Euro-system with the ECB implementing a single monetary policy and a single exchange rate policy, with the absence of exchange controls, Andrew Sheng stressed the need for unified capital markets, fiscal policies and integration of different political views. The success of monetary unions depended on one supra-body or lead member to be LOLR or underwriter of losses within the union.

Andrew Sheng commented on monetary integration in Asia: in fact, there was trade integration with variable geometry but no monetary union. After the 1997/98 Asian financial crises, currencies which had been closely linked to each other were floated against the dollar, reserves increased and bank supervision tightened. The Chiang Mai Initiative of central banks expanded but was never operationalized because one of the conditions for a member State to draw on the facility was to be subject to the IMF conditionality. Insufficient attention was given to the importance of stock markets and of long-term institutional investors to deleverage excess debt since bond markets and local currency bonds only increased the overall debt burden and made countries vulnerable to interest rate shocks.

As concerned the internationalization of the RMB, the creation of an RMB zone had never been the official stance of the Chinese authorities had never been the creation of an RMB zone. The 2009 statement of PBoC Governor Zhou Xiaochuan was in favor of the creation of an international reserve currency disconnected from individual nations, removing the inherent deficiencies caused by using credit-based national currencies. He added: "The reform should be guided by a grand vision and begin with specific deliverables. It should be a gradual process that yields win-win results for all". Similarly, the more recent 20th Party Congress Report had a constructive tone: "We will promote the internationalization of the RMB in an orderly way, deeply involve ourselves in the global industrial division of labor and cooperation, and endeavor to preserve the diversity and stability of the international economic landscape and economic and trade relations". The US dollar dominant role was due to the liquidity and efficiency of the US bond and equity markets: it had taken 70 years for the US dollar to overtake the British pound. The steady progress in RMB internationalization is no threat to US dollar dominance. The RMB share of the SDR and of global foreign exchange reserves was still small. There was a lot of talk about de-dollarization but not a lot of action. Sanctions had prompted demands for deglobalization and de-dollarization: 29% of global trade was under sanctions of some kind; 40% of energy producers were under sanctions and the USA had imposed since the 1990s to more than 20 countries, two-thirds of the world's sanctions. Central Bank Digital Currencies (CBDC) could be used to escape sanctions. There were CBDC pilots by the Hong Kong Monetary Authority (HKMA), the Bank of Thailand, the Central Bank of the United Arab Emirates and the PBoC. The next stage would be netting cross-border payments using CBDCs or Stablecoins.

In conclusion, what were the alternatives to the dollar: ideally, SDRs as a supranational currency, as RTI and Michel Camdessus recommended; gold, which was attractive to investors as it has no counterparty risk; cyber-currencies but they could not survive nuclear war or, in a conventional war, disruption of internet from cutting of fiber-optic cables, satellite disruption or massive energy failure. This led Sheng to the conclusion that the US dollar status was for the US to lose and not easily for others to gain. That meant that, in the foreseeable future, given the primacy of the US in military, technology and finance terms, the IMS would not be reformed without the implicit or explicit consent of the US. Given the current geopolitical tensions, it was unlikely that in the next five years a major agreement for reform could be reached among the major shareholders of the Bretton Woods institutions. But there was no reason to abandon a very active debate at the academic level on what should be done.

In the debate that followed, Professor Jorge Braga de Macedo, former Minister of Finance of Portugal (1991–1993), came back on the importance of geopolitics, first of all, in the context of the Community of Portuguese Speaking Countries (CPLP), which were given special emphasis in the conference and, second, in the historical context of the relations between Portugal and Spain. When Portugal joined the European Economic Community, it benefited from the EFTA experience, but it did not have the geopolitical weight of Spain. The fact that the Spanish government was very quick in stabilizing the peseta and in joining the ERM of the EMS obliged Portugal to follow suit with the escudo during its first presidency, just after the conclusion of the Maastricht Treaty. As a former director in the Directorate General responsible for economic and financial affairs, Professor Jorge Braga de Macedo was able to show credibility very early on thanks to the competent team of officials in the Ministry of Finance in 1991–93, led by Hervé Carré. As it turns out, this would happen a second time in 2012 when the Troika, in which Hervé Carré was also involved, had to help a number of countries of the eurozone to overcome their debt problems. In this case, there is econometric evidence that the interest rate spread between Portuguese and German bonds fell in the first half of 2012, well before the famous speech by Mario Draghi committing the ECB to do "whatever it takes" to maintain the integrity of the Euro-zone. The effect of the good advice and management had appeared in a paper presented at the Academy of Science and included in Jorge Braga de Macedo's *Festschrift* edited by Luis Brites Pereira, Maria-Eugenia Mata and Miguel Rocha de Sousa, Springer, 2021, with the title "The peculiar first semester of 2012", written by Antonio Pinto Barbosa and Luis Catela Nunes, pp.165–174.

Hung Tran, Senior Fellow at the Atlantic Council, observed that the SDR, as it was organized now, was as vulnerable as the CBDCs in case of conflict. It was nothing more than a unit of account representing a claim on the five currencies that were composing it. If anyone of the five countries issuing these currencies refused to pay their part, the SDR would disappear. As organized now, the SDR could not be a reserve currency. Christian Ghymers intervened, however, to make clear that, when RTI was talking about the future role of the SDR, it did not have in mind the present basket currency but the genuine multilateral reserve currency that the IMF could issue if there was a change in its statutes. The IMF would buy eligible safe assets from its members in exchange for bonds it would issue, denominated in SDR.

Vassil Karaivanov, Secretary General of ELEC-Bulgaria, observed that the value all alternatives currently proposed to replace the dollar, SDRs or digital currencies, was always expressed in dollars. So he did not see the need to look for any other reserve currency.

Anoop Singh agreed that, as it was currently conceived, the SDR was not really functioning, but things were moving. A number of advanced countries were thinking of transferring their SDRs to other institutions, in particular MDBs, which could use them as equity to raise market finance. The question under discussion was whether this transfer to other institutions would make the SDRs lose their character of reserve asset. France, the United Kingdom and 9 other IMF shareholders were considering such a move. This could be a small but historic step.

Dinner Speech by Vice-Governor Raposo

At the dinner, kindly hosted by Banco de Portugal at the end of the first day of the conference, the Vice-Governor Clara Raposo started thus *Aren't we all somehow children of Bretton Woods? None of our lives would have been what they are, had the IMF and the World Bank not been created, had multilateralism not been a meaningful term*. She recalled that the agreement emerging from Bretton Woods was still a cornerstone of today's international monetary and financial system. Although the exchange rate peg that was the symbol of the Bretton Woods system was abandoned in 1973, the IMF and the World Bank remained pillars of the international economic landscape, providing technical and financial assistance to many countries around the globe.

She acknowledged that the floating exchange regime that followed the abandonment of fixed parities in 1973 might have induced the idea that competitive devaluations could be a solution to structural problems limiting economic progress. Portugal had learnt it the hard way as the economy went through two deep balance of payments crises in the early stages of its democratic regime requiring the assistance of the IMF in 1977–78 and again in 1983. It was only after Portugal joined European Economic Community in 1986 that it decisively conducted important structural reforms that paved the way to a more prosperous future. In this context, regional monetary integration had provided synergy gains and imposed the necessary discipline. In this context, she celebrated the success story of the first 25 years of the euro. She recognized that the euro project was initiated without a fully completed architecture and somewhat partial accession criteria. The lack of a system to deal with asymmetric shocks and current account crises, the absence of common supervision and insolvency mechanisms to deal with banks of systemic importance, the absence of fiscal federalism traits and totally credible fiscal rules were items that had been left to be done later. In the meantime, the sovereign debt crisis had tested the limits of the European integration but in the end the European project emerged stronger: the EU institutional framework was strengthened. More recently, policy support at the European level had been crucial to overcome first the health and economic crisis triggered by the pandemic and second the difficulties and disruptions in the global energy market triggered by the invasion of Ukraine. The ECB had reacted to the inflation surge by removing the exceptional level of accommodation that characterized the previous years and moved interest rates to restrictive territory.

Support for the euro had increased during the recent period. Nevertheless, to keep the euro together, we needed to make the euro better equipped to deal with the medium-term challenges such as population ageing, the climate change and geo-economic fragmentation. Progress in the integration and development of EU capital markets and the banking sector were key to mobilize private investments needed to carry out the green and digital transitions and to enhance EU's productivity and competitiveness. Central banks could contribute by supporting the development and integration of pan-European financial markets infrastructures.

She concluded with words of optimism: "Despite the fact that there is strong antagonism and polarization in today's world, the Bretton Woods institutions are still core, for the multilateral approach that must be adopted to reach a global solution to the challenges of our times". She referred to the enthusiastic mood she had perceived at the 2024 spring meetings of the IMF and World Bank Group in Washington, with a special event "Celebrating 80 years of Bretton Woods: What's Next?". Better — or different — dialogue was the way to reach multilateral solutions. To honor the principles that had underpinned Bretton Woods, there was no other way than "together, at last, build trust and join forces to jointly solve global problems; For the sake of our children".

Day 2: Tuesday 7 May 2024
Venue: Academia das Ciências de Lisboa

Introduction

In his introductory remarks, Professor José Luís Cardoso, President of the Academy of Sciences of Lisbon, said that, through his lenses of an historian of economic ideas, he had always been interested in the outcomes of the Bretton Woods Conference, especially due to the essential role played by John Maynard Keynes in the organization of the conference and of its several preparatory meetings. He stressed the innovative nature and inspired vision of the Keynes Plan, which involved: a) a multilateral compensation mechanism integrated into an international organization, aiming at multi-lateralizing intergovernmental payments; b) an international currency disconnected from any country's money supply; and c) an adjustment process in which creditor countries also had their share of responsibility in keeping the sustainability of the system. The issues raised by Keynes were still present in the sessions of the conference.

Professor Cardoso made also reference to the founding father of modern economics in Portugal, Professor Antonio Manuel Pinto Barbosa, who, in a conference held at the Academy in 1977 had conveyed his appreciation of Keynes' role in the preparation of the Bretton Woods Agreement. Pinto Barboso was a distinguished member of the Academy of Sciences and had also served as Governor of Banco de Portugal. This made the Academy a particularly appropriate place for a conference addressing the new challenges 80 years after Bretton Woods.

Session 3: The State of Regional Economic and Monetary Cooperation in Africa

Lessons from the past and issues for the future

The session was moderated by Professor Jorge Braga de Macedo, Treasurer of the Academy, who is also the successor of Professor Pinto Barbosa, the longest serving Minister of Finance of Portugal, one of the founders of Nova School of Business and Economics.

The first speaker was Zenaida Cassama, National Director for Guinea Bissau, BECEAO. She stated that since the conquest of independence, the African countries had put emphasis on economic and monetary cooperation and on regional integration as a key part of their strategy of structural transformation but that they had to overcome three important obstacles, namely the small size of their national economies, the absence of structural complementarity and the dependence on the import of intermediate products. Inter-regional trade on the African continent represented only 15% of its total trade, compared to 62% for the European Union and 23% in the case of ASEAN. She mentioned the eight existing Regional Economic Communities (REC) in Africa. Unfortunately, the successive shocks of COVID-19 and the Russian-Ukrainian conflict had affected significantly their development in terms of macroeconomic convergence and structural change.

As concerned the WAEMU, of which Guinea-Bissau was a member since 1997, a number of positive developments had been the establishment of infrastructure for regional payments, the adoption of a regulatory framework for the issue of digital currency and the implementation of the project of interoperability of digital financial services. The accession of Guinea-Bissau to the WAEMU had made possible to control inflation, to reduce the budgetary and balance of payments deficits and to reinforce the resilience of the financial sector.

Maria Esperança Mateus Majimeja, Board Member of Banco de Moçambique, was expected to speak in the same session. At the last minute, she had to remain in Mozambique but she sent the text of her prepared remarks. She was focusing on the challenges and stages of policy coordination, a single currency being the final stage in the process, one which for African countries was still far away. The incentive for coordination was depending on the existence of interdependency between the economies of the countries concerned. In her view, Africa faced three main challenges:

- a low level of commercial and macro-financial integration.
- high asymmetries between African economies in terms of openness to international trade and poor development and integration of the national financial market; and
- weak institutional frameworks for implementing policies: even the WAEMU had no direct authority to coordinate fiscal policy.

Maria Esperança Mateus Majimeja mentioned lessons for the future such as:

- the primacy to be given to the need for coordination: this had to happen first at the level of the RECs; the General Assembly of Governors of the Association of the African Central Banks established in 2023 the need for each REC to define a roadmap for the harmonization of monetary policies so that integration would gradually take place.
- the creation of regional institutions, programs and other key enablers of the economic integration process: examples included the creation of the Pan-African Bank (Afreximbank, 1993), the Program for Infrastructure Development in Africa (2009), the Pan-African Payment and Settlement System (2022).

In conclusion she stated: "Experience shows that monetary unions have not only emerged from the recognition of economic benefits; political will has always played an important and decisive role". Incentives had to be created for political actors such as the availability of funding for infrastructure and structural reforms.

Professor Óscar Évora Santos, Governor of Banco de Cabo Verde, spoke about Cabo Verde participation in ECOWAS and the objective of ECOWAs to go beyond monetary cooperation towards a common currency, the Eco. He was concerned that the fundamentals in terms of economic integration were not there, given the low degree of interregional trade in Africa (except in the case of landlocked countries). The Eco was work in progress, but its introduction had been postponed several times. The new deadline was 2027. Four main convergence criteria had been established: budget deficit of less than 4% of GDP, inflation not exceeding 5%, no central bank financing of fiscal deficit beyond 10% of tax revenue, external reserves above three months of imports. Cabo Verde was meeting these criteria but only a handful of other ECOWAS countries were meeting them. Cabo Verde had a currency cooperation agreement with Portugal, signed in 1998, pegging the Cabo Verde escudo to the Portuguese escudo (one of the founding currencies, now the euro). Using the exchange rate as a nominal anchor had allowed Cabo Verde to liberalize its current account and subsequently its capital account. The question now was; is the country ready to leave the escudo to join the Eco? The governor had doubt as Cabo Verde citizens had more confidence in the escudo and ECOWAS' future required also the respect of political criteria (no military coup) and stronger institutions.

The moderator quoted his work on Cabo Verde and Mozambique showing both CPLP members from African countries where governance issues had been tackled, as showed in a project of study by the National Bureau for Economic Research (NBER) in Cambridge Mass., US, published in 2016. Referring to his long association with the Catholic University of Angola, through Professor Manuel Alves da Rocha, a foreign member of the Academy, he introduced the next speaker Osvaldo Victorino João, who gave a comprehensive picture of the process of regional integration in Africa and of its most important milestones, under the auspices of the African Union:

- in 1980, the Lagos plan of action for self-sustained economic development
- in 1991 the Abuja Treaty on the African Economic Community (AEC), proposing integration through Regional Economic Communities (RECs). Each REC was to move successively from the creation of a free trade zone

to a customs union, then a single market, a common central bank and a common currency, thus ending up with an Economic and Monetary Union
- in 1994, the Common Market for Eastern and South-eastern Africa (COMESA) for integration through trade and investment.
- in 2001, the African Union Development Agency (NEPAD) as a socio-economic development framework
- in 2002, the African Union succeeding the Organization of African Unity to accelerate the process of integration; and
- in 2018, the African Free Trade Area, creating the world's largest free trade area by number of countries.

Despite valuable efforts, the process of regional integration in Africa has been fragmented and redundant, with eight RECs, most of them existing prior of the AEC. Most of the African countries are in more than one REC. The East African Community (EAC) is the most integrated one and the Southern Africa Development Community (SADC) the least integrated. The most advanced dimensions of integration are the free movement of people and the convergence of macroeconomic variables. As concerned the integration score of individual countries, South Africa is the highest performer and Angola is among the worst performers. The reasons for Angola lagging behind are the long period of war, which ended only in 2002, the high inflation rate, the excessive dependence on oil and vulnerability to oil shocks, erratic politics, public debt exceeding 100% of GDP; after the COVID and war in Ukraine shocks, the inflation rate exceeded 20%.

The handicaps preventing integration were political instability, lack of political will, lack of domestic support, low level of competitiveness in the private sector, poor regional infrastructure to connect the continent and the high level of disparities among African countries in macroeconomic terms. The economic integration design that had been adopted did not seem to be the right one. There was lack of a common convergence agenda.

In conclusion, Osvaldo Victorino João suggested abandoning the REC approach in favor of several constructive proposals such as:

- the integration process in Africa should be de-fragmented. What was happening with the proposed African Trade Area was a good step but had to be accelerated.

- the convergence criteria would only be met if there were penalties for the countries that failed to achieve them and benefits for those who did.
- the Bretton Woods institutions should improve their cooperation and support the African Union instead of working only country by country.
- the Debt Service Suspension Initiative (DSSI) was a good example of the challenges faced by the African countries in the present context of geo-political fragmentation
- the biggest economies of the continent had to lead the integration process in order to achieve step by step the monetary union.

The last speaker in this session was Maria-Eugenia Mata, economic historian and Jubilee Professor of Nova School of Business and Economics. She talked about the research that had led to her book: *The Portuguese Escudo Monetary Zone: Its impact in Colonial and Post-Colonial Africa*(published in 2020 by Palgrave). The Portuguese Escudo Monetary Zone (EMZ) was set up in 1961 as a macro-political experiment, drawn to promote economic growth and economic integration of Portugal and the countries of its empire and take advantage of the new international opportunities created by European economic integration, Portugal being a member of EFTA. The EMZ was a star shaped trade, labor, capital and monetary market with Portugal at its center and seven very unequal territories at its periphery. The Bank of Portugal was the central bank of the EMZ and gathered all the means of international payment (gold and foreign currencies) of the EMZ. An Escudo Monetary Fund (EMZ Fund) was created in the Banco de Portugal to enable the concession of loans to overseas territories in order to make possible the inter-territorial and international payments of all territories under Portuguese administration. However, the system suffered from the distance among its components, the large differences in size of the local economies, rigidities and asymmetric shocks. The evolution of the EMZ illustrates the consequences of war for an entire financial and monetary system, the impact of increasingly negative investors' expectations about the possibilities of transferring their savings, the perception that the mainland's currency was safer than the currencies of the territories, considering the rising success of political and military groups fighting for decolonization.

Professor Mata explained how the Treaties of independence of the five former Portuguese territories in Africa had led to the creation of new currencies, namely the Guinean peso (Guinea-Bissau in 1978), the metical (Mozambique, 1980), the Cabo Verdian escudo (Cabo Verde, 1977), the kuanza (Angola, 1976) and the dobra (Sao Tomé e Principe, 1976). In many territories, nationalizations took place of properties, plantations, stores, equipment and even bank deposits of the former colonizers. The independence agreements included financial and monetary agreements to which were added technical cooperation agreements, covering a wide array of sectors, with emphasis on training in banking and finance as in most of the former colonies, there were no banking network at the time of the independence. The EMZ Fund continued its operations until the 1980s, supporting the payment system for Portuguese exports to the new countries.

In the ensuing debate, Antoine Vivant asked whether some countries (Sahel countries) were not making a less positive assessment of their participation in the WAEMU than Guinea-Bissau and were not considering to leave the WAEMU. The answer given was that if they would really leave the WAEMU, it would be much more for political rather than economic reasons.

Another question was how to get out of the vicious circle: countries had no incentive to join a regional monetary union if there was no interdependence; but there was no interdependence because there was no regional trade. Osvaldo Victorino João agreed that incentives were needed: the African Union or the RECs should have funding mechanisms for countries that would take the step to embark in a regional integration process.

Another question by Vassil Karaivanov related to the use of gold to implement transfers out of Mozambique. Professor Mata acknowledged that this might have happened during some periods when Mozambique had exhausted its foreign exchange reserves. Mozambique was close to South Africa and parallel markets might have developed using gold to transfer resources. We should have in mind the tremendous impact of a long and devastating war on the economy of the former Portuguese colonies.

Governor Óscar Évora Santos concluded in saying that, while Africa today represented only a small fraction of the Global GDP, its importance was steadily increasing in geopolitical and demographic terms: there were today 800 million young Africans and by 2050, the population of Africa would reach 2.5 billion. In this connection, Jorge Braga de Macedo pointed to the need for closer cooperation between the European Union and the African Union, which was now a member of the G20.

Session 4: The State of Regional Economic and Monetary Cooperation in Latin America and in Asia

Lessons from the Past and Issues for the Future

This session, moderated by Professor Maria-Eugenia Mata, began with a *magistral* presentation of Christian Ghymers, Vice Chairman of RTI and President of the Interdisciplinary Institute for Relations between Europe, Latin America and the Caribbean (IRELAC), who started by making reference to the Portuguese age of Enlightenment and the role played by José Correia da Serra (1750–1823), its first secretary, who was also a member of other European academies, including the Liège Academy, and who was considered by Thomas Jefferson as the most erudite man he had ever encountered.

He went on to the conditions under which regional monetarism could play a positive role of lever towards the broader objectives of regional integration and reform of the IMS.

The trend to regional monetarism could be explained by a number of factors: deterioration of the geopolitical context, global financial instability, weakening of the multilateral order and opportunities offered by new technologies applied to payments such as blockchain; more recently, the primary motivation was to lessen dependence on the dollar, limiting the spillovers of monetary policy by the Federal Reserve Board and the "weaponization" of the dollar. Two trends were becoming obvious: the increasing use of local currencies for cross-border payments and a strategy of internationalization of the Chinese RMB as both reserve and invoicing currency.

Though regional monetarism entailed high risks of monetary fragmentation and more protectionism. It did not mean in itself that the international monetary system was being de-dollarized, in other words, even though at some point de-dollarization was ineluctable and even desirable, the solution was not to substitute other national currencies to the dollar. A multi-currency IMS would reproduce the flaws of the present system and even make it worse. History showed that a multi-key-currency system would be highly unstable, given the indeterminacy of the exchange rate equilibrium. Furthermore, it could not solve the Triffin dilemma as it could not ensure the adequate supply of stable safe assets. Indeed, any country willing to provide a key reserve currency would need to become borrower/consumer of last resort to issue the needed level of safe assets. To compete with the dollar to become a key currency meant to try to be a larger debtor than the US. Instead, the right objective of the reformed IMS should be to issue safe assets which are not the debt of a national economy but the liability of the multilateral system as counterpart of national liquid assets. One had to realize that it was becoming impossible to issue sufficient stable safe assets denominated in national currencies. An additional point was that financing the decarbonization of the planet under the current IMS appeared impossible.

According to Ghymers, Regional Monetary Arrangements (RMAs) could become a game changer for the IMS in two main steps:

- RMA as a catalyzer of regional integration: RMAs were the proof that cooperation was easier among like-minded partners, sometimes subject to a common external threat, than at the multilateral level. RMAs could spur regional integration if the right method was followed by obliging technicians from different countries (rather than diplomats or ministers) to meet on a regular basis, behind closed doors, speaking informally (under Chatham House rules), not for taking decisions but for monitoring the national policies, analyzing alternatives, reporting collegially to Ministerial Councils, stimulating economic cooperation and policy coordination, triggering a virtuous circle of better governance and above all enhancing mutual trust to escape the "Prisoners' dilemma " (distrust among partners when uncertainty prevails). This was a matter of psychology more than economics: human being facing technical issues under a common threat tend to cooperate. The issue of exchange rates implied monitoring of the national policy mix, improvement of mutual knowledge, awareness that national interests converge to regional interest. Coordination had to be perceived as the self-interest of each participant by reaching a common objective (such as escaping spillovers or dependence from the dollar), helping creating consensus. We should not forget that the successful integration of Europe started thanks to a regional monetary arrangement, the European Payments Union (EPU), in the creation of which Robert Triffin played a crucial role. In addition to a collegial technical committee meeting regularly behind closed doors, there was the US generous Marshall Plan as the carrot promoting cooperation. Other historical cases included the Monetary Committee (combining Central Bank and Treasury representatives) doing the technical monitoring of the ERM in the EU convergence process towards the euro, and the CFA organization of regional surveillance of national policies under the WAEMU and CAEMU Treaties as well as the Macroeconomic Dialogue Network Experiment (REDIMA), which was conceived and implemented from 2000 to 2006 by ECLAC. These regional experiences demonstrated the capacity to solve the prisoners' dilemma through closed-doors exchanges between macroeconomic experts. In particular, Brazil was able to cushion the regional financial turmoil of the beginning of the years 2000s and to cooperate informally despite numerous regional conflicts at that time. The Brazilian experience might be useful for the CPLP. Drawing upon these experiments, Ghymers proposed to organize in all regions similar "Monetary Committees";

- RMAs as facilitators of inter-regional cooperation: the discussions of the RMA Monetary Committees had to include cross-border payments systems, with regional clearing houses. In his view, they should propose moving to CBDCs for applying tokenization in SDR with almost no transaction cost. General tokenization would foster the development of private SDRs for financing national debts. This would be combined with the creation of Regional Monetary Funds (RMFs) in SDR, representing a given percentage of the national reserves, complemented by multilateral resources with conditionalities, the access to which would be linked to technical propositions submitted by the Monetary Committees to their respective Ministerial Councils. In this way, some IMF missions would be decentralized to the RMFs. These RMFs could become a lever for implementing macroeconomic dialogues both inside each region and with the other regions as well as with the IMF. This would lead also to regions speaking with one voice in the discussions concerning the reform of the IMS. Hopefully this would lead to consensual views on common interests. A coalition could be forged for changing the IMF statutes, supported by pressures for merging the private and the official SDRs, the interventions of central banks taking place more and more in SDRs. Ghymers thinks that this would make the hegemon realize that sharing its power would be beneficial. The ultimate objective would be to turn the IMF into a global federal LOLR. Each region would bargain with the IMF for the award of specific mandates against the creation of SDR complementary multilateral resources.

The second speaker was Rodolfo Lavrador, General Manager for International Business, Caixa Geral de Depósitos, former Secretary of State at the Portuguese

Ministry of Finance after the 1995 elections, representing Banco Nacional Ultramarino, Macau.

He addressed how could Macau positions itself in the East Asia Monetary Cooperation around China), starting by explaining that BNU is one of the local commercial leading banks and also, together with the Bank of China, the issuing bank (but it did not have any competence in defining Macau's monetary policy, which belonged to the AMCM — Macau Monetary and Exchange Authority). Although it had its own currency (the Pataca), pegged to the US dollar, it seemed to him obvious that Macau's position in this, as in other matters, of international monetary cooperation, would depend on the political position of the authorities in mainland China. The current local priority seemed to be the project to digitize the Pataca, which fell within the scope of the Macau Government's program for modernization of its financial sector in conjunction with the priority of the bond market, improving the financial legal framework, payment systems as Easy Transfer fast payment and its real time settlement system for HKD payments and tax incentives to attract more asset management companies, all with the ambition of transforming Macau's financial sector into a platform that connected mainland China to the world and that supported the internationalization of the Chinese currency. Macau's positioning and possible role in any monetary cooperation process would depend very much on what it could offer in terms of added and differentiated value. In this sense, the differentiating factor might be Macau's directive to act as the facilitator in cooperation between China and Portuguese speaking countries.

Looking to China's position, it seemed clear to Rodolfo Lavrador that the main priority, in terms of international monetary policy, continued to be the process of internationalization of the renminbi, through its acceptance in commercial exchanges in general and in Asia in particular. There was a relationship between power and currency, which certainly involved the internationalization of the domestic currency, but also the creation and membership of international monetary institutions. From this perspective, China had promoted monetary cooperation through its accession to monetary stability mechanisms, regional swaps arrangements, such as the CMI (Chiang Mai Initiative) and the later CMIM (+Multilateralization). Another instance was the creation of the AIIB Asian Infrastructure Investment Bank, linked to OBOR — One Belt One Road Initiative. Or even being part of the

AMU — Asian Monetary Unit. To him China (and Macau by extension) would be an active protagonist in greater monetary cooperation in the region if it achieved a dominant monetary position among Asian countries and exerted greater influence at an international level through the use of the renminbi. However, he did not believe it was realistic to think that a monetary union could be achieved in the region, with for example the AMU evolving from a mere basket currency to a currency, as this depended on factors that were very difficult to combine, such as political will, economic convergence, institutional structure (it would be a process that would require the construction of collective institutions) and popular support. It would always depend on geopolitics and the global economy.

When asked questions related to the Pataca's peg to the US dollar being able to evolve, for example, into a pegging to the renminbi, he gave as a personal opinion that, although in the long term such an evolution would certainly not displease the Chinese authorities, in the short term, the reasons why the peg to the US dollar existed remained valid, so any short-term change in this direction would be a surprise to him. He believed that China saw such an evolution as an outcome of a possible future total or greater internationalization of the renminbi and not as a way or a mean of achieving it

Manuel Clarote Lapão, Director of Development Cooperation of CPLP, started by explaining that, rather than regional, CPLP was a transcontinental community, with an intergovernmental nature. There were great geographical distances among its members so that oceans served the member States common borders to many members. CPLP as a maritime platform, accounts for 4% of world GDP and ranks as the 4th oil producer. CPLP is an immense repository of resources, biodiversity, population, fresh waters, maritime resources, sun and wind, agricultural products, minerals and geothermal sources, etc. CPLP has 10 members and 29 countries are associated observers. CPLP countries are members of regional communities such as the EU, the Mercosur, the ASEAN, the ECOWAS the Economic Community of Central African States and the Southern Africa Development Community.

CPLP's areas of activity are political-diplomatic coordination, cooperation in all sectors, projects aiming at the promotion of the Portuguese language, reinforcement of civil society and economic and business cooperation, promoting trade and investment; CPLP cooperation was transversal since it promoted interconnection between various thematic areas and sectors and aligned with the commitments expressed in the 2030 Agenda for Sustainable

Development and with the Sustainable Development Goals. CPLP followed closely the activities of the World Bank Group and of the other MDBs. However, Lapao was concerned about statements in the minutes and reports of the recent spring meeting of the Bretton Woods institutions, indicating that countries in the Global South were paying more in debt service than they were getting in development aid and that $50 billions of promised international aid flows had not reached their intended beneficiaries in 2024. He drew attention to the fact that 60% of low-income countries were at risk of debt distress; not enough money was available to sustain the achievement of the 2030 Agenda and matters could get worse with the multiplicity of challenges and crises.

Speaking at the end of the session, Professor Jorge Braga de Macedo, expressed how committed he was to fostering the links between the Academy and CPLP countries. This all began at the turn of the century in Macau, when a CPLP meeting was held by China for the first time and he represented the OECD, having followed through with CPLP Secretariat and IICT, a *Tropical Research Institute* in Lisbon he run until 2015, when it was taken over by the greater University of Lisbon, which subsequently created a *Tropical College.* providing many opportunities to developing its links with the CPLP. Special attention was given to Macau, where a CPLP meeting had given China for the first time the opportunity to develop its links with the CPLP. Special attention was given to another small member, namely East-Timor: after a difficult beginning, East Timor has been accepted as an observer in ASEAN since 2022 but its participation as a full member has been delayed by requirements such as the absence of a building sufficiently large to host meetings for all members. There was also an association of the African countries for which Portuguese was one of the official languages. This included Equatorial Guinea. There was active cooperation with Lusophone universities. Like the *Académie française* for the French language, the Lisbon Academy claims authority on the Portuguese language. it is divided into a Sciences class and a "Letters" which includes Literature and Social Sciences, including Economics and Finance, of which he is Acting Dean.

Vassil Karaivanov asked Christian Ghymers how long he thought that the US could increase its Government deficit, which was a condition for the continued supply of the dollar safe asset that the dollar-based IMS needed. Ghymers answered that we could not count indefinitely on the US debt. This was why it would become at some point necessary to move to a multilateral institution issuing a multilateral liability in SDR strictly equivalent to national assets being accumulated.

Bernard Snoy suggested that the experience of the negotiations leading to the Treaties of Rome and of Maastricht showed the necessity not only of building trust and complicity among national technicians but also the need at some crucial points for strong political leadership. He referred to the Belgian Minister of Foreign Affairs Paul-Henri Spaak, who had chaired the Committee of Experts set up after the Messina Conference. Ghymers agreed that we needed a two-tier system where Committees of national technicians made technical analyses and proposed solutions and Councils of Ministers made decisions. Jorge Braga de Macedo mentioned the leadership role of Jacques Delors, who led the group of Central Bank Governors who produced the Delors Report, and added that he revealed a profound understanding of the two Iberian countries having recently joined the European Economic Community. He also evoked the Italian Prime Minister Giulio Andreotti who had found the way, at the European summit of Rome in October 1990, to go around the reluctance of UK Prime Minister Margaret Thatcher to agree to the launching of the intergovernmental conference that led to the Maastricht Treaty. Her positions were so well known that he simply omitted to ask her individually whether she agreed. When he asked around the table, she did not use her veto.

Keynote speech by Vitor Gaspar
Director of the IMF Fiscal Department

The speech by former Minister Gaspar was introduced by his former deputy and successor as Minister of Finance, Maria Luis Albuquerque, now member of the Supervisory Board of Morgan Stanley. She recalled Vitor's brilliant career with Banco de Portugal, the ECB as Director General of Research, and the European Commission, where he headed the European Bureau of European Policy Advisers. She concentrated on the difficult years when he was Minister of Finance, between 2011 and 2013, and had to restore Portugal's credibility after serious imbalances in the Portuguese economy had been allowed to accumulate for a number of years. There were difficult negotiations with the IMF and the European Commission. Many hurdles had to be overcome to deliver on the rescue plan. Vitor Gaspar had to work under immense pressure; he was the most hard-working member of the team and showed a great sense of humor. Maria Luis Albuquerque recalled an amusing anecdote about the first press conference given by Vitor Gaspar as Minister of Finance: it started on time, while most of the journalists were late, and it finished on time. She still thinks that Vitor Gaspar is not getting the credit he deserves for the way in which he got Portugal out of its sovereign debt crisis.

Vitor Gaspar chose the topic of *the impact of geopolitics on fiscal policy* for his keynote address. He started his presentation by showing that the fault lines are growing across the world. *Polarization* and *fragmentation* appear in headline news everywhere. However, he showed that the global trade-to-GDP ratio has not declined so far. No sign of deglobalization is found at the aggregate level. The geopolitical risk index is also not particularly high compared with the past. The geopolitical uncertainty index has been flat for the U.S., although it has risen for China and Germany. Nonetheless, he highlighted that geopolitics has shifted trade patterns. The U.S. trades more with Mexico and Vietnam, while China trades more with India, Indonesia, and Brazil. He also showed that global power has shifted in the long run. The share of the EU in global GDP has decreased, while China's share has increased. More worryingly, productivity growth in the EU has been falling behind the U.S. since 1995. Then he argued that geopolitics are already having substantial fiscal policy implications. The governments are now facing a difficult policy trilemma amid rising geopolitical tensions. First, rising spending pressures (with higher interest payments, pension and health care, defense, climate, SDGs, and industrial policy). Second, political red lines on taxation. And third, the imperatives of debt sustainability and financial stability. As in all policy trilemmas, policymakers can have two but not all three elements. Something has to give.

In conclusion, he made four policy recommendations. The governments should (i) spend better; (ii) ensure that revenue keeps up with spending; (iii) rely on strong fiscal rules, frameworks and institutions; and (iv) recognize that fiscal policy is a structural policy crucial for competitiveness and growth.

In the question time, Bernard Snoy wondered how the huge investment expenditures required for the ecological transition could be financed, taking into consideration the red lines on taxation. Hung Tran pointed out that, if fiscal policy was industrial policy, which would mean changes in how we work and live, it would encounter strong resistance. Christian Ghymers raised the issues of increases in the relative price of energy and the possibility to cut the annual $1 trillion of subsidies to fossil fuels. Jorge Braga de Macedo asked about the concept of income tax neutrality. Vitor Gaspar answered that cutting fossil energy subsidies has been a long-standing recommendation of the IMF. If current energy subsidies continue, public debt levels would become unsustainable in many countries. The political economy needs to be taken into consideration when implementing fiscal reforms, such as energy subsidy reforms, and carbon pricing and taxation. In this context, income tax neutrality remains the benchmark to evaluate tax reforms around the world. It is also important to recognize that the general public dislikes inflation and budget deficits much more than economic professionals consider. Future research should engage more with political economy aspects.

Session 5: *Where do we go from here?*

80 Years after Bretton Woods, what kind of regional initiatives could contribute to a more stable and equitable international monetary system? If Robert Triffin were alive, what kind of initiative would he promote at the regional and global level?

This session was moderated by Antonio Martins da Costa, President of the American Chamber of Commerce of Lisbon. Having attended the discussion on changes in the patterns of trade, he wondered if we were not just exchanging our previous dependence on oil and other sources of fossil energy for a new dependence on critical raw materials. He drew attention to the importance of the transatlantic relation between the US and the European Union. Trade between the two blocks amounted to 800 billion dollars, which was more than the US-China trade or the EU-China trade. The two blocks accounted for one third of global GDP and one half of personal consumption in the world.

Fabio Masini, summarizing his discussion note "Building Multilateral and Multi-layered Global Economic Governance: The Role of Regional Integration" recalled first the key points of his analysis of the last 80 years with the emergence and persistence of a historical flaw in the IMS: the Triffin Dilemma, particularly in its form of Built-in Destabilizer, causing basic imbalances and obliging developing countries to accumulate reserves, reducing their possibilities for domestic investment. Efforts to get rid of the hegemonic dollar-based system and to build a more balanced and multilateral system had repeatedly failed. The US had hindered the IMF attempt to boost the role of the SDR after the first oil shock in the 1970s, dissuading

Saudi Arabia to invoice oil in SDR. When in 1994, the IMF Managing Director Michel Camdessus had tried to issue $50 billion in SDRs to help face multiple financial threats, the USA, assisted by Germany and the UK, had vetoed him. in 2010, Stiglitz had stated: "the US is exporting Treasury bills to be held in reserves — partly at the expense of automobiles.... This means that the government must run a fiscal deficit to keep the economy at full employment". There had been illusions that, with the advent of the euro, the EU would be willing to develop the international reserve currency role of the euro, but the EU was not willing to be the consumer of last resort. Before the weaponization of the dollar that followed the Russian invasion of Ukraine, pressures towards multilateralism in the IMS became increasingly manifest. The acceptance of the renminbi in the SDR basket in 2016 and the issue of $650 billion in SDRs in August 2021 were a testimony of this. Nevertheless, SDRs continued to be relegated to be parked as a reserve asset in central banks instead of being used as a multiplier for actions devoted to the development and the provision of global public goods. Inaction was not an option. Weaponization of other currencies to resist to the hegemon as proposed by Professor Renato Flôres could become even riskier.

Faced with this unsatisfactory situation at the global level, Fabio Masini was putting on the table two very concrete initiatives:

1. a regional safety net for Latin America: a regional monetary fund would be established pooling 30% of the reserves in gold and foreign assets of the countries of the region, as a first line of defense in case of national financial crisis. This would be a first line of defense and be part of a global multi-layered system of safety nets. This would oblige central banks and treasuries to be more transparent between one another and coordinate their economic policies.
2. an EU-Africa Plan for Next Generation: the idea is that the EU countries would pool the about €150 billion in SDRs attributed to them in 2021 and channel them to multilateral development banks (the African Development Bank and the European Investment Bank) as prescribed holders of SDRs, and collateralize them to issue €750 billion bonds to be used for a jointly designed development plan, targeting six main objectives: energy independence, digital infrastructure, health infrastructure, green transition. This would constrain African countries to

agree on common priorities and strategies and would also strengthen European identity as a global actor thus contributing to multilateralism. and climate change, education and a regional safety net.

The message of Hung Tran, Senior Fellow, Atlantic Institute, former Assistant Director in the IMF Capital Markets Department, was that the future was Asia. It represented already 54% of the global GDP. The ASEAN trade exceeded dollar 1 trillion. Next to China, other giants were emerging: India, Indonesia and other ASEAN countries. Demand for financial integration and monetary cooperation were bound to increase with trade. Asian countries, in line with the spirit of the time, were increasing the use of domestic currencies for the settlement of trade and foreign investment. The landscape of the regional economy would evolve, with three pillars growing quickly: 1) each country would develop its payment and settlement system, having in mind interoperability; 2) central banks would open bilateral swap lines to each other; China had already swap lines with 44 countries; 3) the countries were investing heavily in technology, *for example* mobile phone payments, while the US remained behind, working still with checks. These developments were reaching a critical mass and setting examples for other countries in the world.

Ousmène Jacques Mandeng, Senior Advisor Global Blockchain Technology, Accenture, said that the most problematic aspect of the Bretton Woods system as it had evolved over the last 80 years was that only very few currencies served in international payments, producing a high dependency on the so-called key currencies. Under Article VIII of the statutes of the Articles of Agreement of the IMF, member countries had to abstain from discriminatory currency arrangements for current transactions comprising international trade and interest payments. In reality, only a few were commonly used. This was the biggest shortcoming, already identified by Robert Triffin, that would need to be addressed. The IMF today still considers only five currencies, the dollar, euro, sterling, yen and renminbi, as freely usable currencies out of about 145 currencies in circulation. The narrow set of currencies seemed particularly problematic as large emerging markets, representing about half of the world's real economy, remained significantly constrained in using their own currencies in international payments.

Fortunately, a new willingness to adopt unconventional approaches was pointing in the right direction. CBDCs initiated a new fundamental debate about the use of money. New approaches were being tested on how new technologies could facilitate foreign exchange settlement, establish more direct monetary relations and reduce risk in particular in foreign transactions. The European Union is at the forefront with important work being done on the digital euro; this was in line with the EU's increasing emphasis on open strategic autonomy and the enhanced role of the euro. Recent initiatives like the BIS Innovation Hub CBDC project mBridge aimed at conducting international payments using local currencies to advance currency diversification. There is no doubt that Triffin would be pleased with these new technological solutions solving many old problems.

Marc Uzan, Founder and Executive Director of the Reinventing Bretton Woods Committee (RBWC) expressed appreciation for the many occasions when RTI and RBWC had worked together. RBWC was following since three decades the evolution of the Bretton Woods institutions. In the past, we took for granted that the Bretton Woods institutions were here to stay. Today, our first priority should be to make sure that we would be able to continue to treasure them in the future. A multiplicity of new challenges (pandemia, climate change, biodiversity, concerns for supply chains, cost of living, etc.) and increased polarization (Ukraine, Middle-East, US-China conflict) have dramatically increased geopolitical risk and global uncertainty. We are coming out of decades of supportive demographics, globalization and technological advances, which have resulted in high growth, but many of these trends are now reversed: the assumptions of growth through trade, ever expanding supply chains and financial globalization have been disrupted by the pandemia. The war in Ukraine has ruptured the rules that governed the international order. International cooperation is at its lowest point since the end of the Cold War and the peace dividend has evaporated as defense spending has risen across the world. A poly crisis (*i.e.* disparate crises interacting such that their overall impact far exceeds the sum of each of them), as described by the Columbia University historian Adam Tooze, has now emerged. These developments have led to a rush for energy and food security, re-shoring of supply chains and the adoption of protectionist policies. In this changed environment, we are facing a new debate about the Bretton Woods institutions and their global role in policy coordination. Do they have the right mandate, governance, policies and staffing to continue securing global economic prosperity? Were the institutions fit for financing the ecological transition and managing our global commons? Could they adapt their operations to new areas, without forgetting their core mandate and mission creep?

A lot of reflection on these issues was taking place in the two institutions. The problem was to navigate between two forms of global governance: the first was Bretton Woods driven under US leadership, but the second was spearheaded by China with partners in the Global South, forging new or parallel institutions such as the Asian Infrastructure investment Bank. Up to now, China was quiet and prudent at the global level and showed commitment to the good functioning of the Bretton Woods framework, despite an unsatisfactory representation.

In this context, the RBWC was initiating in 2024 a series of international events (a first event had already taken place in Austria and was followed by an event in China with others to come in Latin America, Asia and Nordic countries), trying to understand better geo-economic fragmentation and the emergence of different perspectives at the regional level. RBWC was also always ready to assist the successive G20 presidencies, helping them to showcase some topics and produce *deliverables*. The overall objective remained to keep multilateralism alive, despite *blockalization*.

Jorge Braga de Macedo concentrated his final remarks on some of his most fundamental convictions and on the economists who had most influenced him. He remembered when his teacher and friend Paulo de Pitta e Cunha (1937–2022), mentioned in the opening session, introduced him to Robert Triffin at the 1971 IMF annual meeting and was the dean of the economics session of the Academy over the last ten years. James Peaslee, lawyer with Cleary Gottlieb Steen & Hamilton, was co-author in 1977 of Triffin's piece on *Monetary and Political Aspects of Optimal Economic Interdependence* Jorge Braga de Macedo's conviction was that, for regional initiatives to play a positive role in containing financial instability, they needed to be embedded in the relevant institutions of global surveillance. The architecture of the world economy in the new millennium could benefit from Robert Triffin's vision of Europe 50 years ago. Other sources of inspiration were Ralph C. Bryant (Brookings Institution) and Richard Cooper (Professor of International Economics at Yale, later Under-Secretary of State for Economic Affairs), his teacher and lifelong friend. He had followed a seminar given by Cooper on "the politics of the international economy" and written a paper on how his ideas could apply to Portugal. Cooper was less radical than Triffin and had brought Robert Triffin out of his ivory tower. Jorge Braga de Macedo regretted that the IMF and the World Bank had shown incapacity to work with the WTO. He reiterated the importance of close cooperation between the European Union and the African Union.

In his conclusions, Bernard Snoy thanked again all those who had cooperated to the preparation and the implementation of the conference. Jorge Braga de Macedo, who had been a student of Robert Triffin at Yale, had inspired the program. His experience as Minister of Finance who had signed the Maastricht Treaty and made sure, with the assistance of Hervé Carré, that Portugal would join the euro at its inception, was particularly relevant for the discussions over the two days of the conference. It was not possible to give justice to the contributions of all the speakers and moderators. Among the "deliverables" of the conference Bernard Snoy singled out a few important ideas:

- "we are all the children of Bretton Woods" as said by Vice-Governor Raposo in her dinner speech. We all needed to be grateful for a framework and for institutions that had for so long underpinned global growth and prosperity. José Luís Cardoso had stressed our intellectual debt to John Maynard Keynes, even if his main ideas had not prevailed at Bretton Woods.
- there was recognition that Robert Triffin and his followers had correctly identified a fundamental flaw at the heart of the IMS since Bretton Woods and even more since the abandonment of the dollar's convertibility in gold: this was the TD, which was taking a number of forms:a more and more unsustainable indebtedness of the United States, financial instability, insufficiency of safe assets, *built-in destabilizer* effect on emerging countries, multiple asymmetric and unequitable features, limited number of currencies used in international transactions, etc.
- we needed change and reform of the IMS and of the Bretton Woods institutions but, as underlined by Ricardo Mourinho Félix and Marc Uzan, this was made difficult by the multiple new challenges and crises, generating fragmentation and polarization, increasing geopolitical risk and global uncertainty. The priority was to preserve and enhance the capacity of the Bretton Woods institutions to deliver on their core mandate and to adapt to new ones. The superb keynote speech by Vitor Gaspar showed

the extent to which geopolitics has impacted fiscal policy, which requires countries to strengthen their fiscal frameworks in the face of a difficult policy trilemma.

- there was not the same consensus on how to proceed to reform the IMS. Nevertheless, contributions by several speakers, in particular Christian Ghymers, Fabio Masini, Luiz Awazu Pereira da Silva, Jose Antonio Ocampo and Anoop Singh were pointing to a concrete path under which regional monetary arrangements, instead of leading to an unstable multi-reserve currency model, would help create trust and solidarity among "like-minded" countries. They could create "multilateral funds" in SDRs and decentralize a number of IMF function, facilitating the move to a "green and fair Bretton Woods", including the transformation of the IMF into a genuine LOLR. De-dollarization was not per se the solution although it would become unescapable. The flaw in the system would not be solved but made worse if several countries were genuinely competing to promote the international use of their currency and become LOLR, which meant also debtor of last resort. But it was not even sure that China aspired to such a role. Fabio Masini had put on the table two concrete proposals that could create a positive dynamic: a regional safety net for Latin America and a EU-Africa Plan for Next Generation.
- other speakers such as Professor Renato Flôres expressed skepticism about any possibility for reform at the global level. Andrew Sheng had concluded that "the US dollar status was for the US to lose and not easily for others to gain". Renato Flôres, particularly concerned at the way in which the United States was weaponizing the dollar, proposed to concentrate efforts on a broader use of national currencies, particularly from emerging countries, for the settlement of cross-border trade. This would be facilitated through technological innovations such as CBCDs, as shown by Ousmène Jacques Mandeng. In fact it could be complementary and not incompatible with the development of regional monetary arrangements.
- the past and present experience with regional monetary arrangements and regional monetary unions turned out to be encouraging, even though all of them still needed to be consolidated and required a minimum of political consensus. Governor Kassi-Brou of the BCEAO confirmed the positive impact of monetary unions, where they existed, in terms of macroeconomic and structural policy convergence. The experience of the African countries belonging to the CPLP was particularly illuminating.

The presentations by Governor Óscar Évora Santos, Zenaida Cassama, Maria-Esperança Mateus Majimeja confirmed the support of their respective central banks to the process of regional integration, without ignoring the need for convergence. Osvaldo Victorino Joao gave a comprehensive picture of the milestones of regional integration on the African continent and made constructive proposals, including a greater support from the Bretton Woods institutions to the African Union, while Manuel Clarote Lapão emphasized the commitment of the CPLP Secretariat towards its consulting members such as the Academy so as to improve mutual knowledge about member states. There were important lessons to draw from the history escudo zone as described by Professor Maria-Eugenia Mata.

- Asia was perceived by Hung Tran and Andrew Sheng as the continent where change was taking place at the fastest pace. Rodolfo Lavrador gave an interesting insight from Macau, which seemed a particularly important place to observe regional integration and the cooperation of China with its ASEAN neighbors.

Concluding Remarks

Fabio Masini

The draft of this book is being completed in the early afternoon of July 1st, 2024, exactly 80 years after the start of the Bretton Woods international monetary conference that would attempt to define a path of economic and financial governance for the post-WWII world. A path dominated, first *de jure*, then *de facto*, by the United States and dollar hegemony. After all, this hegemony reflected the dominant role that the United States had acquired as the decisive military power that would put an end to the war and establish a network of alliances that shaped the following decades.

That world trembled between the early 1970s, when the system collapsed and new players emerged on the global scene, and the late 1980s, when the Berlin Wall was torn down and the USA eventually emerged as the winning liberal democracy, suggesting that we were facing the *end of history*.

Paradoxically, since then, the global system of power has been quickly evolving and is currently navigating unexplored waters, under manyfold threats to global security and stability. No longer tenable global imbalances, increasing problems to finance the US debt and the issue of a $-denominated safe assets, the emergence of payment systems alternative to the SWIFT, the advent of digital currencies, are only among the most manifest features of a changing financial context. While the institutions of global governance are (or appear to be) still the same as those established 80 years ago, tensions are rising between the international economic and political governance and the new balance of power being struggled for.

The parallel rise of awareness concerning the global nature of a few, crucial public goods and the risk of fragmented responses, designed upon national or block logics, is further adding uncertainty to a very unstable framework. Hence, we believe, the need to restore a path towards multilateralism. In turn, this requires the creation and consolidation of ambitious regional integration projects, without which multilateralism would be bound to degenerate into a dualistic confrontation, with all its related dangers and inefficiencies.

The workshop held in Lisbon was precisely meant to collect ideas and suggestions from academics and policymakers on how to recover a path towards regional integrations, aimed at building a global multilateral governance.

The texts collected in the volume mostly represent papers prepared for — and presented in — Lisbon. Some of them, though, are revised and longer contributions on the topic, that authors decided to expand for this specific volume. A few other authors were not able to provide their written texts, but thanks to Snoy's last chapter, which is in fact a wrap up of the debates held at the initiative, readers may have an idea of the whole thread followed.

Commonly shared analyses and goals concerned mainly the acknowledgment that the international monetary system is flawed, and that there is not only a systemic risk connected to the Triffin Dilemma, but one further worry related to the potential shortage of safe assets due to constraints in US budgetary procedures. Major divides concerned the degree of urgency of a systemic change (within a short-mid-or-long-term perspective?), the degree of change needed (adjustment or reform?) to tackle effectively the shortcomings of the present system, the tactics to be implemented to secure some change in the right direction (is currency competition a solution?).

Such differences may suggest that not enough consensus may emerge even within informed circles of professionals, making the task of both adjustments and reform virtually unviable. Europe is still an unfinished project, and euro-skepticism is on the rise again. Africa and Latina America may be seen as frameworks in which action towards monetary and financial integration is impossible. The past and current state of regional integration there seem to support such pessimism.

At the same time, if one goes through all the contributions, a substantial and widespread awareness emerges on the main lines of change needed to make the international monetary system be ready for the next 80 years: multilateralism, comparable dignity for more than one major actor, recognition of the increasing importance of emerging markets in international political economy, need for increasing regional *cooperation* (even if a few authors consider *integration* a too ambitious goal).

The aim of the workshop was not to acknowledge obstacles and simply stare at them. There are indeed major political hindrances to change. But there are also powerful movements in history leading to a reshuffle of the whole balance of power. The issue is therefore if we, and the USA first, want to guide such change or be subject to it. If we can create a reasonably stable and efficient framework for change without further exacerbating conflicts, or if change will take place in an unstable and volatile, unpredictable manner, opening scenarios that might be detrimental to the whole humankind.

Anchoring expectations is crucial in economics. Resuming a path towards regional financial, monetary and economic integration might be one of the keys towards a smooth evolution of the international monetary system. Regional integration might be a more interesting alternative to a logic of confrontation between two blocks, one under the hegemony of the USA and another one under the Chinese influence. Which is currently the most likely and dangerous outcome.

We dare to hope that the reflections and proposals presented in this workshop may be of inspiration for policymakers to avoid surrendering to the logic of *Realpolitik*. After all, politics is about making unlikely things happen.

Attendees' and Authors' Profiles

(alphabetical order)

Jorge Braga de Macedo was a student of Robert Triffin in Yale where he got his Ph.D. in Economics. He was head of the OECD Development Center and Director at the European Commission in charge of analyzing the economies of EU member States, before being elected to the Portuguese Parliament and becoming Minister of Finance of Portugal in 1991. He signed for Portugal the Treaty of Maastricht and was the architect of the policies that enabled Portugal to join the euro-zone from the very beginning. He has been teaching at the Nova University of Lisbon as well as for Sciences Po in Paris and at the Catholic University of Angola. He is Treasurer of the Academy of Sciences of Lisbon and Member of the Belgian Royal Academy.

José Luís Cardoso is research professor at the Instituto de Ciências Sociais da Universidade de Lisboa where he served as Deputy Director (2010–2014) and Director (2014–2018) and is President of the Lisbon Academy of Sciences. Until 2008 he was full professor of economics and history of economic thought at ISEG, University of Lisbon. He collaborates with several foreign universities as visiting professor. He is author and editor of several books on the Portuguese history of economic thought from a comparative perspective, with special emphasis on the study of the processes of diffusion and assimilation of economic ideas. He is the general editor of the series Classics of Portuguese Economic Thought (20 titles in 30 volumes) and founding editor of the European Journal of the History of Economic Thought and of the e-journal of Portuguese history. He has been President of the European Society for the History of Economic Thought (ESHET) in 2014–2016.

Hervé Carré, a French national, had a brilliant career at the European Commission, specializing in international economic and monetary affairs. He was one of the architects of the European Monetary System, of the ECU and the euro. In 1991 he was seconded to the Federal Reserve in Washington. In 1992–93 he worked for the Portuguese Government, as Adviser of the Minister of Finance, Jorge Braga de Macedo. He went back to the European Commission in 1994 as Director of Monetary Affairs and in 1999 as Director overseeing the economy of the Eurozone and the smooth introduction of the euro coins and notes. From 2002 to 2005 he was Minister for Economic and Financial Affairs and Development in the Delegation of the European Commission in Washington. His last positions were Deputy Director General of ECFIN and Director General of Eurostat.

Zenaida Cassamá, Graduate in Management and Master in Finance at ISCTE in 1995. With over 27 years professional experience in banking, she was Director-General of Banco Regional de Solidariedade during five years; a position she retained for two more years after the bank became part of ORABANK. She was President of the Bank Association of Guinea-Bissau and second Vice-President of the Federation of UEMOA bank employees, council of the National Director (2015–17) and led large projects as Fiduciary Diretor-General of BCEAO in Dakar (Senegal). She has been National Director since 9 May 2022.

Óscar Évora Santos was the President of Praia city council from 2016 to 2020 and became Governor of Banco de Cabo Verde on 4 January 2021.

Renato Galvao Flores Junior is Professor at the Escola de Pos-Graduaçao em Economia in Rio de Janeiro and Director of the International Intelligence Unit of the Fundaçao Getulio Vargas. He has until recently been Member of the Permanent Group of Experts of the Committee on Subsidies and Countervailing Measures at the World Trade Organization as well as Member of the Academic Committee of the Centro Brazileiro de Relaçoes Internacionais (CEBRI) and President of ECSA-Brasil, the Brazilian chapter of the European Community Studies Association. He is associated to Research Centers in many European Universities.

Vitor Gaspar is Director of the Fiscal Affairs Department at the IMF. Before that, he was Portuguese Minister of State and Finance from 2011 to 13 and has held various positions in European and Portuguese institutions, including head of BEPA at the European Commission, director-general of research at the European Central Bank, director of Economic Studies and Statistics at the Central Bank of Portugal, and Director of Economic Studies at the Portuguese Ministry of Finance. Mr. Gaspar holds a Ph.D. and a post-doctoral agregado in Economics from Universidade Nova de Lisboa; he graduated from Universidade Católica Portuguesa.

Christian Ghymers is Professor of International Economics with tenure at ICHEC — Brussels Management School, Vice-President of the RTI — Robert Triffin International/University of Louvain-la-Neuve, Belgium, President of IRELAC. He is specialized in international monetary issues, regional integration, and Latin American policy issues. His had a career of adviser at the European Commission (DG Economic and Financial Affairs), the Joint Vienna Institute (IMF Institute), the ECLAC/CEPAL- United Nation Secretary (Santiago), the Research Department of the National Bank of Belgium, and used to be Visiting Professor or Lecturer in various Universities (UCL — Louvain-la-Neuve, Belgium, IESEG Lille, Aix-Marseille II, Ecole Nationale d' Administration — ENA — Strasbourg, France, and University of Chile).

Osvaldo João, Former Treasury and Finance Secretary in Angola, is Ph.D. candidate at Instituto Superior de Ciências do Trabalho e da Empresa (ISCTE) in Lisbon.

Jean-Claude Kassi Brou is since 2022 the Governor of the *Banque Centrale des Etats d'Afrique de l'Ouest* (BECEAO), which brings together eight countries of Western Africa. He earlier was for four years the President of the ECOWAS (*Economic Community of Western African States*) Commission, which brings together fifteen countries cooperating on a range of economic and political affairs. Before that, Governor Kassi Brou was for six years *Minister of Industry and Mining* in his country, Ivory Coast. He worked 13 years in the IMF, including being the Resident Representative of the IMF in Senegal and two years in the World Bank, as Resident Representative in Chad. He has a profound understanding of issues linked to regional cooperation in Africa.

Ousmène Jacques Mandeng is a Visiting Fellow at the School of Public Policy at the *London School of Economics and Political Science*. He is a Senior Advisor with *Accenture's*

Global Blockchain Technology Practice with a focus on digital currencies and writes a blog on international monetary affairs. He worked more than 20 years in the financial sector and international institutions, including as Managing Director with Prudential Financial and UBS. He was Deputy Division Chief with the IMF working on IMF financial resources and Latin America. He is a member of RTI.

Fabio Masini is Professor of *Theories and History of International Political Economy*, Jean Monnet Chair of *European Economic Governance* and Director of the Master in *The Economics of Interdependence* at the University of Roma Tre. Advisor for local development in many projects involving Local Authorities and Civil Society Organizations, he was Secretary General and Vice-President of the *European Movement* in Italy. He is now serving as Secretary General of *Robert Triffin International*. His main areas of research concern regional and global economic and monetary governance and integration.

Maria Eugénia Mata is Full Professor at the Faculdade de Economia of the *Universidade Nova de Lisboa*, Nova SBE, teaching Economic History, History of Globalization, and History of Economic Analysis. Visiting scholar at Brown University, Rhode Island, 2000. Alfred Chandler Jr. Scholar at the Harvard Business School, 2007. She was awarded the Oliveira Marques Prize, by the Association of Spanish and Portuguese Historical Studies in 2010, and *Mulheres na Ciência* (Women in Science) prize in 2017. Ex-President of the *Portuguese Economic and Social History Association*, she is the author or editor of some books.

Maria Esperança Mateus Majimeja holds a Postgraduate Degree in Financial Economics from the *University of London*, England (1997) and a Degree in Economics (1992) from the Universidade Eduardo Mondlane. She worked as an economist at the *Ministry of Cooperation* and was a member of the *Technical Group for Negotiations* with the IMF, the *Technical Group for External Trade Statistics* and the *Road Transport Committee*.

Jose Antonio Ocampo was until recently *Minister of Finance of Colombia*. He had been previously *Minister of Agriculture and Rural Development* and a Member of the Governing Board of the *Central Bank of Colombia*. He was Director at the *School of International and Public Affairs of Columbia University*, New York. Ocampo has held in the past several prominent positions in the United Nations, most notably as *Under-Secretary General for Economic and Social Affairs* and *Executive Secretary of the Economic Commission for Latin America and the Carribean* (ECLAC). He is a member of Robert Triffin International.

Luiz Awazu Pereira da Silva retired recently from the *Bank for International Settlements* (BIS), where he was Deputy General Manager since 2015. Before that, he had been Deputy-Governor of the *Central Bank of Brazil* and Chief Economist of the *Ministry of Planning and Budget* and *Deputy Finance Minister of Brazil for International Affairs*. He has been Regional Director for Southern Africa at the *World Bank* and Director of the Country Risk Department at the *Japan Bank for International Cooperation*. He still teaches in a Japanese University on international affairs.

Clara Raposo is Vice-Governor of the *Banco de Portugal*. Dean of *ISEG Lisbon School of Economics and Management — Universidade de Lisboa* since 2018, and Full Professor of Finance at this institution since 2010. She was in charge of the scientific area of Finance in the Management Department, coordinated the Master courses both in *Finance and Management* (MiM), the Post-Graduate Degree in *Financial Analysis* and the *Sustainable Finance: Green and Climate Finance Executive Program*. She holds a PhD in Finance from *London Business School — University of London* (1998), a Master's Degree in Economics from *Westfield College — Queen Mary University of London* (1994) and a degree in Economics from the *Nova School of Business and Economics — Universidade Nova de Lisboa* (1992).

Anoop Singh, an Indian national, was successively Director of the *Western Hemisphere Department* and Director of the *Asia and Pacific Department* of the *International Monetary Fund*. His additional work experience include special Advisor to the Governor of the *Reserve Bank of India*, Adjunct Professor at *Georgetown University*, Lecturer in Bombay and more recently Member of the 15th *Fiscal Commission of India* (2018–2021). Anoop Singh is the author of many publications. He recently was invited to deliver lectures on International Monetary Reform and on SDRs at *Renminbi University, China*.

Bernard Snoy et d'Oppuers is Professor at the *Institute of European Studies* at the Catholic University of Louvain, Chairman of *Robert Triffin International* and Honorary Chairman of the *European League for Economic Cooperation*. He studied Law, Economics and Philosophy at the Catholic University of Louvain and holds a Ph.D. in economics from Harvard University. He started his career at the World Bank in 1974. In the 1980s, he worked for two years in the Economic and Monetary General Directorate of the European Commission in Brussels. Subsequently, he was Chief of Cabinet of the Belgian Minister of Finance, Executive Director of the World Bank (where, in addition to Belgium, he represented Austria, Belarus, the Czech Republic, Hungary, Kazakhstan, Luxembourg, Slovakia, Slovenia and Turkey), Member of the Board of Directors of the European Bank for Reconstruction and Development, Director of the Economic Table of the Stability Pact for South-Eastern Europe, and Coordinator of the Economic and Environmental Activities of the Organization for Security and Cooperation in Europe. His publications cover a wide variety of subjects, linked to developing countries indebtedness, transition economics, European Union enlargement and international monetary reform.

Hung Tran is a nonresident senior fellow at the *Atlantic Council's Geoeconomics Center*, former Executive Managing Director at the *Institute of International Finance* and a former Deputy Director at the *International Monetary Fund*, where he played an important role: coordinating the negotiations of the Private Creditor-Investor Committee for Greece with the European Commission, the Eurogroup, the ECB and the IMF. Before that, he served at the IMF as Deputy Director for the Monetary and Capital Markets Department. Hung Tran is a member of RTI.

Marc Uzan is the Executive Director and Founder of the *Reinventing Bretton Woods Committee*, a not-for-profit organization established in 1994 that focuses on addressing issues related to the international financial architecture. Marc Uzan serves also as consultant helping private and public sector clients plan high-level conferences across the globe. He has edited several large volumes on international finance, including *Bretton Woods: the next 70 years*, with contributions by major economic experts.

Federalism

VOL. 34

The book series Federalism, run by the Centro Studi sul Federalismo (CSF), aims to disseminate knowledge in the field of studies on federalism, as well as to feed the academic and public debate and support the activity of decision- makers, confronted with demands for autonomy by local governments, along with forms of regional and world integration needed to govern global processes.

The book series is divided into two sub- series: Studies and Classics. The former mostly contains the research outcome and the proceedings of conferences and seminars promoted by the CSF, while the latter consists in reprints of the federalist classic works and English translations of Italian federalists' works.

The CSF is a think tank that carries out activities of interdisciplinary research, documentation, information regarding domestic and supranational federalism, developments in the area of regional and continental integration – first and foremost the European Union – and problems related to global governance and the democratization process of the international system.

The CSF has been founded in November 2000. Since 2012 it is a Foundation under the auspices of Fondazione Compagnia di San Paolo and the Universities of Turin, Pavia and Milan, with Politecnico di Torino as co-founder.

Centro Studi sul Federalismo
Piazza Vincenzo Arbarello 8
10122 Torino - Italy
Tel. + 39 011 15630 890
E-mail: info@csfederalismo.it
Website: www.csfederalismo.it

Series Editor: Lucio Levi, Former Professor of Political Science and Comparative Politics at the Turin University, Editor of The Federalist Debate and Scientific Director of the International Democracy Watch

Editorial Board

Series Titles

NO. 1 Giovanni Finizio and Ernesto Gallo (eds.), Democracy at the United Nations. UN Reform in the Age of Globalisation, 2013.

NO. 2 Roberto Castaldi (ed.), Immanuel Kant and Alexander Hamilton, the Founders of Federalism. A Political Theory for Our Time, 2013.

NO. 3 Claudio Giulio Anta (ed.), Lord Lothian: The Paths of Federalism. Writings and Speeches, 2014.

NO. 4 Filippo Maria Giordano and Stefano dell'Acqua (eds.), "Die Welt war meine Gemeinde". Willem A. Visser 't Hoof – A Theologian for Europe between Ecumenism and Federalism, 2014.

NO. 5 Giampiero Bordino (ed.), A New Right for Democracy and Development in Europe. The European Citizens' Initiative (ECI), 2015.

NO. 6 Filippo Maria Giordano, Unity through Diversity. An Insight into Federalism and Ecumenism within Italian Protestantism, 2016.

NO. 7 Lucio Levi, Giampiero Bordino and Antonio Mosconi (eds.), Federalism. A Political Theory for Our Time, 2016.

NO. 8 Lorenzo Vai, Pier Domenico Tortola and Nicoletta Pirozzi (eds.), Governing Europe. How to Make the EU More Efficient and Democratic, 2017.

NO. 9 Korwa G. Adar, Giovanni Finizio and Angela Meyer (eds.), Building Regionalism from Below. The Role of Parliaments and Civil Society in Regional Integration in Africa, 2018.

NO. 10 Alberto Majocchi, European budget and sustainable growth. The Role of a Carbon Tax, 2018.

NO. 11 Elena Flor, SDR: from Bretton Woods to a world currency, 2019.

NO. 12 Lucio Levi (ed.), Albert Einstein from Pacifism to the Idea of World Government, 2020.

NO. 13 Alberto Majocchi (ed.), Africa and Europe: a Shared Future, 2020.

NO. 14 Olimpia Fontana, Investing in Europe. Old problems and new opportunities, 2022.

NO. 15 Hilda Monte, The Unity of Europe. With an introduction by H. N. Brailsford. Edited by Andreas Wilkens, 2023.

NO. 16 Fabio Masini (ed.), 80 Years after Bretton Woods. Relaunching Multilateralism through Regional Monetary Unions, 2025.

www.peterlang.com

www.ingramcontent.com/pod-product-compliance
Ingram Content Group UK Ltd.
Pitfield, Milton Keynes, MK11 3LW, UK
UKHW020710041026
15590UKWH00002B/589

9 783034 354448